First Joint Workshop on Narrative Understanding Storylines, and Events 2020

Online
9 July 2020

ISBN: 978-1-7138-1386-6

ACL 2020

Narrative Understanding, Storylines, and Events

Proceedings of the First Joint Workshop

July 9, 2020

Introduction

Welcome to the 1st Joint Workshop on Narrative Understanding, Storylines, and Events!

This workshop brings together an interdisciplinary group of researchers from NLP, ML, and other computational fields with authors and scholars from the humanities to discuss methods to improve automatic capabilities for narrative understanding, storylines, and event recognition and modeling.

We are happy to present 15 papers on this topic (along with 2 non-archival papers to be presented only at the workshop). These papers take on the complex challenges presented by diverse texts including spoken narratives, dialogue, literature, and journalism as they look to improve methods for event extraction, emotion and bias recognition, discourse evaluation, script induction, quality assessment, cross-document event coreference, and other tasks related to the workshop theme. We would like to thank everyone who submitted their work to this workshop and the program committee for their helpful feedback.

We would also like to thank our invited speakers for their participation in this workshop: Angela Fan, Mark Finlayson, Andrew Gordon, Alexander Hauptmann, Kathleen McKeown, Ellen Riloff, and Ted Underwood.

We are excited to showcase this work and for this opportunity to bring together researchers working on challenges in understanding narratives, storylines, and events. Thank you to the ACL Workshop Co-Chairs, Milica Gašić, Saif M. Mohammad, Dilek Hakkani-Tur, and Ves Stoyanov, and to all who made this workshop possible.

—Claire, Tommaso, Snigdha, Elizabeth, Ruihong, Mohit, Alejandro, Heng, Lara, Ben, Teruko, Nanyun, and Joel

Organizers:

Claire Bonial, Army Research Lab
Tommaso Caselli, University of Groningen
Snigdha Chaturvedi, University of North Carolina, Chapel Hill
Elizabeth Clark, University of Washington
Ruihong Huang, Texas A&M University
Mohit Iyyer, University of Massachusetts Amherst
Alejandro Jaimes, Dataminr
Heng Ji, University of Illinois at Urbana-Champaign
Lara J. Martin, Georgia Institute of Technology
Ben Miller, Emory University
Teruko Mitamura, Carnegie Mellon University
Nanyun Peng, University of Southern California
Joel Tetreault, Dataminr

Program Committee:

Akiko Aizawa
Alexandra Balahur
Ann Bies
Annemarie Friedrich
Ari Holtzman
Balaji Vasan Srinivasan
Baotian Hu
Chenliang Li
Chris Kedzie
Chuhan Wu
Cyril Goutte
Danqing Wang
Daphne Ippolito
David Caswell
Di Lu
Diego Esteves
Donald Metzler
Eduard Hovy
Enamul Hoque
Faeze Brahman
Faisal Ladhak
Florian Boudin
Fumiyo Fukumoto
Gaël Lejeune
Georg Rehm
George Giannakopoulos
German Rigau
Giannis Nikolentzos
Giorgio Maria Di Nunzio
Guillermo Garrido
Hao Zheng

Haoran Li
Hou Pong Chan
Ioannis Konstas
Irene Russo
Jessica Ouyang
Jia Zhu
Jiacheng Xu
Jiaming Shen
Jinfeng Rao
Jin-ge Yao
John Conroy
Jonathan Stray
Junnan Zhu
Junwen Duan
Kapil Thadani
Karl Pichotta
Kentaro Torisawa
Kevin Duh
Koji Murakami
Kuan-Yu Chen
Laure Thompson
Liqiang Xiao
Lucie Flek
Maarten Sap
Marc Verhagen
Margot Mieskes
Marina Litvak
Mark Finlayson
Martha Palmer
Maxime Peyrard
Melissa Roemmele
Natalia Vanetik
Nathanael Chambers
Nichola Lubold
Pavel Pecina
Piji Li
Po Hu
Prasenjit Mitra
Prodromos Malakasiotis
Qiang Ning
Reinald Kim Amplayo
Rik Koncel-Kedziorski
Roser Morante
Ruifang He
Saadia Gabriel
Sadid A. Hasan
Sanjeev Kumar Karn
Sara Tonelli
Seraphina Goldfarb-Tarrant
Shen Gao
Tim O'Gorman

Tobias Falke
Tomohide Shibata
Tong Wang
Tracy Holloway King
Udo Kruschwitz
Vahed Qazvinian
Vidas Daudaravicius
Weifeng Su
Wojciech Kryscinski
Xiuying Chen
Yacine Jernite
Yang Zhao
Yangfeng Ji
Yao Zhao
Yi Tay
Yimai Fang
Yllias Chali
Youzheng Wu
Yufan Guo
Zhaochun Ren
Zhunchen Luo
Ziqiang Cao

Invited Speakers:

Angela Fan, Facebook Research
Mark Finlayson, Florida International University
Andrew Gordon, University of Southern California
Alexander G. Hauptmann, Carnegie Mellon University
Kathleen McKeown, Columbia University
Ellen Riloff, University of Utah
Ted Underwood, University of Illinois, Urbana-Champaign

Table of Contents

Workshop Program

Thursday, July 9, 2020

8:15–8:30   **Opening Remarks**

8:30–9:30   **Q+A (Session 1)**

10:00–11:00   **Speaker Panel (Session 1)**

12:00–13:30   **Annotation Exercise**

15:00–16:00   **Speaker Panel (Session 2)**

16:00–17:00   **Q+A (Session 2)**

17:00–17:15   **Closing Remarks**

Keynote Talks

Keynote 1
Angela Fan

Keynote 2
Mark Finlayson

Keynote 3
Andrew Gordon

Keynote 4
Alexander G. Hauptmann

Keynote 5
Kathleen McKeown

Thursday, July 9, 2020 (continued)

Exploring aspects of similarity between spoken personal narratives by disentangling them into narrative clause types
Belen Saldias and Deb Roy

Extracting Message Sequence Charts from Hindi Narrative Text
Swapnil Hingmire, Nitin Ramrakhiyani, Avinash Kumar Singh, Sangameshwar Patil, Girish Palshikar, Pushpak Bhattacharyya and Vasudeva Varma

Emotion Arcs of Student Narratives
Swapna Somasundaran, Xianyang Chen and Michael Flor

Frustratingly Hard Evidence Retrieval for QA Over Books
Xiangyang Mou, Mo Yu, Bingsheng Yao, Chenghao Yang, Xiaoxiao Guo, Saloni Potdar and Hui Su

On-The-Fly Information Retrieval Augmentation for Language Models
Hai Wang and David McAllester

Detecting and understanding moral biases in news
Usman Shahid, Barbara Di Eugenio, Andrew Rojecki and Elena Zheleva

Paper Talks (Non-Archival)

Bringing Stories Alive: Generating Interactive Fiction Worlds
Prithviraj Ammanabrolu, Wesley Cheung, Dan Tu, William Broniec and Mark Riedl

CompRes: A Dataset for Narrative Structure in News
Effi Levi, Guy Mor, Shaul Shenhav and Tamir Sheafer

New Insights into Cross-Document Event Coreference:
Systematic Comparison and a Simplified Approach

Andres Cremisini & Mark A. Finlayson
School of Computing and Information Sciences
Florida International University
11200 S.W. 8th Street, CASE Building, Room 362, Miami, FL 33199
`{acrem003,markaf}@fiu.edu`

Abstract

Cross-Document Event Coreference (CDEC) is the task of finding coreference relationships between events in separate documents, most commonly assessed using the Event Coreference Bank+ corpus (ECB+). At least two different approaches have been proposed for CDEC on ECB+ that use only event *triggers*, and at least four have been proposed that use both *triggers* and *entities*. Comparing these approaches is complicated by variation in the systems' use of gold vs. computed labels, as well as variation in the document clustering pre-processing step. We present an approach that matches or slightly beats state-of-the-art performance on CDEC over ECB+ with only event trigger annotations, but with a significantly simpler framework and much smaller feature set relative to prior work. This study allows us to directly compare with prior systems and draw conclusions about the effectiveness of various strategies. Additionally, we provide the first cross-validated evaluation on the ECB+ dataset; the first explicit evaluation of the pairwise event coreference classification step; and the first quantification of the effect of document clustering on system performance. The last in particular reveals that while document clustering is a crucial pre-processing step, improvements can at most provide for a 3 point improvement in CDEC performance, though this might be attributable to ease of document clustering on ECB+.

1   Introduction

Cross-Document Event Coreference (CDEC) is a clustering problem with a seemingly straightforward objective: Assign every event mention in a corpus to exactly one set in which every mention in the set refers to the same real-world event. CDEC

The data and code for the experiments described herein is available at https://doi.org/10.34703/gzx1-9v95/FQVNQY.

is often contrasted with *Within-Document Event Coreference* (WDEC), where all the event mentions are drawn from the same document. All systems previously described in the literature approach CDEC in two steps: first, grouping documents into topical clusters (*document clustering*), followed by grouping events within each document cluster (*event clustering*). The CDEC literature defines events (probably incompletely) as linguistic objects comprised of a *trigger* and a set of *arguments*. The trigger is the word or phrase (usually a verb, though also commonly a noun phrase) that most closely describes the event, and the arguments are modifiers that would distinguish two events with identical triggers. Arguments are always entities, including things like times, locations, and human or non-human participants.

For example, consider the statements *"Yanitza went for a run"* and *"Juan went for a run,"* describing two distinct events. Note that names of the human participants, *Yanitza* and *Juan*, are arguments that distinguish otherwise identical events. The events often also have internal structure: the event trigger contains a light verb construction using *went* in combination with *run*. Add the complexity that these event mentions might be found in completely different contexts from completely different documents, and this simple example illustrates why event annotation—and the related task of event coreference, cross-document or not—is difficult and prone to error.

In seeking to build a CDEC system for our own use, we began with a thorough review of prior work. We discovered that prior systems were not well compared or evaluated, and that the performance of the key step of document clustering was often not reported. On the basis of these insights, we developed a system with a focus on simplicity and explainability. We identify issues in the CDEC literature that make comparing prior work difficult

1

Proceedings of the 1st Joint Workshop on Narrative Understanding, Storylines, and Events, pages 1–10
July 9, 2020. ©2020 Association for Computational Linguistics

and suggest best practices to remedy this situation going forward. Our system is modeled on the BAG OF EVENTS system described by Vossen and Cybulska (2018), primarily because of its simplicity and strong performance. However, we use a different and significantly smaller feature set to predict pairwise event coreference (4 features instead of 19), we employ a different document clustering scheme independent of gold-standard annotations, we ingest only event trigger annotations (instead of both triggers and entities), and we develop a different event clustering technique while maintaining comparable state-of-the-art performance.

The paper proceeds as follows. We begin with an extensive review of the area: the two major corpora, prior work in CDEC, as well as some relevant WDEC work (§2). We then describe our own, simplified approach, with careful attention to evaluating all stages of the pipeline (§3). We discuss our cross-validated results for various scenarios (§4) and conclude with a list of contributions (§5).

2 Prior Work

2.1 Data: The ECB & ECB+ Corpora

Most CDEC systems have been developed and evaluated on the EventCorefBank (ECB) and EventCorefBank+ (ECB+) corpora, with most using ECB+ because it is larger. ECB was the first corpus developed specifically for CDEC (Bejan and Harabagiu, 2010). It comprises 482 documents selected from GoogleNews, clustered into 43 topics, with each topic containing documents on a specific event, such as the 2009 Indonesian earthquake or the 2008 riots in Greece over a teenager's death. The corpus is annotated using a "bag of events" and entities approach, where co-referring events are all placed into the same group along with their related entities, but relationships between specific entities and events are not recorded. A limitation of this annotation scheme is that it makes it impossible to differentiate events based on their arguments.

ECB+ extends ECB with 500 articles (bringing the total to 982) that refer to similar but unrelated events across the same 43 topics (Cybulska and Vossen, 2014). For example, the topic with the 2009 Indonesian earthquake was expanded with texts referring to the 2013 Indonesian earthquake. These extra texts were marked with a different subtopic. In the release notes of ECB+, the authors recommend using a subset of 1,840 sentences that were additionally checked for correctness of coref-

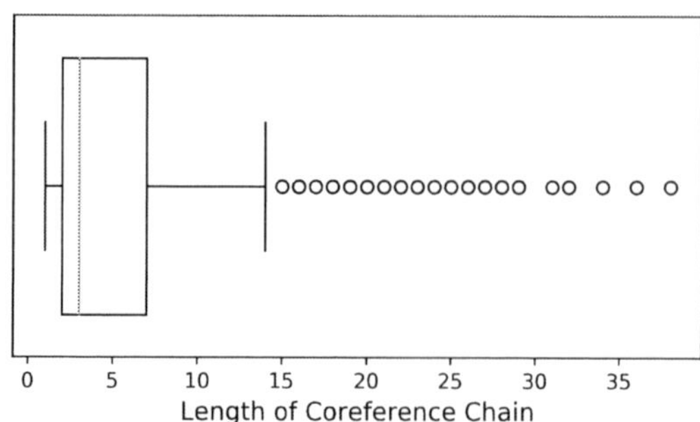

Figure 1: Boxplot of Coreference Chain Lengths in ECB+

erence annotations. We restrict our experiments to these double-checked sentences; they contain 5,726 events and 897 coreference chains with an average length of 5.5 events per chain ($\sigma = 6.1$). Figure 1 shows a boxplot of chain lengths, which shows that most coreference chains in the data are quite short, with only a handful (around 20) greater than 15 events in length.

Other datasets are available for the WDEC task only, namely KBP and ACE (Getman et al., 2018; Doddington et al., 2004). These datasets employ a different, richer event annotation than ECB/+, including types of events and temporal relationships between events. However, these corpora provide only WDEC annotations (and are also not free, being distributed by the Linguistic Data Consortium).

All extant CDEC systems begin with document clustering followed by event clustering, either by computing document clusters or using gold-standard topic or sub-topic labels. Most CDEC systems approach document clustering with off-the-shelf algorithms, and in the experimental setups used with the ECB+ corpus these algorithms tend to work quite well, though we discuss some subtleties in Section 4.2. All approaches make use of event trigger or event trigger combined with entity information, either gold-standard or computed.

2.2 Early Approaches

Early CDEC resolution systems used approaches that have not been carried into more recent work. Bejan and Harabagiu (2010) used a Bayesian approach that used a Dirichlet Process with a Chinese Restaurant prior to find the configuration of event clusters with greatest probability given the data. They used gold-standard document clusters, but did not make use of gold-standard event annotations, rather using an event and entity extractor developed in earlier work and augmenting the predicted events using a semantic parser. They tested their model on the ECB dataset, and achieved an overall performance of 0.52 CoNLL F_1. Notably, this is the only system in prior work that reports cross-validation results, but they did not report the performance of their event detection system.

Chen and Ji (2009), in contrast, developed an approach that formulates *Within-Document* Event Coreference (WDEC) as a spectral graph clustering problem. Although this system was tested on the ACE dataset, which only includes WDEC annotations (not CDEC), its performance of 0.836 Constrained Entity-Alignment F-measure (Luo, 2005) (CEAF, a.k.a., the ECM, or Entity Constrained-Mention, F-measure) is of interest to work on CDEC.

2.3 Later Approaches

All recent CDEC systems divide into *event-only* clustering and *joint event-entity* clustering. Event-only systems only perform event clustering (though some use entity information to augment their feature sets) while joint event-entity systems resolve event and entity coreference simultaneously.

2.3.1 Event-Only Clustering

Kenyon-Dean et al. (2018) describe an event-only clustering approach that generates event embeddings for clustering within the hidden layer of a neural network. The paper does not specify if document clustering was performed before CDEC, or if they used gold-standard labels. Using only event trigger annotations, the authors trained a neural network with a single hidden layer to predict the event cluster of an event given its feature representation (e.g. *word2vec* embeddings). Since their interest was clustering and not classification, however, they constrained the training loss function in such a way as to produce more clusterable event embeddings in the model's hidden layer. As a final step, they use the event embeddings of test set events as input to an agglomerative clustering algorithm.

Vossen and Cybulska (2018) describe two event-only systems, NEWSREADER and BAG OF EVENTS. The NEWSREADER system is a pipeline designed to track events in the news, with extensive use of rule-based components as well as machine-learning-based components. The *Bag of Events* system is a simpler, event-only clustering approach that achieves strong performance on ECB+; because of this we chose it as the starting point for our

system, and as such we describe it in greater detail than other prior work. BAG OF EVENTS is based on a pairwise decision tree classifier trained at both the document and event level. The document-level classifier is trained to predict if two documents contain at least one pair of coreferring events, and the event-level classifier is trained to predict if two events corefer. The first step of BAG OF EVENTS is to run the document-level classifier on every pair of documents in the test set, placing those documents that are predicted as coreferent together in the same set. Once documents are clustered, the event-level classifier is run on every pair of events in the cluster, followed by computing the transitive closure to find the final event clusters.

Both the document-level and event-level classifiers use the same features, but are computed at different levels of granularity by comparing a pair of document or event "templates." A *template* is defined by the "bag of events" principle, where each event is represented as a collection of slots (action, time, location, etc., see Table 1) where each slot contains the union of items that fill slot across all event mentions in the relevant unit of discourse. A document template's unit of discourse is the document itself, and an event's unit of discourse are the sentence where it appears. For example, if we take the two sentences in Example (1) as a document, we can derive the document and event templates as shown in Table 1.

(1) *The "American Pie" actress has entered Promises for undisclosed reasons. The actress, 33, reportedly headed to a Malibu treatment facility on Tuesday.*

The feature vector for a pair of templates is derived by computing 19 overlap features between the corresponding slots of each template. 5 features are derived from event triggers, and the remaining 14 from entities. This approach is attractive because of its conceptual uniformity and simplicity, essentially repeating the same step at two levels of granularity. The drawbacks are a large feature set, dependence on both trigger and entity annotations, and an extremely simple clustering procedure; we designed our system to address these issues.

2.4 Joint Event-Entity Clustering

In contrast to event-only clustering, joint event-entity clustering attempts to resolve event and entity coreference simultaneously, using information

| | **Templates** | | |
Slot	Event 1	Event 2	Document
Action	*entered*	*headed*	*entered, headed*
Time	-	*on Tuesday*	*on Tuesday*
Location	*Promises*	*Malibu treatment facility*	*Promises, Malibu treatment facility*
Human Partici-pant	*actress*	*actress*	*actress*
non-Human Partici-pant	-	-	-

Table 1: Event and Document Templates in Example (1)

from either step to inform the decisions made by the other. Lu and Ng (2017) described a system that jointly learns event triggers, anaphoric event relationships, and non-anaphoric event coreference relationships. They only perform *Within-Document* Event Coreference (WDEC) and evaluate their model on the KBP 2016 English and Chinese datasets for event coreference. Their formulation makes explicit use of discourse information within the document to construct a conditional random field (CRF) that performs the classification. Given the conceptual differences between KBP 2016 and ECB+ it is difficult to compare results across the two datasets. However, Lu and Ng (2017) reported state-of-the-art performance on KBP 2016 at the time.

Lee et al. (2012) described a system that computes event triggers and entities using a publicly available system that performs nominal, pronominal, and verbal mention extraction. After extracting all candidate event or entity mentions, they make use of a publicly available WDEC resolution system that applies a series of high precision deterministic rules to decide coreference. Using this initial clustering, they trained a linear regressor that predicts the quality of merging two clusters (where quality is defined as the number of correct pairwise links divided by the number of total pairwise links),

merging clusters in decreasing order of predicted quality. They did not distinguish between events and entities at clustering time, but rather perform cluster merges using features derived from the relationships between the mentions in two candidate clusters, relying heavily on a semantic role labeler (SRL). They use the ECB dataset, adding a series of event and entity coreference annotations.

Barhom et al. (2019) describe a system inspired by Lee et al. (2012), developed on ECB+. The system performs document clustering using K-means and then uses gold-standard event trigger and entity annotations to generate vector embeddings for events and entities, including both character-, word-, and context-embeddings (ELMo is used for the context embeddings; Peters et al., 2018). Together with these vectors the system uses a *dependency vector*, which is the concatenation of a set of vectors designed to capture inter-dependency between event and entity mentions. For entities, this set includes an embedding for the event head that the entity modifies as well as the embeddings for the event heads of all coreferring events. For events, the set includes entity embeddings for each of four event roles (ARG0, ARG1, TMP, LOC) that combine the embedding for the modifying entity mention and the embeddings of all other entity mentions that corefer with the modifying entity. The system computes event and entity clusters iteratively, recomputing the dependency vectors as clusters are merged. They employ an agglomerative clustering algorithm furnished with two trained pairwise prediction functions that output the likelihood that two pairs of events or entities corefer.

3   Simplified Approach

We based our approach on the BAG OF EVENTS system described by Vossen and Cybulska (2018) and discussed above in Section 2.3, primarily because of its simplicity and strong performance. However, we made several modifications based on what we learned in our literature survey:

- We use a different and significantly smaller feature set to predict pairwise event coreference (4 features instead of 19);
- We employ a different document clustering scheme independent of gold-standard annotations;
- We ingest only event trigger annotations, instead of both triggers and entities; and,
- We developed a different event clustering tech-

nique.

These modifications simplified the approach while maintaining comparable performance. At a high level, our pipeline first performs document clustering and then uses a trained pairwise event coreference classifier as the essential component in an event clustering procedure that generates CDEC chains.

3.1 Document Clustering

Like all extant systems, we first perform document clustering to assemble clusters within which event coreference will be performed. We represent our documents as a bag-of-words vector with *tf-idf* weights and perform clustering using affinity propagation (Frey and Dueck, 2007) with the damping parameter set to 0.5. On the test set used by Vossen and Cybulska (2018)$_{BoE}$ we achieve near perfect document clustering performance, as detailed in Section 4.2. This strong document clustering performance is reported by other researchers as well (Barhom et al., 2019; Choubey and Huang, 2017); Vossen and Cybulska (2018)$_{BoE}$ do not provide these numbers. The document clustering step, employed in some form by all CDEC systems, is essentially a high recall, low precision class balancing scheme that significantly reduces the number of false event coreference pairs while retaining a high percentage of true coreference pairs. This reduces the search space of event pairs before building CDEC chains and makes it easier to train a classifier with a more balanced training set.

3.2 Pairwise Event Coreference Classifier

The training data for our pairwise event coreference classifier comprises all possible event pairs within a gold-standard ECB+ sub-topic document cluster, labeled as either coreferring or not. We use a shallow, fully-connected neural network with one hidden layer composed of two nodes to predict coreference between two events. We choose this classifier because neural networks of this sort are adept at modeling the class probability of a prediction, which is a feature we make use of in our event clustering scheme by picking a cutoff for true predictions (Scikit-Learn, 2019). We tried a number of other classifier types (e.g., RDF, SVM, regression, more complex MLP architectures), but they all equivalent or worse performance. After training the classifier we use a held-out development set (20% of the training samples) to perform grid search to find a confidence threshold that max-

imizes the classifier's F_β score. The value of β we used and the reasoning behind our choice is detailed in Section 4.4. Note that at testing time, we use computed document clusters to generate the dataset of event pairs, inevitably losing some corefering event pairs that are erroneously placed in different document clusters. The classifier uses four features, listed below, to predict pairwise event coreference.

Feature 1: Head Phrase Word Similarity (Vec) This feature captures the semantic similarity of two events by measuring the average cosine similarity of each word in two events' triggers using pre-trained Fasttext word embeddings (Bojanowski et al., 2016). Our experiments (shown below) indicate that this feature accounts for the majority of the performance of the pairwise classifier.

Feature 2: Event Word Distribution (WD) This feature captures the lexical similarity between the overall textual expression of the event, including modifiers and slot fillers. Starting from the gold-standard trigger annotations provided by ECB+, we identify the *event text*—the set of words related to each event—by collecting all of the event's trigger words and their dependent words as found in the dependency graph of the sentence (we computed the dependency graphs using Stanford CoreNLP; Manning et al., 2014). For both events we construct a vector where each element represents a surface form found in the union of both sentences, and the value of each cell is the term frequency of that form: the number of tokens of that form found in the event text, divided the total number of tokens across both sentences. We found that term frequency worked better than a *tf-idf* type measure. The feature itself is the cosine similarity between the two vectors. This is the second most useful feature.

Feature 3: Relative Sentence Similarity (SS) Whereas the event word distribution feature is meant to capture the relative lexical similarity of events themselves, relative sentence similarity is designed to capture the relative lexical similarity of their sentence contexts. The sentences in each event's document are treated themselves as documents in order to compute a *tf-idf* vector for each event's sentence. For example, if two events appear in the same sentence their *tf-idf* vectors are identical. As for the event word distribution feature, the relative sentence similarity feature itself is the

Feature Set	B^3			$CEAF_e$			MUC			$CoNLL$
	P	R	F_1	P	R	F_1	P	R	F_1	F_1
POS only	99.9	18.2	30.7	9.6	51.5	16.1	20.0	0.1	0.2	15.6
SS only	23.7	82.7	36.7	25.6	13.3	17.5	74.5	83.4	78.7	45.9
WD only	38.3	75.5	50.6	36.2	32.0	33.8	81.9	83.8	82.8	55.7
VEC only	78.6	74.4	76.1	52.2	68.9	59.2	92.2	85.4	88.7	74.6
All except Vec	61.4	66.0	63.2	37.4	57.6	45.3	87.6	76.9	81.8	63.4
All except SS	80.9	72.6	76	50.3	70.5	58.5	92.7	84.2	88.2	74.3
All except POS	80.6	73.0	76.2	51.2	70.1	59.1	92.4	84.4	88.2	74.5
All except WD	80.5	73.3	76.4	51.4	70.7	59.3	92.5	84.8	88.4	74.7
All (Vec, WD, SS, POS)	**82.2**	**72.5**	**76.8**	**51.3**	**71.2**	**59.4**	**92.5**	**84.5**	**88.3**	**74.8**

Table 2: Feature Ablation Study on CDEC Performance (5-fold CV), using Gold triggers and Gold document clusters.

cosine similarity between the vectors of the two sentences. This is the third most useful feature.

Feature 4: Head Phrase Part of Speech (POS) This is a binary feature that is assigned a value of 1 if two events' triggers have the same part of speech (*noun*, *verb*, or *other*) and a 0 if they differ. This is the least useful feature.

3.3 Event Clustering

Final event clustering relies on the pairwise event classifier prediction confidence. First, we use the pairwise event classifier to predict a coreference confidence for all event pairs in the set and rank the pairs in decreasing order of classifier confidence. Confidences above a certain the cutoff are clustered using transitive closure. We chose the cutoff to maximize an intermediate measure, F_β, where β is chosen by tuning on the development set. All events not assigned to a cluster in this step were assigned to singleton clusters. We attempted to use affinity propagation as a clustering scheme with our trained classifier as a distance function, but this performed significantly worse. Nevertheless, one drawback of relying on pairwise distances (rather than embedding in a metric space) for clustering is that we cannot use clustering algorithms that perform vector arithmetic between single instances, significantly limiting our design choices.

The relative contributions of the different features to the overall performance is shown in Table 2. We performed this ablation study with gold event triggers and gold document clusters.

4 Results

4.1 CDEC

Table 3 shows results for all combinations of gold and computed labels using 5-fold cross validation. We use 5-fold cross validation because it generates test sets of roughly the same size as a commonly used test set amongst systems that use ECB+ (topics 36-45). Ours is the first study to report cross-validated results on ECB+, though we report our system's performance on two different test sets in Section 4.6 in order to compare with prior work.

4.2 Document Clustering

Our experiments show that on average, document clustering on ECB+ is responsible for about 3 CoNLL F_1 points, as shown in the difference between rows 1 and 2 in Table 3. Despite this modest performance loss, there is cause to doubt that this generalizes to document collections "in the wild," since ECB+ document clusters correspond to fairly distinct events with little lexical overlap that are probably relatively easy to cluster. In any case, document clustering is an important step for CDEC resolution. Without document clustering, the testing false/true ratio on ECB+ over 5 cross-validation folds is 89:1 (544,157 false pairs and 6,113 true pairs) on average. With document clustering, the false/true ratio drops to 6:1 (26,416 false pairs and 4,836 true pairs); the cost is that we lose some corefering event pairs—13% on average—but we gain a procedure with a tractable running time and higher performance. Details of the clustering performance are shown in Table 4.

Doc. Clust.	Ev. Trig.	B^3			$CEAF_e$			MUC			$CoNLL$
		P	R	F_1	P	R	F_1	P	R	F_1	F_1
Gold	Gold	82.2	72.5	76.8	51.3	71.2	59.4	92.5	84.5	88.3	**74.8**
Pred.	Gold	78.5	68.4	72.8	48.3	68.8	56.6	90.5	81.8	85.8	71.7
Gold	Pred.	44.3	26.2	32.9	18.8	37.0	24.8	64.3	34.3	44.6	34.1
Pred.	Pred.	45.2	24.6	31.7	18.1	37.9	24.4	64.0	32.4	42.8	33.0

Table 3: CDEC Performance (5-fold CV)

ARI	V-Measure	Homogeneity	Completeness
0.85	0.94	0.97	0.91

Table 4: Document Clustering Performance (5-fold CV)

Feature	Coef.	Std. Err.	p-value
Vec	7.12	0.068	0.000
WD	0.89	0.072	0.000
SS	-0.50	0.069	0.000
POS	-0.31	0.045	0.000
constant	-3.18	0.045	0.000

Table 5: Logistic Regression Coefficients (all ECB+). The p-value is computed for $\alpha = 0.05$.

4.3 Computed Event Triggers

The most striking performance drop occurs when we remove gold-standard event triggers, showing that trigger detection is a major performance bottleneck for CDEC, responsible for about 40 CoNLL F_1 points on average. To detect triggers we use the freely available pre-trained CAEVO Event Trigger extraction system (Chambers et al., 2014), which achieves modest performance on ECB+ of 0.62 precision, 0.43 recall, and 0.51 F_1. The CAEVO system achieved state-of-the-art performance at time of publication, and was in our experience the simplest event extraction system to integrate.

4.4 Pairwise Event Coreference Classifier

Using a cutoff of 0.72, the pairwise event classifier achieved a maximum *in vitro* performance (that is, in isolation from the rest of the system) of 0.64 precision, 0.55 recall, 0.59 F_1, and 0.95 accuracy. The cutoff is the confidence level above which a pairwise event coreference judgement is retained. We tuned the cutoff on the development set[1].

4.5 Feature Analysis

We perform logistic regression on the entire ECB+ dataset in order to investigate the predictive power of our feature set. While we do not use logistic regression as our classifier, given that our shallow neural network is a concatenation of gated logistic regressions trained by minimizing overall classifi-

cation error, analysis of logistic regression provides useful insight into our feature set.

The regression coefficients in Table 5 clearly show that the most powerful feature is the word vector feature (Vec), the word embedding head phrase similarity. In fact, training a simple logistic regression with only an intercept and the word vector feature gives a 5-fold cross-validated CoNLL F_1 of 70.7 and 69.2 on topics 36-45.

4.6 Comparison with Prior Work

Comparing the performance of existing ECB+ CDEC systems is unfortunately quite difficult due to a wide variation in testing schemes and usage of gold-standard annotations. Because of this, it is not possible to clearly determine which system achieves state-of-the-art performance. In an attempt to provide a fair comparison amongst existing systems, Table 6 shows performance of all prior work evaluated on ECB+ grouped by test sets and gold-standard annotations. Minding these conditions, we can currently only determine state-of-the-art performance on a given test set using a given set of gold-standard annotations.

4.6.1 Test Sets and Gold-Standard Annotations

Unfortunately, none of the existing CDEC papers provide a reasoning behind their choice of test set; in fact, the choices seem quite arbitrary. Standard practice in NLP suggests that multi-fold cross val-

---

[1] An interesting aside is that, through additional experimentation we found that if one wished to tune the pairwise event coreference classifier in isolation to maximize CDEC performance, the appropriate metric to maximize is $F_{0.8}$ for the pairwise classifier, rather than F_1.

	Gold	Test	B^3			$CEAF_e$			MUC			$CoNLL$
			P	R	F_1	P	R	F_1	P	R	F_1	F_1
OURS	T	36–45	74.3	69.2	**71.6**	49.6	60.7	54.6	89.4	84.9	**87.1**	**71.1**
KD2018			71	67	69	71	67	**69**	67	71	69	69
OURS	T	24–43	73.6	65.8	**69.5**	40.8	60.3	48.7	88.7	80.7	**84.5**	**67.6**
CH2017			56.2	66.6	61	59	54.2	**56.5**	67.5	80.4	73.4	63.6
Bh2019	T+E	36–45	76.1	85.1	**80.3**	81	73.8	**77.3**	77.6	84.5	**80.9**	**79.1**
CV2018 (BoE)			71	78	74	-	-	64	71	75	73	73
CV2018 (NwR)	T+E	24–43	72.8	64.2	**68.3**	55	65.4	**59.7**	77.4	69.7	**73.3**	**67.1**
YC2015*	-	24–43	78.5	40.6	53.5	38.6	68.9	49.5	80.3	67.1	73.1	**58.7**

Table 6: CDEC Performance on Single Test Set. KD2018 = Kenyon-Dean et al. (2018); CH2017 = Choubey and Huang (2017); Bh2019 = Barhom et al. (2019); CV2018 = Vossen and Cybulska (2018); YC2015 = Yang et al. (2015). *YC2015 computes event triggers and entities

idation (CV) should clearly be used. In our experiments, we used 5-fold CV, after noting that our system performed similarly using 10-fold cross validation as well as with 10 runs of randomized 5-fold and 10-fold cross validation, respectively. 5-fold cross validation is also useful for comparison with published systems because it generates test sets of roughly the same size as the previously used test set of topics 36-45. Using 2-fold cross validation to approximate the size of test set 24-43 (the other previously used test set) seems less useful.

Comparing the performance between trigger-only CDEC systems and CDEC systems that use triggers & entities is more difficult. Computing entities as well as event triggers adds an additional potential source of error, and if researchers did not report evaluation of their entity extraction systems independently of the rest of the pipeline, the contribution of those components cannot be separated from the whole. Current state-of-the-art entity detection systems perform at around 0.90 F_1 on the OntoNotes 5.0 corpus (Strubell et al., 2017), whereas state-of-the-art trigger detection systems perform at around 0.80 F_1 on the ACE2005 dataset (Yang et al., 2019). Of course, finding implementations of state-of-the-art systems or implementing them from scratch is a task onto itself. There is currently no evaluation of trigger or entity detection performance on the entire ECB+ dataset. Yang et al. (2015) describe the only system that makes exclusive use of computed trigger and entity labels on ECB+. They report that their trigger and entity detection system correctly identifies 95% of actions, 90% of participants, 94% of times and

74% of locations, but these results apply only to a development set comprised of topics 21-23; they do not provide the system's performance on any other subset of ECB+. Despite these difficulties, the results of Barhom et al. (2019) do seem to suggest that adding in entities results in a substantial improvement in performance.

4.6.2 Document Clustering

Reporting of the source of document cluster labels is inconsistent across the literature. Yang et al. (2015) is the the only ECB+ system that does not use document clustering as a pre-processing step, instead using gold-standard labels to restrict the search space for CDEC. Kenyon-Dean et al. (2018) do not specify if they use computed or gold-standard document clusters. We believe it is reasonable to separate document clustering performance from CDEC performance—events and documents are fairly distinct objects with different structures that require different techniques to determine their similarity. Practically, however, it seems that document clustering is a necessary pre-processing step in order to make CDEC tractable, as outlined in Section 4.2. For these reasons, we suggest that future CDEC systems report on performance both with and without gold-standard document clusters.

5 Contributions

We have presented a simple, event-trigger-only CDEC system that achieves strong performance on ECB+ compared with other trigger-only CDEC systems. We have compared our approach, where possible, with prior work and highlighted the difficulties in comparing existing ECB+ systems, providing suggestions for evaluation criteria in future work. We presented performance results of all components of our pipeline and quantified how error on each component propagates to downstream CDEC performance. We also provided cross validated results, the first ECB+ CDEC study to do so.

Acknowledgments

This work was supported by Office of Naval Research (ONR) grant number N00014-17-1-2983.

References

Shany Barhom, Vered Shwartz, Alon Eirew, Michael Bugert, Nils Reimers, and Ido Dagan. 2019. Revisiting Joint Modeling of Cross-document Entity and Event Coreference Resolution. *arXiv*, 2.

Cosmin Bejan and Sanda Harabagiu. 2010. Unsupervised Event Coreference Resolution with Rich Linguistic Features. *Proceedings of the 48th Annual Meeting of the Association for Computational Linguistics*, pages 1412–1422.

Piotr Bojanowski, Edouard Grave, Armand Joulin, and Tomas Mikolov. 2016. Enriching word vectors with subword information. *arXiv preprint arXiv:1607.04606*.

Nathanael Chambers, Taylor Cassidy, Bill McDowell, and Steven Bethard. 2014. Dense Event Ordering with a Multi-Pass Architecture. *Transactions of the Association for Computational Linguistics*, 2:273–284.

Zheng Chen and H Ji. 2009. Graph-based event coreference resolution. *Proceedings of the 2009 Workshop on Graph-based Methods for Natural Language Processing*, pages 54–57.

Prafulla Kumar Choubey and Ruihong Huang. 2017. Event Coreference Resolution by Iteratively Unfolding Inter-dependencies among Events. *arXiv*.

Agata Cybulska and Piek Vossen. 2014. Using a sledgehammer to crack a nut? Lexical diversity and event coreference resolution. *Proceedings of the Ninth International Conference on Language Resources and Evaluation (LREC'14)*, pages 4545–4552.

George Doddington, Alexis Mitchell, Mark Przybocki, Lance Ramshaw, Stephanie Strassel, and Ralph Weischedel. 2004. The automatic content extraction (ace) program-tasks, data, and evaluation. *Proceedings of LREC*, 2.

Brendan J. Frey and Delbert Dueck. 2007. Clustering by passing messages between data points. *Science*, 315(5814):972–976.

Jeremy Getman, Joe Ellis, Stephanie Strassel, Zhiyi Song, and Jennifer Tracey. 2018. Laying the groundwork for knowledge base population: Nine years of linguistic resources for TAC KBP. In *Proceedings of the Eleventh International Conference on Language Resources and Evaluation (LREC 2018)*, Miyazaki, Japan. European Language Resources Association (ELRA).

Kian Kenyon-Dean, Jackie Chi Kit Cheung, and Doina Precup. 2018. Resolving Event Coreference with Supervised Representation Learning and Clustering-Oriented Regularization. *arXiv*.

Heeyoung Lee, Marta Recasens, Angel Chang, Mihai Surdeanu, and Dan Jurafsky. 2012. Joint Entity and Event Coreference Resolution across Documents. *(EMNLP-CoNLL 2012) Proceedings of the 2012 Joint Conference on Empirical Methods in Natural Language Processing and Computational Natural Language Learning*, pages 489–500.

Jing Lu and Vincent Ng. 2017. Joint Learning for Event Coreference Resolution. In *Proceedings of the 55th Annual Meeting of the Association for Computational Linguistics (Volume 1: Long Papers)*, pages 90–101.

Xiaoqiang Luo. 2005. On coreference resolution performance metrics. In *Proceedings of Human Language Technology Conference and Conference on Empirical Methods in Natural Language Processing*, pages 25–32, Vancouver, Canada.

Christopher D Manning, Mihai Surdeanu, John Bauer, Jenny Finkel, Steven J Bethard, and David McClosky. 2014. The {Stanford} {CoreNLP} Natural Language Processing Toolkit. In *Association for Computational Linguistics (ACL) System Demonstrations*, pages 55–60.

Matthew E. Peters, Mark Neumann, Mohit Iyyer, Matt Gardner, Christopher Clark, Kenton Lee, and Luke Zettlemoyer. 2018. Deep contextualized word representations. *CoRR*, abs/1802.05365.

Scikit-Learn. 2019. Scikit-learn probability calibration. https://scikit-learn.org/stable/modules/calibration.html. Accessed: 2019-11-23.

Emma Strubell, Pat Verga, David Belanger, and Andrew McCallum. 2017. Fast and accurate entity recognition with iterated dilated convolutions. In *EMNLP*.

Piek Vossen and Agata Cybulska. 2018. Identity and Granularity of Events in Text. In *Lecture Notes in Computer Science*, volume 9624 LNCS, pages 501–522. Springer-Verlag.

Bishan Yang, Claire Cardie, and Peter Frazier. 2015. A Hierarchical Distance-dependent Bayesian Model for Event Coreference Resolution. *arXiv*.

Sen Yang, Dawei Feng, Linbo Qiao, Zhigang Kan, and
Dongsheng Li. 2019. Exploring Pre-trained Language Models for Event Extraction and Generation.
In *Proceedings of the 57th Annual Meeting of the
Association for Computational Linguistics*, pages
5284–5294, Florence, Italy. Association for Computational Linguistics.

Screenplay Quality Assessment: Can We Predict Who Gets Nominated?

Ming-Chang Chiu   Tiantian Feng   Xiang Ren   Shrikanth Narayanan
Department of Computer Science
University of Southern California
Los Angeles, CA 90089, USA
{mingchac,tiantiaf,xiangren}@usc.edu
shri@sipi.usc.edu

Abstract

Deciding which scripts to turn into movies is a costly and time-consuming process for filmmakers. Thus, building a tool to aid script selection, an initial phase in movie production, can be very beneficial. Toward that goal, in this work, we present a method to evaluate the quality of a screenplay based on linguistic cues. We address this in a two-fold approach: (1) we define the task as predicting nominations of scripts at major film awards with the hypothesis that the peer-recognized scripts should have a greater chance to succeed. (2) based on industry opinions and narratology, we extract and integrate domain-specific features into common classification techniques. We face two challenges (1) scripts are much longer than other document datasets (2) nominated scripts are limited and thus difficult to collect. However, with narratology-inspired modeling and domain features, our approach offers clear improvements over strong baselines. Our work provides a new approach for future work in screenplay analysis.

1 Introduction

The motion picture industry is a multi-billion dollar business worldwide (Lash and Zhao, 2016). Decisions in selecting movies to be produced are critical to the profitability of a movie studio. However, the selection of the screenplay that happens at the initial phase of a movie production pipeline and has a large influence on the financial budget and quality of the final movie production, has a large subjective element. For example, a typical script review service costs a studio $80 to $150 to receive a report containing a short summary of the script and opinion as to its quality (Follows et al., 2019). Considering the amount of scripts a studio needs to filter through, it can be overwhelming. Thus, an objective and reliable tool to help evaluate and narrow down the candidate scripts is of vital importance to aid the "green-lighting" (deciding which scripts to turn into movies) process.

Consider this scenario, if a tool can facilate the script review process and provide the chance of success, wouldn't this make an impact and cut down lots of budgeting decisions in the production process? The main idea of this work is to develop such a tool which gather custom analyses from various aspects, e.g., screenplay writing theory, character-focused linguistic behavior, to help assess the quality of the script.

In general, movie script writing can follow a well-defined *Three Act* structure (Field, 2007; McKee, 1997). Also, Weiland (Weiland, 2013, 2018) specifies a more fine-grained storytelling plan, starting from *hook, inciting event, 1st plot point, 1st pinch point, midpoint, 2nd pinch point, 3rd plot point, climax* to *resolution*, what are called Structural Points (SP). We believe knowledge like the above in strucuring a screenplay can bring benefits in selecting the most relevant textual properties for the prediction of script quality.

Aside from the event positioning, Follows et al. (2019) reported that how writers develop characters and events, i.e., *Characterization* and *Plot*, are two main foci of industry reviewers. We thus devise our domain specific features in these two aspects. We hope to offer an enhanced understanding of the essential elements in high-quality movie scripts.

To perform quality assessment, based on an assumption that the nominated scripts are recognized writings and thus should have had higher chance of passing green-lighting, we propose to perform an evaluation in a two-fold approach. First, we use award-nomination prediction as a proxy to the green-lighting process. Second, we examine our domain features and models by integrating them into existing document classification methods.

We acknowledge the constraints of our metric in that the number of award venues has its limits, and

Proceedings of the 1st Joint Workshop on Narrative Understanding, Storylines, and Events, pages 11–16
July 9, 2020. ©2020 Association for Computational Linguistics

not necessarily those without nomination would be any worse than the nominated. But due to the difficulty in collecting unproduced scripts with peer reviews, we adopt our current approach.

Our main contributions are as follows: (1) We defined a quality metric for screenplays and collected ground truths from peer-reviewed venues. (2) Based on structural knowledge of screenplay narratology, we developed a simple narratology-inspired model for our task. (3) Motivated by industry opinions and narratology, we devised domain-specific features to achieve our objective. (4) We tested that for long document classification, a simple feature-based approach can work better than state-of-the-art models.

2   Related Works

Literary works-related research has gained interest in recent years. Bamman et al. (2013, 2014) have succeeded to learn latent character types in film and novels; Iyyer et al. (2016); Chaturvedi et al. (2016); Elson et al. (2010) try to model character relations in novels. Papalampidi et al. (2019) analyze narrative structure of movies by using turning points, and Chambers and Jurafsky (2008); Sims et al. (2019) seek to detect events in narratives. On text quality assessment, Mesgar and Strube (2018) encode local change patterns to assess readability and score essays; Toledo et al. (2019) collect argument pairs that was originally built for an automatic quality assessor for debate.

A noteworthy attempt in measuring quality of literary works we know of is made by Kao and Jurafsky (2012), who quantitatively analyze various indicators for discerning professional poems from amateurs'. However, in script writing, the cinematic success criteria lack evaluative consensus (Simonton, 2009) — previous works on evaluation of movies have largely focused on forecasting revenue or profit of movies using production, distribution, and advertising data (Ghiassi et al., 2015; Lash et al., 2015) or basic textual and human annotated features (Eliashberg et al., 2014).

The main differences between our work and previous works are: (1) our approach aims to process automatically without human annotated features. (2) our metrics and methods are geared towards evaluation that based solely on textual properties.

3   Data and Problem Setting

Data collection. We evaluated our method using ScriptBase (Gorinski and Lapata, 2018) and Movie Screenplay Corpus (MSC) Ramakrishna et al. (2017) datasets. ScriptBase provides 917 scripts and MSC contains 945 Hollywood movies. We kept 897 and 868 suitable ones which have enough character utterances for our approach from each dataset respectively. Similar to Underwood (2019), which analyzes high-prestige novels as works that have been reviewed by top journals, we collected the screenplays that have histories of nominations as quality "ground truth". The venues we collect from are well-known professional prizes, which include "Writers Guild of America Award", "Academy Awards", "Golden Globe Awards", and "British Academy of Film and Television Arts Awards". We assume the nominated scripts are of higher quality by professional standards. Since we focus on textual properties for success, we only gleaned nominations in the "original screenplay" and "adapted screenplay" categories. In the end, we obtained 212 (23.6%) movies out of ScriptBase and 113 (13.0%) from MSC as quality "ground truth" labels.

Problem Setup. Our work focuses on measuring quality as whether or not a movie would be nominated at a peer-reviewed venue. The basic assumption for using this approach as success metrics is simple — a screenplay that receives nominations by critical reviewers should have had higher chance of getting through green-lighting.

Challenges. By nature, a movie should be tough to be cleanly categorized, due to its length, complex storyline and turns, and the lack of evaluative criteria. Prior works in document classification (Yang et al., 2016; Liu et al., 2017; Adhikari et al., 2019; Johnson and Zhang, 2015) evaluated on datasets with small document size (Reuters, IMDB, Yelp, etc.). However, our document size on average is at least 65 times longer, which may be challenging for NN-based models to train due to long sequences and the associated computational burden. Besides, the number of training data we have is at most 1000 times smaller than other datasets. With our datasets being **long**, **fewer** and **skewed**, state-of-the-art deep learning techniques may not work well. Summary of the comparisons is shown in Table 1.

Dataset	documents	average #w	%pos
Reuters	10,789	144.3	-
IMDB	135,669	393.8	-
Yelp 2014	1,125,457	148.8	-
ScriptBase	897	27,539.7	23.6
MSC	868	27,067.4	13.0

Table 1: **Dataset statistics and comparisons of datasets.** #w denotes the number of words and %pos denotes the percentage of positive class.

4 Analysis of Domain Features

In this section, we introduce our domain features that are divised to achieve our goal and provide analysis based on our problem setup.

Characterization and *Plot* are major aspects of focus in the industry; inspired by which, we devised 6 novel features. For each, we provide intuitive motivations, and then detail how we converted them computationally. We chose the top two most speaking characters of each movie to analyze for *characterization*.

According to Weiland (2018), a script can place 9 SPs roughly equally distributed, creating eight equal-lengthed development segments (DS) in between. We hypothesize that such structural hints should help to achieve our objective. Based on the statistics of both datasets, to leverage the SPs, we collected a context window of 1% ($\sim$270 words) centered at SPs for all scripts. Larger windows may contain more information and should improve the results, and we leave that for future experiments.

By the definition of characterization, we hypothesized that by measuring pattern change of characters, we may see how writers develop the characters' personality. We sought pattern change via two kinds of changes writers would make between SPs - linguistic (speaking pattern) change and emotional change. To do this, we proposed *Linguistic & Emotional Activity Curve*.

Linguistic & Emotional Activity Curve (*ling, emo*). For linguistic change, we extracted the dependency trees of characters; for emotional change we used normalized Empath (Fast et al., 2016) to get characters' emotion status. We combined the linguistic distribution, Empath distribution of sentences in each DS with *activity curve* (Dawadi et al., 2016), which uses a Permutation-based Change Detection in Activity Routine (PCAR) algorithm, to measure the change between two DSs of distribu-

tions.

Type-token ratio (*tt*). As Kao and Jurafsky (2012) show, in poetry, the *type-token ratio* related most positively to the quality of a poem. We believed this concept should work similarly on character analysis, and can show how much effort writers devoted in characterization. We defined this feature as the number of unique words used by a character divided by the total number of words.

Valence-Arousal-Dominance (*VAD*). Mohammad (2018a) performed extensive study in getting an objective score for words in VAD dimensional space (Russell, 1980, 2003). We used average scores over the context window of each SP to represent level of emotion.

Emotion Intensity (*int*). Similar to *VAD*, we used the NRC Affect Intensity Lexicon (Mohammad, 2018b) over the SPs to score emotion intensity along four basic emotion classes (Plutchik, 1980).

Also, since events are usually addressed in units of scenes, we wanted to get a picture of how many different emotionally similar scenes across the dataset appear in a movie.

Empath Clustering (*clus*). We retrieved lexical categories for each uttrance from Empath and then clustered the lexical category distributions of all utterances with deep embedded clustering (Xie et al., 2016). We obtained the cluster distribution based on the lexical categories within a movie as a feature representation.

We visualized partial features in a "nomination vs non-nomination" fashion, as in Fig. 1, to show the potential of our features. For some we can easily observe clear differences from one to the other, while some are more subtle. For instance, in *VAD*, the *arousal* of MICA is ambiguous between the two, and yet we can easily discern nominated scripts along the same axis for ScirptBase.

5 Predictive Modeling

In this section, we define our prediction task, and then propose our base model and then move on to a paradigm which integrates domain features proposed in previous section.

Task Formulation. As a proxy to the original quality assessment task, we define a binary classification task as to predicting the nomination of a script.

Narratology-inspired Model. Inspired by narratology, we propose *Tfidf-SVM$_{narr}$* — instead of using all texts in an entire document, we extract words in context window of SPs for each docu-

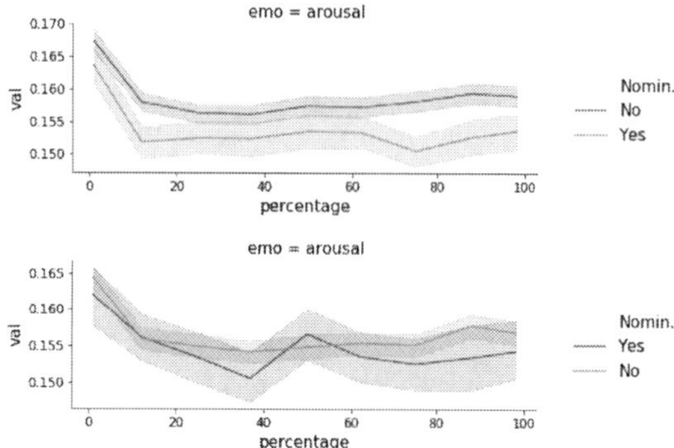

Figure 1: **Nomination vs Non-nomination of arousal level along percentage of scripts.** *Upper:* ScriptBase. *Lower:* MSC.

ment, compute the tf-idf representations, and feed them into a SVM classifier. The main components of *Tfidf-SVM$_{narr}$* are shown in Fig. 2. Due to the large amount of unique tokens, we chose only the top 500 important features ranked by Tf-idf to represent a document. We test the results without choosing 500 features and our setting is better.

Feature-based Prediction. To examine the predictive power of proposed features, on top of *Tfidf-SVM$_{narr}$*, we add domain features along with tf-idf to SVM to see the efficacy of domain features.

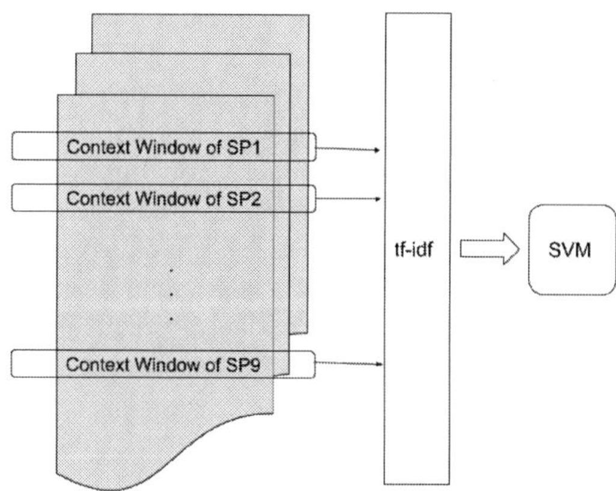

Figure 2: **Narratology-inspired model workflow.**

6 Experimental Setups

Dataset usage. We performed random sampling on both datasets such that 80% is used for training, 10% for validation, and 10% for test.

Baselines. We adopted HAN (Yang et al., 2016), BERT$_{base}$, BERT$_{large}$ (Devlin et al., 2019) as our baselines. Since a script is subdivided into scenes,

Method / Dataset	ScriptBase	MSC
HAN$_{scene}$	45.12	45.62
BERT$_{base}$	42.67	46.29
BERT$_{large}$	42.67	46.29
Tfidf-SVM	47.01	59.21
TFIDF-SVM$_{narr}$	**57.43**	**59.21**
+ emo + VAD	56.52	55.29
+ ling + emo + tt	**62.35**	62.73
+ int + ling + emo + clus	60.87	**64.79**

Table 2: **F1 scores (%) of model predictions.**

our HAN implementation, HAN$_{scence}$, uses scence as the second hierarchy instead of sentence.

Implementation details. We use Scikit-learn 0.21.3 to implement feature-based models, and PyTorch 1.3.1 for deep neural models. With Hugginface (Wolf et al., 2019), we overcome BERT's 510-token limit by applying averaging pooling on the sequence of BERT $h_{[CLS]}$ hidden states of sub-chunks of the script to get a global context vector, and then fine-tune the task end-to-end. And since the binary labels in both datasets are imbalanced, we weight the positive class by inverse frequency of class labels in the training set.

Hyper-parameters. To ensure a fair comparison, we tuned the hyper-parameters for all models. On feature-based models, we performed grid search. For NN models, we use embedding size 100 and Adam optimizer with 0.001 learning rate.

7 Results and Discussion

We report the macro-averaged F1 scores of each model in Table 2, interestingly, from which we see that NN-based document classification methods are no better than our proposed simple narratology-based model. We suppose the length of document could be the main reason, RNNs or transformers may not handle "super long-term depdendencies" well for complex compositions like movie scripts. For NN models, both BERT$_{large}$ and BERT$_{base}$ are better than HAN$_{scene}$, which is expected provided the capacity of BERT is significantly larger than HAN; we are not sure why BERT$_{large}$ did not outperform BERT$_{base}$ by even a slight margin.

In Fig. 3, we show the effect of each individual feature. *Linguistic & Emotional Activity Curve* show improvements on both datasets, and yet the rest do not consistently help, especially on MSC, we think it may be because (1) the tfidf has 500 dimensions so individual feature may be overwhelmed, but, more features combined such as adding *int+ling+tt* can generate consistent improvements, (2) the efficacy of feature can be dataset-dependent, e.g., we do not observe significant differences in *Arousal* of MSC as in its Script-Base counterpart (Fig. 1), and so does the classifier. Besides, adding features with negative correlations can damage the performance, e.g., adding *emo & vad*.

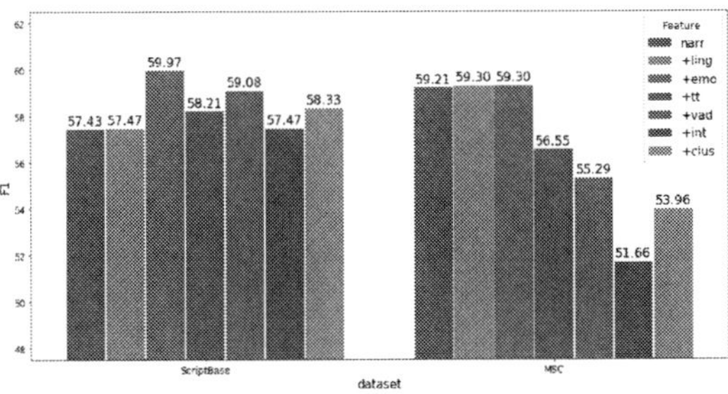

Figure 3: **Individual feature effect.** F1 scores of *Tfidf-*SVM_{narr} and adding proposed features individually.

8 Conclusion and Future Work

We present a novel approach and features to systematically analyze the quality of a screenplay in terms of its festival nomination-worthiness. This can serve as a preliminary tool to help filmmakers in their decision-making, or on the other hand, an objective way for writers to compare their works with others. Our results also show that simple lightweight approach can outperform state-of-the-art document classification methods. This also points out the current deficiency for long document classification research in the community.

In the future, in addition to textual properties, we intend to develop a more fine-grained approach by incorporating more metadata such as gender of characters, film genres, and then experiment on different award categories to evaluate our approach and gain more insights.

References

Ashutosh Adhikari, Achyudh Ram, Raphael Tang, and Jimmy Lin. 2019. Rethinking complex neural network architectures for document classification. In *NAACL-HLT*.

David Bamman, Brendan O'Connor, and Noah A. Smith. 2013. Learning latent personas of film characters. In *Proceedings of the 51st Annual Meeting of the Association for Computational Linguistics (Volume 1: Long Papers)*, pages 352–361, Sofia, Bulgaria. Association for Computational Linguistics.

David Bamman, Ted Underwood, and Noah A. Smith. 2014. A Bayesian mixed effects model of literary character. In *Proceedings of the 52nd Annual Meeting of the Association for Computational Linguistics (Volume 1: Long Papers)*, pages 370–379, Baltimore, Maryland. Association for Computational Linguistics.

Nathanael Chambers and Dan Jurafsky. 2008. Unsupervised learning of narrative event chains. In *Proceedings of ACL-08: HLT*, pages 789–797, Columbus, Ohio. Association for Computational Linguistics.

Snigdha Chaturvedi, Shashank Srivastava, Hal Daumé III, and Chris Dyer. 2016. Modeling evolving relationships between characters in literary novels. In *AAAI*, pages 2704–2710.

Prafulla N Dawadi, Diane J Cook, and Maureen Schmitter-Edgecombe. 2016. Modeling patterns of activities using activity curves. *Pervasive and mobile computing*, 28:51–68.

Jacob Devlin, Ming-Wei Chang, Kenton Lee, and Kristina Toutanova. 2019. Bert: Pre-training of deep bidirectional transformers for language understanding. In *NAACL-HLT*.

J. Eliashberg, S. K. Hui, and Z. John Zhang. 2014. Assessing box office performance using movie scripts: A kernel-based approach. *IEEE Transactions on Knowledge and Data Engineering*, 26(11):2639–2648.

David Elson, Nicholas Dames, and Kathleen McKeown. 2010. Extracting social networks from literary fiction. In *Proceedings of the 48th Annual Meeting of the Association for Computational Linguistics*, pages 138–147, Uppsala, Sweden. Association for Computational Linguistics.

Ethan Fast, Bin Bin Chen, and Michael S. Bernstein. 2016. Empath: Understanding topic signals in large-scale text. In *CHI*.

Syd Field. 2007. *Screenplay: The foundations of screenwriting*. Random House LLC.

Stephen Follows, Josh Cockcroft, and Liora Michlin. 2019. Judging screenplays by their coverage: An analysis of 12,000+ unproduced feature film screenplays and the scores they received, revealing what professional script readers think makes a good screenplay.

M. Ghiassi, David Lio, and Brian Moon. 2015. Pre-production forecasting of movie revenues with a dynamic artificial neural network. *Expert Systems with Applications*, 42(6):3176 – 3193.

Philip John Gorinski and Mirella Lapata. 2018. What's this movie about? a joint neural network architecture for movie content analysis. In *NAACL-HLT*.

Mohit Iyyer, Anupam Guha, Snigdha Chaturvedi, Jordan Boyd-Graber, and Hal Daumé III. 2016. Feuding families and former Friends: Unsupervised learning for dynamic fictional relationships. In *Proceedings of the 2016 Conference of the North American Chapter of the Association for Computational Linguistics: Human Language Technologies*, pages 1534–1544, San Diego, California. Association for Computational Linguistics.

Rie Johnson and Tong Zhang. 2015. Effective use of word order for text categorization with convolutional neural networks. In *Proceedings of the 2015 Conference of the North American Chapter of the Association for Computational Linguistics: Human Language Technologies*, pages 103–112, Denver, Colorado. Association for Computational Linguistics.

Justine Kao and Dan Jurafsky. 2012. A computational analysis of style, affect, and imagery in contemporary poetry. In *Proceedings of the NAACL-HLT 2012 Workshop on Computational Linguistics for Literature*, pages 8–17, Montréal, Canada. Association for Computational Linguistics.

Michael T. Lash, Sunyang Fu, Shiyao Wang, and Kang Zhao. 2015. Early prediction of movie success - what, who, and when. In *SBP*.

Michael T. Lash and Kang Zhao. 2016. Early predictions of movie success: The who, what, and when of profitability. *Journal of Management Information Systems*, 33(3):874–903.

Jingzhou Liu, Wei-Cheng Chang, Yuexin Wu, and Yiming Yang. 2017. Deep learning for extreme multi-label text classification. In *SIGIR*.

Robert McKee. 1997. *Substance, Structure, Style, and the Principles of Screenwriting*. New York: HarperCollins.

Mohsen Mesgar and Michael Strube. 2018. A neural local coherence model for text quality assessment. In *Proceedings of the 2018 Conference on Empirical Methods in Natural Language Processing*, pages 4328–4339, Brussels, Belgium. Association for Computational Linguistics.

Saif M. Mohammad. 2018a. Obtaining reliable human ratings of valence, arousal, and dominance for 20,000 english words. In *Proceedings of The Annual Conference of the Association for Computational Linguistics (ACL)*, Melbourne, Australia.

Saif M. Mohammad. 2018b. Word affect intensities. In *Proceedings of the 11th Edition of the Language Resources and Evaluation Conference (LREC-2018)*, Miyazaki, Japan.

Pinelopi Papalampidi, Frank Keller, and Mirella Lapata. 2019. Movie plot analysis via turning point identification. *ArXiv*, abs/1908.10328.

Robert Plutchik. 1980. Chapter 1 - a general psycho-evolutionary theory of emotion. In Robert Plutchik and Henry Kellerman, editors, *Theories of Emotion*, pages 3 – 33. Academic Press.

Anil Ramakrishna, Victor R. Martinez, Nikos Malandrakis, Karan Singla, and Shrikanth Narayanan. 2017. Linguistic analysis of differences in portrayal of movie characters. In *ACL*.

James Russell. 1980. A circumplex model of affect. *Journal of Personality and Social Psychology*, 39:1161–1178.

James A Russell. 2003. Core affect and the psychological construction of emotion. *Psychological review*, 110 1:145–72.

Dean Keith Simonton. 2009. Cinematic success, aesthetics, and economics: An exploratory recursive model.

Matthew Sims, Jong Ho Park, and David Bamman. 2019. Literary event detection. In *Proceedings of the 57th Annual Meeting of the Association for Computational Linguistics*, pages 3623–3634, Florence, Italy. Association for Computational Linguistics.

Assaf Toledo, Shai Gretz, Edo Cohen-Karlik, Roni Friedman, Elad Venezian, Dan Lahav, Michal Jacovi, Ranit Aharonov, and Noam Slonim. 2019. Automatic argument quality assessment - new datasets and methods. *ArXiv*, abs/1909.01007.

T. Underwood. 2019. *Distant Horizons: Digital Evidence and Literary Change*. University of Chicago Press.

K.M. Weiland. 2013. *Structuring Your Novel: Essential Keys for Writing an Outstanding Story*. PenForASword.

K.M. Weiland. 2018. Story structure q&a: 6 outstanding questions about structure.

Thomas Wolf, Lysandre Debut, Victor Sanh, Julien Chaumond, Clement Delangue, Anthony Moi, Pierric Cistac, Tim Rault, R'emi Louf, Morgan Funtowicz, and Jamie Brew. 2019. Huggingface's transformers: State-of-the-art natural language processing. *ArXiv*, abs/1910.03771.

Junyuan Xie, Ross Girshick, and Ali Farhadi. 2016. Unsupervised deep embedding for clustering analysis. In *International conference on machine learning*, pages 478–487.

Zichao Yang, Diyi Yang, Chris Dyer, Xiaodong He, Alexander J. Smola, and Eduard H. Hovy. 2016. Hierarchical attention networks for document classification. In *HLT-NAACL*.

Improving the Identification of the Discourse Function of News Article Paragraphs

Deya Banisakher, W. Victor H. Yarlott, Mohammed Aldawsari,
Napthali D. Rishe, & Mark A. Finlayson
School of Computing and Information Sciences
Florida International University
11200 S.W. 8th Street, CASE 362, Miami, FL 33199 USA
{dbani001,wyarl001,malda021,rishe,markaf}@fiu.edu

Abstract

Identifying the discourse structure of documents is an important task in understanding written text. Building on prior work, we demonstrate an improved approach to automatically identifying the discourse function of paragraphs in news articles. We start with the hierarchical theory of news discourse developed by van Dijk (1988) which proposes how paragraphs function within news articles. This discourse information is a level intermediate between phrase- or sentence-sized discourse segments and document genre, characterizing how individual paragraphs convey information about the events in the storyline of the article. Specifically, the theory categorizes the relationships between narrated events and (1) the overall storyline (such as MAIN EVENTS, BACKGROUND, or CONSEQUENCES) as well as (2) commentary (such as VERBAL REACTIONS and EVALUATIONS). We trained and tested a linear chain conditional random field (CRF) with new features to model van Dijk's labels and compared it against several machine learning models presented in previous work. Our model significantly outperformed all baselines and prior approaches, achieving an average of 0.71 F_1 score which represents a 31.5% improvement over the previously best-performing support vector machine model.

1 Introduction

News articles usually follow strong principles of journalistic structure. By design, they often begin with a introductory summary of main events, followed by detailed exposition of the main events and consequences, interspersed in a stereotyped fashion with relevant background information, current and past evidence, and reported speech. Yarlott et al. (2018) demonstrated the feasibility of detecting this type of discourse structure for news articles using an established hierarchical theory of news discourse (van Dijk, 1988). In their study, they showed that it was feasible to identify the discourse function of news paragraphs using a support vector machine (SVM) model and a small set of simple linguistic features, with a performance of 0.54 F_1.

Similar to Yarlott et al.'s (2018) approach, we demonstrate an improved approach to automatically labeling news article paragraphs with the van Dijk discourse functions Yarlott et al. (2018) applied in their study. Our work uses a conditional random field (CRF) model, along with new features, to obtain an improved performance of 0.71 F_1. Most importantly, our model is able to precisely capture the interdependencies between the various discourse label types, which flows from our hypothesis that each paragraph in an article is dependent not only on the previous one but rather on a longer sequence of previous paragraphs.

The remainder of this paper is structured as follows. We first provide a definition of van Dijk's theory as was presented in (Yarlott et al., 2018) (§2). Second, we describe the dataset we used in training and testing our CRF model (§3). We then detail the discourse label identification methods, including the CRF model and how it captures both section ordering and section content, how the model is trained, and the features it leverages (§4). We next compare the performance of the CRF model with various baselines, demonstrating that it performs better than prior models (§5). We then discuss related work (§6), and conclude with a summary of contributions (§7).

2 Van Dijk's Theory of News Discourse

Van Dijk (1988) described a hierarchical theory of news discourse, the categories of which are shown in Figure 1, which we apply to a subset of the news articles of the ACE Phase 2 corpus. In this section,

Proceedings of the 1st Joint Workshop on Narrative Understanding, Storylines, and Events, pages 17–25
July 9, 2020. ©2020 Association for Computational Linguistics

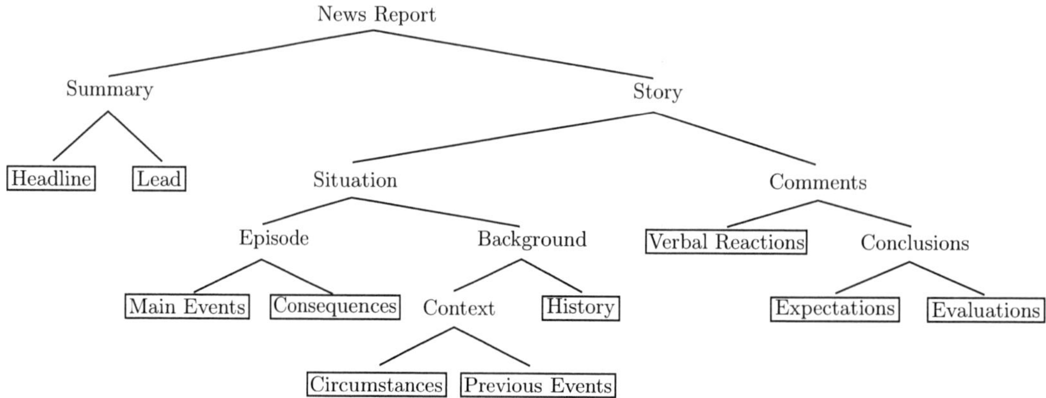

Figure 1: The hierarchical discourse structure of news proposed by van Dijk (van Dijk, 1988). Boxes indicate labels that were directly annotated on the documents; other labels can be inferred. From Yarlott et al. (2018), Figure 1.

we repeat our descriptions of the leaf categories from our prior paper, as well as their parent categories when appropriate, for ease of reference.

SUMMARY elements express the major subject of the article, with the HEADLINE being the actual headline of the article, and the LEAD being the first sentence, which is often a summary of the main events of the article.

SITUATION elements are the actual events that comprise the major subject of the article. EPISODES concern MAIN EVENTS, which are those events that directly relate to the major subject of the article, and the CONSEQUENCES of those events. The BACKGROUND provides important information about the relation of each paragraph with respect to the central events of a news story. Background includes the CONTEXT, of which CIRCUMSTANCES are temporally or spatially non-specific states that contribute to understanding the subject, while PREVIOUS EVENTS are specific recent events that enhance understanding of the main events. HISTORY paragraphs are another type of Background describing events that have not occurred recently, typically referenced in terms of years prior, rather than months, weeks, or days.

COMMENTS provide further supporting context for the central events of an article. Comments may include VERBAL REACTIONS solicited from an external source, such as a person involved in the events, or an expert. CONCLUSIONS, by contrast, are comments made by a journalistic entity (the newspaper, reporter, etc.) regarding the subject. Conclusions can be separated into EXPECTATIONS about the resolution or consequences of an event, or EVALUATIONS of the current situation.

3 Dataset

We used a gold-standard corpus previously developed by Yarlott et al. (2018) of van Dijk's labels applied to a subset of the Automated Content Extraction (ACE) Phase 2 corpus (NIST, 2002). The ACE Phase 2 corpus is a major standard corpora of news articles that boasts three advantages: it is widely-used, has relevance to other tasks, and was readily available to researchers. This dataset comprises 50 documents containing 28,236 words divided in 644 paragraphs.Table 1 shows the corpus-wide statistics for the number of words and paragraphs, where each paragraph is given a single type in accordance to van Dijk's theory.

	Words	Paragraphs
Total	28,236	644
Average	564.7	12.9
Std. Dev.	322.1	4.9

Table 1: Corpus-wide statistics for the annotated data. Adapted from Yarlott et al. (2018), Table 1.

Yarlott et al. (2018) doubly annotated 50 randomly selected news articles, divided into ten sets of five documents each. Within these sets, documents were swapped or replaced in order to obtain uniform sets in terms of total document lengths. The majority of texts were already divided into paragraphs in an obvious manner, either with empty lines or with indentation. The remaining texts were divided by the adjudicator based on either contextual or structural clues, such as abrupt change in topic or unnatural line breaks. The authors report an all-around high agreement with the gold standard ($F_1 = 0.85$, $\kappa = 0.75$) which demonstrates that the gold-standard was not dominated by a single annotator.

Although the dataset discussed was annotated for all labels discussed here, the HEADLINE label could be computed automatically from the structure of ACE Phase 2 corpus, as the files has the headline separate as part of its markup scheme.

Table 2 provides the resulting distribution of van Dijk's labels. Verbal reactions and circumstances dominate the labels. Although the distribution of labels is highly skewed, we find that this is roughly in-line with the style of reporting featured in the ACE Phase 2 corpus, which seeks comments and analysis from experts within the field as well as explaining the immediate context that has an effect on the main event.

Label	Count	Label	Count
HEADLINE	50	LEAD	42
MAIN EVENTS	60	CONSEQUENCES	19
CIRCUMSTANCES	103	PREVIOUS EVENTS	64
HISTORY	27	VERBAL REACTIONS	252
EXPECTATIONS	21	EVALUATIONS	56

Table 2: Distribution of the labels within the annotated corpus, with 644 labels total. The majority of paragraphs fall under the categories of verbal reactions or circumstances. From (Yarlott et al., 2018)

4 Identifying Discourse Labels

In contrast to the approach reported by (Yarlott et al., 2018), we the treated label identification for paragraphs as a sequence modeling task. Formally, the task is as follows: given a news report with n discourse labels and m paragraphs, where the paragraphs are unlabeled, identify the optimal sequence (order) of discourse labels $H^* = (L_1^*, \ldots, L_n^*)$ from among all possible label sequences, and assign every paragraph a discourse label $H^* = (H_1, \ldots, H_m)$ consistent with L^*. Sequence labeling problems in NLP, medical informatics, and discourse parsing have been studied by both generative and discriminative approaches, including Hidden Markov Models (HMMs; generative) and Conditional Random Fields (CRFs; discriminative). Li et al. (2010) used HMM and n-gram models to detect the orders or labels of

sections within clinical reports, while modeling the observation probabilities at the section level. Sherman and Liu (2008) used HMMs as well as n-gram models to detect topic shifts in meeting minutes, and, in contrast to Li et al., modeled the observation probabilities on the sentence level.

Our approach was inspired by the method described in Banisakher et al. (2018) which identifies section labels in clinical psychiatric reports. Their approach combined a *Hierarchical* Hidden Markov Model (HHMM)—which used section statistics as the model's transition probabilities—with n-grams for the observation probabilities of words. In this paper we substitute a CRF for the HHMM. Generative models such as HMMs have more explanatory power when compared with their discriminative counterparts such as CRFs. However, HMMs, rely on the assumption that observations are statistically independent from one another. For our problem, this means that an HMM assumes that the presence of certain paragraphs corresponding to a certain discourse label or function A is independent from other paragraphs within another section B. In practice, however, this is not the case: for example a paragraph following the MAIN EVENTS are often either CONSEQUENCES or CIRCUMSTANCES.

4.1 Linear Chain Conditional Random Fields

Conditional Random Fields (CRFs) are undirected graphical models (Lafferty et al., 2001; Konkol and Konopík, 2013) that can be used for discriminative sequence labeling. CRFs have proved useful for many sequence labeling problems in NLP and computer vision (Lin and Wu, 2009), including Named Entity Recognition (NER) and image classification. There are several CRF variations such as the tree CRF and the hierarchical CRF which are mostly used for computer vision related tasks.

We built and trained a linear chain CRF modeled on Banisakher et al.'s HHMM approach. In contrast to an HHMM, the CRF encodes labels as nodes in the CRF graphical representation (instead of HMM states), and uses weighted feature functions for transitions between nodes (instead of the HMM transition and emission probabilities). Additionally, the CRF model captures the "true" desired probability distribution, that is the *conditional distribution* of labels given the observations $P(Y|X)$, instead of modeling the joint distribution of observations and labels $P(X, Y)$. This a known advantage of CRFs in general over HMMs and is mainly due to, again, removing the independence assumption. Thus, CRFs can have an arbitrary number of dependencies as opposed to the limited dependency structure of HMMs. Our model benefits from this as it does not only record the dependence of a discourse label only on its predecessor and observations, but on additional dependencies given the entire sequence of labels (i.e., paragraph discourse functions) and observations (i.e., paragraphs).

The CRF probability distribution is defined by Equation 1. Let $\bar{l}$ be the sequence of discourse labels, $\bar{p}$ be the sequence of paragraphs (i.e., the observations) in a given report, and L be the set of all possible label sequences. Our model follows a typical linear chain CRF where the conditional distribution is:

$$P(\bar{l}|\bar{p},\lambda) = \frac{\exp(\sum_i \sum_j \lambda_j F_j(l_{i-1},l_i,\bar{p},i))}{\sum_{l' \in L} \exp(\sum_i \sum_j \lambda_j F_j(l'_{i-1},l'_i,\bar{p},i))} \quad (1)$$

where λ is a set of model parameters, and each λ_j is a weight associated with each feature function F_j. Each feature function represents a dependency within the model. We used the L-BFGS method to estimate each λ_j (Nocedal, 1980). The model's probability distribution is thus generated by summing over the entire observation sequence, where each observation is indexed by the variable i and the entire feature function space index by the variable j. The denominator sums over all possible label sequences L.

The most critical component in the design of CRF models is the feature function space. In our model, each feature function is:

$$\begin{aligned} F_j(l_{i-1}, l_i, \bar{p}, i) = \\ H_j(l_{i-1}, l_i, \bar{p}, i) \cdot SF_j(l_{i-1}, l_i, \bar{p}, i) \end{aligned} \quad (2)$$

where H_j models the discourse labels' order, and SF_j models the labels' content. These are similar to an HMM's transition and emission probability distributions, respectively. In contrast to HMMs, however, the feature functions are evaluated over the entire observation sequence $\bar{p}$ taking into account the neighboring labels l_i and l_{i-1}. This conditions the probability of a given discourse label type on the content and order of the entire sequence. We outline the intuition behind and implementation of our feature functions in the following sections.

4.2 Modeling the Discourse Labels' Order

The feature function F_j incorporates section ordering through the section ordering function $H(l_{i-1}, l_i, \bar{p}, i)$. As discussed above, there is a feature function for each of the dependencies defined in the model. We encode the interdependent order of labels (i.e., which labels depend upon each other) using a binary matrix. To achieve this, we first used the van Dijk discourse labels shown in Tables 2 and discussed in §2. Then we created a binary matrix V_{l_{i-1},l_i} whose entries represent whether a label follows another or not. For example if label HISTORY (indexed as label 6) was observed in the data directly before VERBAL REACTIONS (indexed as label 7), then the entry $V_{6,7}$ would contain a value of 1. The matrix contained N^2 entries, where N is the total number of labels. Thus our CRF models contained 9 nodes in total. We formulated the section order feature function as follows:

$$H_j(l_{i-1}, l_i, \bar{s}, i) = V_{l_{i-1},l_i} \quad (3)$$

Note that for each label s_i, the model sums the total entries for the entire sequence of labels and observations as shown in Equation 1, thus conditioning each label on the entire sequence.

4.3 Modeling the Discourse Labels' Content

Similarly, the feature function F_j incorporates the discourse label type content via the feature function $SF(l_{i-1}, l_i, \bar{p}, i)$. These functions model the dependency between a label type and its content. Importantly, the feature function should not be confused with the linguistic features that are extracted from the text and input into the section feature function. To capture label content (i.e., to model discourse label type-specific language) we extracted the following set of features:

Features from Yarlott et al. (2018): *Unigrams* (i.e., bag of words), the *tf-idf* count vector of the top 3 words (across the corpus) per label type, bag-of-words, and *paragraph vectors* using the Doc2Vec approach (Le and Mikolov, 2014). As pointed out by Yarlott et al., the *tf-idf* and *paragraph vectors* approximate topics within a given paragraph. Yarlott et al. also used the previous paragraph's label as an explicit feature; this is included by default in the CRF model.

Lexical: *Bigrams* to capture the type of language per discourse label type.

Positional: *Size of paragraphs* represented by number sentences present. As well as the *paragraph position* relative to the document head.

Syntactic: A *POS count vector* which encodes the number of times each part of speech (POS) (specifically, nouns, verbs, adjectives, and adverbs) appears in the paragraph.

Semantic: Here we incorporated four additional features: a *reported speech* feature, a *majority event tense* feature, a *subevent relation* count vector, and *NER vectors* representing a select set of named entities. For the *reported speech* feature, we extracted quotations and sentences with tagged as reported speech by the `textacy` library (DeWilde, 2020) and labeled the containing paragraph as VERBAL REACTIONS. For the *majority event tense* feature, we extracted the events in each paragraph using the CAEVO event extraction system (Chambers et al., 2014), noted their POS tags using a dependency tree, and recorded the majority verb tense in that paragraph. For the *subevent relation* feature, we used Aldawsari and Finlayson's subevent extraction system (2019) to capture relationships between paragraphs. For this, we used a vector for each paragraph corresponding to the number of paragraphs of the article with the maximum number of paragraphs in the corpus. Aldawsari and Finlayson (2019) presented a supervised model for automatically identifying when one event is a subevent of another using narrative and discourse features. For each event relation found by this system between two distinct paragraphs, we recorded a +1 in that corresponding vector cell, while we discarded relationships found within a single paragraph. For the *NER vectors*, we applied Named Entity Recognition (NER) and extracted the first 13 named entity types found by the Spacy library (AI, 2020) including PERSON, LOCATION, DATE, and TIME. These 13 types were represented in a numerical vector for each discourse label type such that, for each type, we recorded the number of entity occurrences.

4.4 Inference

We applied the usual inference process for linear chain CRFs operating at the paragraph level (Forney, 1973). Inference in linear chain CRFs follows a similar algorithm to Viterbi, which is used in decoding HMM models. While not stated explicitly in the Equation 1 above, the normalization factor $Z(S)$ is calculated as is often done using the Gaussian prior as it was introduced in (Chen and Rosenfeld, 1999).

5   Results and Discussion

In order to test our model, we randomly split each corpus into training and testing sets in a cross-validation setup, using five folds, resulting in 40 news reports for training and 10 for testing in each fold. Our model was trained to learn a total of 9 distinct discourse label types as represented in 2 (all leaf labels minus HEADLINE). In this section we describe our baseline comparisons and overall experiments and results.

5.1   Baseline Methods

We followed Yarlott et al. (2018) in their baseline comparisons. We compared our model's performance against five other methods: two baselines including the most frequent class (MFC) and a support vector machine using bag-of-words (SVM+BoW); third, a decision tree classifier; fourth, a random forest classifier; and fifth, Yarlott et al. (2018)'s best performing model, a support vector machine. As described above, the latter three models incorporate a the following set of four features: bag-of-words, *tf-idf*, paragraph vectors, and previous paragraph labels. We used the same experimental setup for all of these models. Yarlott et al. (2018) obtained the best experimental results using grid search to maximize the micro-averaged performance of each classifier, as measured across five folds. Following Yarlott et al. (2018), the SVM classifier uses a linear kernel with $C = 10$ and the class weights balanced based on the training data; the decision tree classifier uses the default parameters with the class weights balanced; the random forest uses 50 estimators with balanced class weights.

5.2   Results

Our CRF model outperformed all other classifiers and baselines achieving a 0.71 F_1 score. Table 3 shows the micro-averaged precision (P), recall (R), and F_1 scores for the five models from (Yarlott et al., 2018) as well as our current CRF approach. Our experimental results show that our CRF approach is a substantial improvement over the previously best performing model.

For CRF, we performed 8 feature combination experiments (shown in Table 3) to evaluate the effect of feature classes as well as the individual semantic features. As discussed before, the SVM as well as the decision tree and random forest classifiers only leveraged Yarlott et al.'s original four

Model	Features	P	R	F_1
MFC	-	0.39	0.39	0.39
HHMM	Bigrams	0.42	0.45	0.43
SVM	BoW	0.46	0.46	0.46
DT	Yarlott et al.	0.41	0.41	0.41
RDF	Yarlott et al.	0.43	0.43	0.43
SVM	Yarlott et al.	0.54	0.54	0.54
CRF	Yarlott et al.	0.58	0.60	0.59
CRF	+Lexical	0.61	0.63	0.62
CRF	+Positional	0.62	0.66	0.64
CRF	+Syntactic	0.65	0.69	0.67
CRF	*+subevent relation*	0.65	0.0.70	0.67
CRF	*+majority event tense*	0.67	0.71	0.68
CRF	*+reported speech*	0.68	0.72	0.70
CRF	All (+Remaining Sem.)	0.69	0.73	**0.71**

Table 3: Experimental results for discourse label identification. All results are micro-averaged across instances, including precision (P), recall (R), and balanced F-measure (F_1). The Decision Tree, Random Forest, and SVM classifiers used the features outlined in (Yarlott et al., 2018). For the middle three lines of the CRF section, these indicate features groups added to the previous line's model. We present the results for the smenatic features individually. The CRF model in the last line (CRF with ALL features) includes all the features from the previous lines as well as all remaining semantic features.

features: bag-of-words, *tf-idf*, paragraph vectors, and previous paragraph labels. While our CRF approach uses a more sophisticated set of features leveraging additional syntactic and semantic features as outlined in 4.3. Most importantly, our model treats the problem as a sequence labeling task and therefore captures the sequential dependencies between the paragraphs as well as the labels within each report. This is evidenced by the CRF model that uses only Yarlott et al.'s features, which achieves a higher performance than the original SVM classifier.

Our CRF model achieved the largest increase in performance after adding the semantic features. This was expected: we anticipated a boost in performance on the VERBAL REACTIONS class given detection of reported speech, and a similar increase in performance on the MAIN EVENTS and PREVIOUS EVENTS classes given the addition of event and subevent features. Of the semantic features, the *reported speech* feature had the biggest impact on the model's performance as the verbal reactions section was predominant in the dataset. Here `textacy` performed quite well in automatically identifying reported speech as the model achieved a 0.91 F_1 score for the VERBAL REACTIONS class.

The *subevent relation* and *majority event tense* features improved the performance by about one point F_1 each, with the second contributing slightly more to the overall performance. The *majority event tense* feature contributed heavily to the PREVIOUS EVENTS and HISTORY, we suspect due to the relatively more frequent use of past tense verbs in paragraphs belonging to those classes. As discussed before, we used automated systems to detect events and subevent relations. Naturally, these systems do not boast a perfect performance and therefore error propagation is expected. Thus, we expect that our model can further achieve higher performance using more refined event detection solutions, as well as a larger corpus.

Table 4 presents the per-label results from our experiments. The relatively strong performance on CIRCUMSTANCES and VERBAL REACTIONS is not surprising, given their relative prevalence in our corpus. Similarly it is not surprising that we have low performance on labels that occur, on average, about once (or less) a document (HISTORY, EXPECTATIONS). However, these label types saw a significant performance boost in our model compared to the previous approaches as our features have captured more of their distinct language. For CONSEQUENCES HISTORY, EXPECTATIONS, and EVALUATIONS, the syntactic and positional features were most helpful. Similar to (Yarlott et al., 2018), we observe an unexpected–but not surprising–level of performance on LEAD paragraphs, given their relative scarcity in the dataset: we find that leads, with a single exception, occur once at the start of the document.

Again, similar to (Yarlott et al., 2018), we expected the tree-oriented methods—decision trees and random forests—to at least outperform the SVM classifier. However, this was not the case in practice and they were outperformed by one of the baselines. We believe that this partially attributed to the fact that these models did not leverage the full set of hierarchical labels in van Dijk's discourse theory: they were only presented with the leaf labels.

6   Related Work

There has been substantial work describing how the structure of news operates with regards to the chronology of real-world events. Much news follows an inverted chronology—called the inverted pyramid (Bell, 1998; Delin, 2000) or relevance

Label Type	F_1	Label Type	F_1
HEADLINE	-	LEAD	0.95
MAIN EVENTS	0.69	CONSEQUENCES	0.29
CIRCUMSTANCES	0.72	PREVIOUS EVENTS	0.51
HISTORY	0.24	VERBAL REACTIONS	0.91
EXPECTATIONS	0.26	EVALUATIONS	0.51
		Macro Average	0.56

Table 4: Per-label F_1 results. The last row shows the macro average over all label types. Best performance occurs for the LEAD, MAIN EVENTS, CIRCUMSTANCES, and VERBAL REACTIONS.

ordering (Van Dijk, 1986)—where the most important and typically the most recent events come first. Bell claims that *"news stories... are seldom if ever told in chronological order"* (Bell, 1994, p. 105), which is demonstrated by Rafiee et al. for both Western (Dutch) and non-Western (Iranian) news (2018). Rafiee et al. also show that many stories follow a hybrid structure, which combines characteristics from both inverted and chronological structures.

Our approach was inspired by Banisakher et al. (2018)'s HHMM approach to section identification in clinical notes. In turn, their work extend an earlier study on section identification of psychiatric evaluation reports that combined the work of Li et al. (2010) on identifying section types within clinical reports and that of Sherman and Liu (2008) on text segmentation of meeting minutes. Li et al. modeled HMM emissions at the section level using bigrams, while Sherman and Liu modeled the emissions at the sentence level and used unigrams and trigrams. Other approaches followed similar strategies in segmenting story text and in creating generative models for detecting story boundaries (Mulbregt et al., 1998; Yamron et al., 1998). More recently, Yu et al. (2016) used a hybrid deep neural network combined with a Hidden Markov Model (DNN-HMM) to segment speech transcripts from broadcast news to a sequence of stories. Similar to our approach, (Sprugnoli et al., 2017) used CRFs and SVMs for the classification of automatic classification of Content Types, a novel task that was introduced to provide cues to access the structure of a document's types of functional content.

Discussing van Dijk's theory of news discourse, Bekalu stated that analysis of *"the processes involved in the production of news discourses and their structures will ultimately derive their relevance from our insights into the consequences, ef-fects, or functions for readers in different social contexts, which obviously leads us to a consideration of news comprehension"* (2006, p. 150). The theory proposed by van Dijk has also been proposed for use in annotating the global structure of elementary discourse units in Dutch news articles (van der Vliet et al., 2011).

Pan and Kosicki (1993), in a similar analysis, presented a framing-based approach that provides four structural dimensions for the analysis of news discourse: syntactic structure, script structure, thematic structure, and rhetorical structure. Of these, the syntactic structure is most closely aligned with van Dijk's theory. In this paper, we chose to focus on van Dijk's theory as Pan and Kosicki do not provide a list or description of the structure that could be readily translated into an annotation scheme.

While White (1998) treats the structure of news as being centered around the headline and lead. White suggests that the headline and lead, which act as a combination of both synopsis and abstract for the news story, serve as the nucleus for the rest of the text: *"the body which follows the headline/lead nucleus—acts to specify the meanings presented in the opening headline/lead nucleus through elaboration, contextualisation, explanation, and appraisal"* (1998, p. 275). We focus on van Dijk's theory for this paper as we find it to provide a higher degree of specificity: White's specification modes serve roughly the same purpose as higher-level groupings in van Dijk's theory.

7   Contributions

We extend earlier work on news paragraph discourse function labeling. We built a linear chain CRF model incorporating various lexical, positional, syntactic, and semantic features that improves detection of the order of discourse labels in a news article at the paragraph level as well as models the paragraph content of each label type. We evaluated our model's performance against two baselines and three existing models with various subsets of features. We showed that the CRF model represents a significant improvement in this task. Most importantly, our work demonstrated the importance of modeling paragraph and discourse label type inter-dependencies.

Acknowledgments

Mr. Banisakher was supported by a Dissertation Year Fellowship from FIU. Mr. Yarlott was supported by DARPA Contract FA8650-19-C-6017. Mr. Aldawsari was supported by a doctoral fellowship from Prince Sattam Bin Abdulaziz University, and thanks Dr. Sultan Aldossary for his advice and support. Dr. Finlayson was partially supported by NSF Grant IIS-1749917.

References

Explosion AI. 2020. Annotation Specifications-SpaCy API Documentation.

Mohammed Aldawsari and Mark Finlayson. 2019. Detecting Subevents using Discourse and Narrative Features. In *Proceedings of the 57th Annual Meeting of the Association for Computational Linguistics*, pages 4780–4790, Florence, Italy. Association for Computational Linguistics.

Deya Banisakher, Naphtali Rishe, and Mark A. Finlayson. 2018. Automatically Detecting the Position and Type of Psychiatric Evaluation Report Sections. In *Proceedings of the Ninth International Workshop on Health Text Mining and Information Analysis*, pages 101–110, Brussels, Belgium. Association for Computational Linguistics.

Mesfin Awoke Bekalu. 2006. Presupposition In News Discourse. *Discourse & Society*, 17(2):147–172.

Allan Bell. 1994. Telling stories. In David Graddol and Oliver Boyd-Barrett, editors, *Media texts: Authors and readers*, pages 100–118. Multilingual Matters, Clevedon, U.K.

Allan Bell. 1998. The Discourse Structure of News Stories. In *Approaches to Media Discourse*, pages 64–104. Blackwell Oxford.

Nathanael Chambers, Taylor Cassidy, Bill McDowell, and Steven Bethard. 2014. Dense Event Ordering with a Multi-Pass Architecture. *Transactions of the Association for Computational Linguistics*, 2:273–284.

Stanley F Chen and Ronald Rosenfeld. 1999. A Gaussian Prior for Smoothing Maximum Entropy Models. Technical report, Carnegie-Mellon University, School of Computer Science, Pittsburgh, Pennsylvania, USA.

Judy Delin. 2000. *The Language of Everyday Life: An Introduction*. Sage, London, UK.

Burton DeWilde. 2020. textacy.

Teun A van Dijk. 1988. *News as Discourse*, chapter Structure of News. Lawrence Erlbaum Associates, Inc., Hillsdale, New Jersey, USA.

G.D. Forney. 1973. The Viterbi Algorithm. *Proceedings of the IEEE*, 61(3):268–278.

Michal Konkol and Miloslav Konopík. 2013. CRF-Based Czech named Entity Recognizer and Consolidation of Czech NER Research. In *Text, Speech, and Dialogue*, pages 153–160, Berlin, Heidelberg. Springer Berlin Heidelberg.

John D. Lafferty, Andrew McCallum, and Fernando C. N. Pereira. 2001. Conditional Random Fields: Probabilistic Models for Segmenting and Labeling Sequence Data. In *Proceedings of the Eighteenth International Conference on Machine Learning*, ICML '01, page 282–289, San Francisco, CA, USA. Morgan Kaufmann Publishers Inc.

Quoc Le and Tomas Mikolov. 2014. Distributed Representations of Sentences and Documents. In *Proceedings of the 31st International Conference on Machine Learning*, pages 1188–1196, Beijing, China.

Ying Li, Sharon Lipsky Gorman, and Noémie Elhadad. 2010. Section Classification in Clinical Notes Using Supervised Hidden Markov Model. In *Proceedings of the 1st ACM International Health Informatics Symposium IHI*, pages 744–750, Arlington, Virgina, USA.

Dekang Lin and Xiaoyun Wu. 2009. Phrase Clustering for Discriminative Learning. In *Proceedings of the Joint Conference of the 47th Annual Meeting of the ACL and the 4th International Joint Conference on Natural Language Processing of the AFNLP*, pages 1030–1038, Suntec, Singapore. Association for Computational Linguistics.

Paul van Mulbregt, Ira Carp, Lawrence Gillick, Steve Lowe, and Jon Yamron. 1998. Text Segmentation and Topic Tracking on Broadcast News Via a Hidden Markov Model Approach. In *Fifth International Conference on Spoken Language Processing*, ICSLP '98, Sydney, Australia.

NIST. 2002. Ace phase 2.

Jorge Nocedal. 1980. Updating Quasi-Newton Matrices with Limited Storage. *Mathematics of computation*, 35(151):773–782.

Zhongdang Pan and Gerald M Kosicki. 1993. Framing Analysis: An Approach to News Discourse. *Political Communication*, 10(1):55–75.

Afrooz Rafiee, Wilbert Spooren, and José Sanders. 2018. Culture and Discourse Structure: A Comparative Study of Dutch and Iranian News Texts. *Discourse & Communication*, 12(1):58–79.

M. Sherman and Yang Liu. 2008. Using Hidden Markov Models for Topic Segmentation of Meeting Transcripts. In *Proceedings of the 2008 IEEE Spoken Language Technology Workshop*, pages 185–188, Goa, India.

Rachele Sprugnoli, Tommaso Caselli, Sara Tonelli, and Giovanni Moretti. 2017. The content types dataset: a new resource to explore semantic and functional characteristics of texts. In *Proceedings of the 15th*

Conference of the European Chapter of the Association for Computational Linguistics: Volume 2, Short Papers*, pages 260–266, Valencia, Spain. Association for Computational Linguistics.

Teun A Van Dijk. 1986. *Studying Writing: Linguistic Approaches. Written Communication Annual: An International Survey of Research and Theory Series, Volume 1.*, chapter News Schemata. Sage, Beverly Hills, California, USA.

Nynke van der Vliet, Ildikó Berzlánovich, Gosse Bouma, Markus Egg, and Gisela Redeker. 2011. Building a Discourse-Annotated Dutch Text Corpus. *Bochumer Linguistische Arbeitsberichte*, 3:157–171.

Peter R White. 1998. *Telling Media Tales: The News Story as Rhetoric*. Department of Linguistics, Faculty of Arts, University of Sydney, Sydney, Australia.

J. P. Yamron, I. Carp, L. Gillick, S. Lowe, and P. van Mulbregt. 1998. A Hidden Mrkov Model Approach to Text Segmentation and Event Tracking. In *Proceedings of the 1998 IEEE International Conference on Acoustics, Speech and Signal Processing*, ICASSP '98, pages 333–336 vol.1, Seattle, Washington, USA.

W. Victor Yarlott, Cristina Cornelio, Tian Gao, and Mark Finlayson. 2018. Identifying the discourse function of news article paragraphs. In *Proceedings of the Workshop Events and Stories in the News 2018*, pages 25–33, Santa Fe, New Mexico, USA. Association for Computational Linguistics.

Jia Yu, Xiong Xiao, Lei Xie, Chng Eng Siong, and Haizhou Li. 2016. A DNN-HMM Approach to Story Segmentation. In *INTERSPEECH 2016*, San Francisco, California, USA.

Systematic Evaluation of a Framework for Unsupervised
Emotion Recognition for Narrative Text

Samira Zad & Mark A. Finlayson
School of Computing and Information Sciences
Florida International University
11200 SW 8th St., Miami, FL 33199, USA
{szad001,markaf}@fiu.edu

Abstract

Identifying emotions as expressed in text (a.k.a. text emotion recognition) has received a lot of attention over the past decade. Narratives often involve a great deal of emotional expression, and so emotion recognition on narrative text is of great interest to computational approaches to narrative understanding. Prior work by Kim et al. (2010) was the work with the highest reported emotion detection performance, on a corpus of fairy tales texts. Close inspection of that work, however, revealed significant reproducibility problems, and we were unable to reimplement Kim's approach as described. As a consequence, we implemented a framework inspired by Kim's approach, where we carefully evaluated the major design choices. We identify the highest-performing combination, which outperforms Kim's reported performance by 7.6 F_1 points on average. Close inspection of the annotated data revealed numerous missing and incorrect emotion terms in the relevant lexicon, Word-NetAffect (WNA; Strapparava and Valitutti, 2004), which allowed us to augment it in a useful way. More generally, this showed that numerous clearly emotive words and phrases are missing from WNA, which suggests that effort invested in augmenting or refining emotion ontologies could be useful for improving the performance of emotion recognition systems. We release our code and data to definitely enable future reproducibility of this work.

1 Introduction

Emotion is a primary aspect of communication, and can be transmitted across many modalities including gesture, facial expressions, speech, and text. Because of this importance, automatic emotion recognition is useful for many applications, including for automated narrative understanding. A narrative is "a representation of connected events and characters that has an identifiable structure, is bounded in space and time, and contains implicit or explicit messages about the topic being addressed" (Kreuter et al., 2007, p. 222), and narratives are often used to express the emotions of authors and characters, as well as induce emotions in audiences. For many narratives—one need only consider romances such as *Romeo and Juliet* or the movie *Titanic*—it is no exaggeration to say that lacking an understanding of emotion leads to a seriously impoverished view of the meaning of the narrative.

Emotion recognition is a challenging problem on account of the complex relationship between felt emotion and linguistic expression. This includes not only standard natural language processing challenges, such as polysemous words and the difficulty of coreference resolution (Uzuner et al., 2012; Peng et al., 2019), but also emotion-specific challenges such as how context can subtly change emotional interpretations (Cowie et al., 2005). These technical challenges are exacerbated by a shortage of quality labeled data addressing this task.

There has been much prior work on emotion recognition. With regard to narrative specifically, Kim et al. (2010) reported a high-performing approach to emotion recognition on a corpus of fairy tales texts (Alm, 2008). This approach involved an unsupervised learning framework for emotion recognition in textual data, using a modified form of Ekman's psychological theory of emotion (joy, anger, fear, sadness; Ekman, 1992b). In that work, they used the WordNetAffect (WNA) and ANEW (Affective Norm for English Words) emotion lexicons to construct a semantic space. Each sentence is placed in the space using *tf-idf* weights for emotion words found in the lexicons. They then tested three methods—Non-negative Matrix Factorization (NMF), Latent Semantic Analysis (LSA), probablistic Latent Semantic Analysis (pLSA)—for compressing the space to extract features of the constructed vector space model, reduce noise,

Proceedings of the 1st Joint Workshop on Narrative Understanding, Storylines, and Events, pages 26–37
July 9, 2020. ©2020 Association for Computational Linguistics

and eliminate outliers. Finally, the framework used cosine-similarity to label sentences by evaluating how similar they are compared to standard vectors generated based on WNA entries strongly associated with emotion lexicon (more specifically an extension of WNA). The best performing method was NMF, which they reported achieved an average emotion recognition F_1 of 0.733.

Close inspection of the work, however, revealed significant reproducibility problems. Despite our best efforts we were unable to reproduce results anywhere near Kim's reported performance; indeed, our best attempt yielded only roughly 0.25 F_1. This was due to several reasons. First, the paper lacked information on model hyper-parameters. Second, the paper omitted descriptions of key NMF steps, including how to identify representative features and what features should be removed before semantic space compression. Third, the paper did not explain how to adapt NMF to deal with the sparse matrices that occur in textual NMF models. Fourth, certain resources associated with WNA either were not correctly identified, or are no longer available. These omissions prevented us from reproducing their models to any degree of accuracy.

Therefore, we undertook to do a systematic exploration of the design space described in Kim et al. (2010). We examined the highest performing vector space compression techniques reported by Kim *et al.* (NMF), as well as Principle Component Analysis (PCA) and Latent Dirchelet Allocation (LDA) which were reported as high-performing techniques in other work. We show that NMF indeed performs the best, and we clearly explain our experimental setup including methods for identifying relevant features and handling sparse text matrices. The PCA and NMF methods implemented in this paper are based on the works of Mairal et al. (2009) and Boutsidis and Gallopoulos (2008) respectively which have implemented mechanisms that works for a large sparse matrix (in our case, $1,090 \times 2,405$). This work resulted in an improvement of performance of roughly 7.6 points of F_1 over Kim's reported results. We release our code and data to facilitate future work[1].

The rest of this paper is structured as follows. We briefly review psychological models of emotions, describe several key emotion language resources, and outline a number of well-known emotion recognition models (§2). We then describe our adapted unsupervised emotion recognition method, giving detailed descriptions of all steps, parameters, and resources needed (§3). We next describe the performance of our method on Alm's corpus of fairy tales (Alm, 2008), which was annotated for emotion on a per-sentence level (§4). Finally, we identify some unsolved challenges that point toward future work (§5), and summarize our contributions (§6).

2   Related Work

2.1   Psychological emotion theories

Theories of emotion go back to the ancient Greeks and Romans, and have been a recurring theme of inquiries into the nature of the human experience throughout history, including famous proposals by Charles Darwin and William James in the 19th century (Darwin and Prodger, 1998; James, 1890). Modern psychological theories of emotion may be grouped into two types: *categorical* and *dimensional* (Calvo and Mac Kim, 2013). Categorical psychological models propose discrete basic emotions, e.g., Oatley and Johnson-Laird's (1987) with five basic emotions, several models with six basic emotions (Ekman, 1992b; Shaver et al., 1987), Parrott's model of six basic emotions arranged in a three-level tree (2001), Panksepp's model with seven emotions (1998), and Izard's with ten (2007).

Dimensional psychological models, by contrast, determine emotions by locating them in a space of dimensions (usually two to four) that might include arousal, valence, intensity, etc. These include two dimensional models such as Russell's circumplex model (1980), Scherer's augmented circumplex (2005), and Whissell's model (Cambria, 2016). Lövheim's model (2012) is an example that uses three dimensions, while Ortony et al. (1990), Fontaine et al. (2007), and Cambria et al. (2012) proposed four-dimensional models.

Finally, there are also models which combine both categorical and dimensional aspects, called *hybrid* models, the most prominent of which is Plutchik's wheel and cone model with eight basic emotions (Plutchik, 1980, 1984, 2001).

Of all the many emotion models that have been proposed, Ekman's 6 category model (anger, disgust, fear, happiness, sadness, surprise) is by far the most popular in computational approaches, partly because of its simplicity, and partly because it has been successfully applied to automatic facial emo-

---

[1]Code and data may be downloaded from https://doi.org/10.34703/gzx1-9v95/03RERQ

tion recognition (Zhang et al., 2018; Suttles and Ide, 2013; Ekman, 1992b,a, 1993). This is despite that some researchers have doubts that Ekman's model is complete, as it seems to embed a Western cultural bias (Langroudi et al., 2018). In our own review of emotion recognition systems, as discussed below, the highest performing system reported for narrative text was described by Kim et al. (2010). In that work, they used a four-label subset of Ekman's model (happiness, anger, fear, and sadness), and this is the model we adopt in this paper.

2.2 Emotion Lexicons

One of the key language resources for emotion recognition in text is an emotion lexicon, which is simply a list of words associated with emotion categories. Emotion lexicons can be used both in rule-based and machine-learning-based recognition methods. There are two types of emotion lexicons. One is general purpose emotion lexicons (GPELs) which specify the generic sense of emotional words. GPELs sometimes express emotions as a score, and can be applied to any domains. Prominent GPELs include WordNet Affect (WNA; Strapparava and Valitutti, 2004), the Wisconsin Perceptual Attribute Rating Database (WPARD; Medler et al., 2005), Linguistic Inquiry and Word Count (LIWC; Pennebaker et al., 2001), and the National Research Council (NRC) and NRC Hashtag lexicons (Mohammad and Turney, 2010; Mohammad et al., 2013). The second type of lexicon are domain specific emotion lexicons (DSELs) which are targeted at specific domains for emotion recognition. Bandhakavi et al. (2014), for example, proposes a domain-specific lexicon for emotional tweets. Table 1 compares the details of several key GPELs.

WordNet Affect Version 1.1 Kim et al. used WordNet Affect (WNA; Strapparava and Valitutti, 2004), which builds upon the general WordNet database (Fellbaum, 1998). WNA classifies 280 WordNet *Noun* synsets into an emotion hierarchy rooted in an augmented version of Ekman's basic emotions, and partially depicted in Figure 1. WordNet links an additional 1,191 *Verb*, *Adverb*, and *Adjective* synsets to this core *Noun*-focused hierarchy. These synsets represent approximately 3,500 English lemma-POS pairs.

2.3 Emotion Recognition Approaches

There have been at least one hundred papers describing approaches to emotion recognition in text

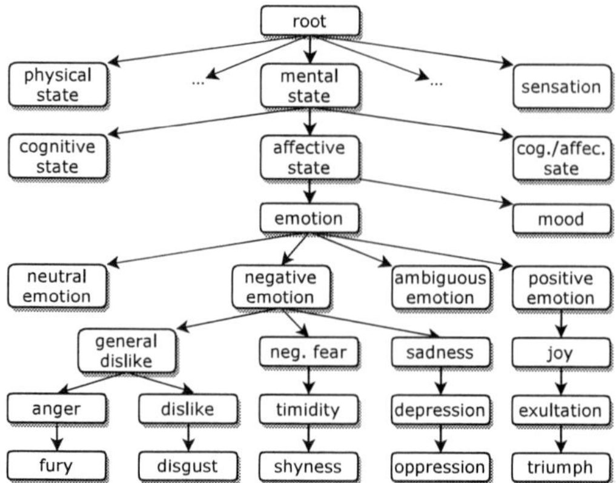

Figure 1: Hierarchy of emotions in WordNet Affect Version 1.1.

(Calefato et al., 2017; Teng et al., 2007; Shaheen et al., 2014). Here we review a selection of approaches that have been applied to narrative-like or narrative-related discourse types. It is important to remember that all of these approaches use different data and different theories, often involving different numbers of labels. All things being equal, classification results usually degrade as the number labels increases; therefore the performance of each system can only be loosely compared.

Strapparava and Mihalcea (2008) described a system for recognizing emotions in news headlines. They extracted 1,250 news headlines from a variety of news websites (such as Google news, CNN, and online newspapers) and annotated them using Ekman's model—anger, disgust, fear, joy, sadness and surprise—splitting the data into a training set of 250 and a test set of 1,000 (this is called the *SemEval-2007* dataset). They tested five approaches: WNA-PRESENCE, LSA-SINGLE-WORD, LSA-EMOTION-SYNSET, LSA-ALL-EMOTION-WORDS, and NAIVEBAYES-TRAINED-ON-BLOGS. WNA-PRESENCE, which looked for headline words listed in WNA, provided the best precision at 0.38. The LSA-ALL-EMOTION-WORDS, which calculated the vector similarity between the six affect words and the LSA representation of the headline, led to the highest recall and F_1, at 0.90 and 0.176, respectively.

Aman and Szpakowicz (2008) used a Support Vector Machine (SVM) trained and tested on blog data for recognition Ekman's emotion classes, plus two additional classes: *mixed emotion*, and *no emotion*. Four human judges manually annotated 1,890 sentences from automatically retrieved blogs to cre-

Emotion Lexicons	Citation	Set of Emotions	Entries
WNA	Strapparava and Valitutti (2004)	A hierarchy of emotions	915 synsets
NRC / Emolex	Mohammad and Turney (2010)	Plutchik basic model 1980, neg./pos.	14,182
LIWC	Pennebaker et al. (2001)	Affective or not, neg./pos. anxiety, anger, sadness	5,690
NRC Hashtag	Mohammad et al. (2013)	Plutchik's basic model	32,400
WPARD	Medler et al. (2005)	Positive or negative	1,402
ANEW	Bradley and Lang (1999)	3D (valence, arousal,dominance)	1,035

Table 1: Emotion-related lexicons table. WNA= WordNet Affect; NRC= National Research Council in Canada; LIWC= Linguistic Inquiry and Word Count; WPARD= Wisconsin Perceptual Attribute Rating Database; ANEW= Affective Norms of English Words

ate the corpus. The features for the SVM were the presence of emotion words listed in Roget's thesaurus and WNA. F_1 measures for each emotion class ranged between 0.493 to 0.751, in each case surpass the baseline performance.

Tokuhisa et al. (2008) described a lexicon-based emotion recognition system for Japanese. They handcrafted emotion lexicon by identifying 349 emotion words from the Japanese Expression Evaluation (JEE) Dictionary classified into 10 different emotions: 3 positive (happiness, pleasantness, relief) and 7 negative (fear, sadness, disappointment, unpleasantness, loneliness, anxiety, and anger). They then used this lexicon to automatically assemble a labeled corpus of 1.3M emotion-provoking (EP) "events" (defined as a subordinate clauses which modifies an emotional statement). They then demonstrated a two-step method for emotion recognition, starting with SVM-based coarse sentiment polarity classification (positive, negative, or neutral) followed by kNN-based classification of non-neutral instances into the appropriate fine-grained emotion classes (3 for positive, 7 for negative). Their reported accuracies of between 0.5 and 0.8 for their best performing model.

Cherry et al. (2012) presented two supervised machine learning models for emotion recognition in suicide note sentences. They used the 2011 i2b2 NLP Challenge Task 2, which comprised 4,241 sentences in the training set, and 1,883 sentences in the test set, which were manually annotated with 13 emotion labels. A one-classifier-per-emotion approach yielded an F_1 of 0.55, while a latent sequence model that applied multiple emotion labels per sentence achieved an F_1 of 0.53. They noted that more than 73% of their training data lacked labels which limited the effectiveness of the training.

Bandhakavi et al. (2017) experimented with unigram mixture models (UMMs) for recognizing emotions in tweets, incident reports, news head-

lines, and blogs. Each corpus was manually annotated with different emotion theories: 280,000 tweets with Parrott's six primary emotions (Parrott, 2001), 1,250 news headlines and 5,500 blogs with Ekman's six emotion set, 7000 incident reports from the ISEAR dataset[2] labeled with a seven emotion set. One goal of the study was to compare the utility of domain-specific emotion lexicons with general purpose emotion lexicons (DSELs vs GPELs). They found that combining DSEL lexicon words with n-grams, part of speech tags, and additional words from sentiment lexicons yielded the highest performance of 0.60 F_1 on the blog data.

Kim et al. (2010) reported the highest performing emotion recognition system on narrative text. Among their data was a set of 176 fairy tales whose 15,087 sentences were labeled by Alm (2008) with a four-emotion subset of Ekman's theory (anger, fear, joy, and sadness). They demonstrated an unsupervised approach, where each sentence is transformed into a vector in a space of emotion words (drawn from WNA and ANEW), and then compressed using a dimension reduction technique (NMF, LSA, or pLSA). These vectors were then compared to reference vectors in the same space that were computed for each of the four emotions. They reported a performance of F_1 of 0.733 for NMF, which was their highest performing model. One advantage of this approach was that it is unsupervised, which means both that significant amounts of training data are not required and that all the annotated data can be used for testing. This is important because of the small size of the corpus on which the technique was tested.

3 Emotion Recognition Framework

We now describe an unsupervised system for emotion recognition modeled on that reported by Kim

---

[2] http://www.affective-sciences.org/researchmaterial

Citation	Corpus	Lexicon	# Emotions	Method	F_1
Kim et al. (2010)	Fairy tales	WNA	4	NMF	0.73
Bandhakavi et al. (2017)	Tweets	UMM+DSEL	6	Lexicon only	0.64
Aman and Szpakowicz (2008)	Blog	-	6	Unigrams	0.57
Cherry et al. (2012)	Suicide notes	-	15	SVM+LS	0.55
Strapparava and Mihalcea (2008)	Headlines	-	6	LSA	0.17
Tokuhisa et al. (2008)	"EP" Events	JEE Dict.	10	SVM+kNN	0.5–0.8 Acc.

Table 2: Emotion recognition approaches on narrative-like text, ordered by performance. LSA = Latent Semantic Analysis; LS = Latent sequence modeling

et al. (2010). While we follow the general pattern of that work, we experiment with a different set of dimension reduction methods (NMF from Lee and Seung, as well as PCA and LDA). The system takes as input the following items:

- A corpus containing n sentences $S : s_1, s_2, \ldots, s_n$;

- A set of emotions $E = \{e_1, e_2, \ldots, e_{l-1}, \text{neu-tral}\}$ for classifying emotions into l different classes, including neutral; and,

- An emotion lexicon $L : \Omega \mapsto E$ which maps each word in the corpus $\omega \in \Omega$ (where Ω has m terms) to an emotion $e \in E$. The word ω is in its lemmatized form and has a specific POS.

A flowchart of the system is shown in Figure 2. The system comprises four consecutive steps. In the first step, **pre-processing**, the system processes the input corpus using the CoreNLP library (Manning et al., 2014) to separate the text into sentences and lemmatized tokens. The second step, **vector space modeling**, uses the lemmatized tokens to generate a vector for each sentence in a vector space whose dimensions correspond to the items in Ω. In the third step, **noise cancellation or dimension reduction**, we explored three different models (Non-negative Matrix Factorization, Latent Dirichlet Allocation, and Principal Component Analysis) to either reduce dimensions or extract features of the vector space. One of our main contributions here is to analyze and explain the effect of this step on the performance of the final emotion recognition system. Finally, the fourth step, **labeling**, compares the vector for each sentence with vectors for each emotion, choosing the closest emotion as the label for the sentence.

Augmenting WNA As mentioned before, WNA 1.1 assigns an emotion label to 1,471 synonym sets (synsets) of WordNet. This corresponds to a lexicon of nearly 3,495 affective lemma-POS pairs. Careful inspection of WNA revealed both incor-

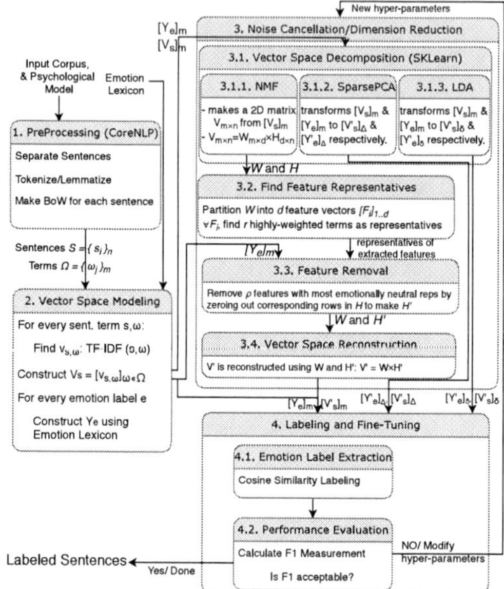

Figure 2: Flowchart of the proposed system. $[V_s]_m$ and $[Y_e]_m$ represent the original m-dimensional sentence and emotion vector model respectively, $[V'_s]_m$, $[V'_s]_\Delta$ and $[V'_s]_\delta$ denote the transformed sentence vector model using NMF, PCA and LDA techniques respectively. $[Y'_e]_\Delta$ and $[Y'_e]_\delta$ denote the transformed emotion vector model using PCA and LDA techniques respectively.

rectly included as well as missing pairs. For incorrectly included pairs, a substantial number were included because all their multiple senses were labeled by emotions related to a secondary affective sense, not their main non-affective sense. We manually reviewed and removed these incorrect labels. Additionally, we identified missing lemma-POS pairs with the help of closely related pairs already labeled by WNA. For example the pair *glorious-JJ* was missing from WNA, but is related (via the *derived-from* relation) to already labeled pair *glorify-VB*. We manually searched for these missing relationships, adding the missing terms, as well as recursively adding their synonyms (e.g.,

30

glorious-JJ resulted in *splendid, magnificent, brilliant,* and *superb* being added as well). In total, we removed 613 and added 814 labels of different lemma-POS pairs, resulting a final count of 4048 lemma-POS pairs.

In general, the technique of using a fixed lexicon of emotion terms to capture highly context-dependent emotional expressions is problematic at best. Although we show here that work on improving the lexicon does improve emotion recognition results, ultimately, any technique will have to move away from a rigid lexicon-based approach to something more flexible. We plan to explore such directions in future work.

Step 1: Pre-Processing

For each sentence $s \in S$ in the given corpus, we construct a bag of words by tokenizing the sentence and lemmatizing each word. We generate a count vector for BoW_s by mapping each lemma to the count in the sentence ($\Omega \mapsto \mathbb{Z}_{\geq 0}$). We do not remove stop words as their effects are minimized by the *tf-idf* computation in the next step.

Step 2: Vector Space Modeling

Using the count vectors constructed in the first step, we compute a *tf-idf* vector for each sentence as well as a standard vector for each emotion class $e \in E$. For each sentence $s_j \in S$, we construct an m dimensional vector where each entry in the vector is the *tf-idf* of term ω_i in sentence s_j; i.e.

$$v_{ij} = \text{TF}_{i,j} \times \text{IDF}_i \quad (1)$$

where $\text{TF}_{i,j} = \text{BoW}_{s_j}(\omega_i)$,

$$\text{IDF}_i = \log \frac{n}{|\{s \in S : BoW_s(\omega_i) > 0\}|}. \quad (2)$$

n is the number of sentences, and $\Omega = \{\omega_i\}_{i=1}^m$.

The constructed vector space model is represented by the following $m \times n$ matrix V:

$$V = [V_{s_1} V_{s_2} \ldots V_{s_n}] \text{ where } V_{s_j} = \begin{pmatrix} v_{1j} \\ v_{2j} \\ \vdots \\ v_{mj} \end{pmatrix} \quad (3)$$

We compute a standard vector for each emotion class $Y_e = (y_{e,\omega_1}, y_{e,\omega_2}, \ldots, y_{e,\omega_m})$ where y_{e,ω_i} is 1 if the term ω_i is mapped to e by the lexicon, otherwise 0.

Step 3: Noise Cancellation or Dimension Reduction

The vectors V_s and Y_e from the previous step are all m-dimensional vectors where m is the total number of terms in the corpus. There are many terms that have little or no effect on the emotion labeling of their sentences. Therefore, dimensional reduction or noise cancellation techniques may improve the performance of the emotion labeling step which comes later. Principle Component Analysis (PCA) has been known for quite some time for noise cancellation (Abdi and Williams, 2010), while Latent Dirichlet Allocation (LDA) was specifically developed for dimension reduction in natural language processing (Blei et al., 2003). Non-Negative Matrix Factorization (NMF) was first introduced for noise cancellation by Lee and Seung (1999).

Step 3.1: Vector Space Decomposition

We can decompose the obtained matrix V in one of the following three ways:

1. Non-negative Matrix Factorization (NMF): we extract d features from the m-dimensional vectors of sentences using NMF.

2. Principal Component Analysis (PCA): We reduce the number of dimensions of V_s vectors from m to $\Delta < m$.

3. Latent Dirichlet Allocation (LDA): We reduce the number of dimensions of V_s vectors from m to $\delta < m$.

When using PCA or LDA we can move directly to fourth step of the system; however, in the case of NMF, we must select important terms (Step 3.2), remove irrelevant features (Step 3.3), and reconstruct the vector space (Step 3.4).

When using NMF for decomposing the vector space model, V is factorized into two matrices $W_{m \times d} = [w_{ij}]$ and $H_{d \times n} = [h_{ij}]$, both with all non-negative entries:

$$V = W \times H \text{ s.t. } w_{ij} \geq 0 \text{ and } h_{ij} \geq 0 \quad (4)$$

Note that d is considered a hyper-parameter in this step and its numerical value can be fine-tuned by maximizing the output of the system on a development set.

The NMF factorization process produces a matrix W whose d columns each represents an m-dimensional feature for each of the original n sentences in the corpus:

$$V = [v_{ij}]_{m \times n} \qquad W = [w_{ij}]_{m \times d} \qquad H = [h_{ij}]_{d \times n}$$

$$
\begin{array}{c}
 \\
\\
t_1 \rightarrow \\
t_2 \rightarrow \\
\vdots \\
t_m \rightarrow
\end{array}
\begin{bmatrix}
v_{11} & v_{12} & \cdots & v_{1n} \\
v_{21} & v_{22} & \cdots & v_{2n} \\
\vdots & \vdots & \ddots & \vdots \\
v_{m1} & v_{m2} & \cdots & v_{mn}
\end{bmatrix}
=
\begin{bmatrix}
w_{11} & w_{12} & \cdots & w_{1d} \\
w_{21} & w_{22} & \cdots & w_{2d} \\
\vdots & \vdots & \ddots & \vdots \\
w_{m1} & w_{m2} & \cdots & w_{md}
\end{bmatrix}
\times
\begin{bmatrix}
h_{11} & h_{12} & \cdots & h_{1n} \\
h_{21} & h_{22} & \cdots & h_{2n} \\
\vdots & \vdots & \ddots & \vdots \\
h_{d1} & h_{d2} & \cdots & h_{dn}
\end{bmatrix}
\begin{array}{l}
\leftarrow\text{weight of } F_1 \\
\leftarrow\text{weight of } F_2 \\
\\
\leftarrow\text{weight of } F_d
\end{array}
$$

(columns $s_1, s_2, \ldots, s_n$ of V; columns $F_1, F_2, \ldots, F_d$ of W)

Figure 3: Non-negative matrix factorization (Step 3.1) to extract features of sentence vector model V. The results of this process is given by matrices W and H. Columns of W are corresponding to the extracted features $F_1, F_2, \ldots, F_d$ of the model and rows of H are called the weights of these features.

$$
\begin{array}{ll}
\text{rep}_1 \rightarrow & \\
\text{rep}_2 \rightarrow & \\
\text{rep}_3 \rightarrow & \\
\vdots &
\end{array}
\begin{bmatrix}
\text{NN kindness} & \text{VB leap} & \text{NN sorrow} \\
\text{JJ beloved} & \text{NN chicken} & \text{VB pay} \\
\text{NN chance} \ \cdots & \text{NN lion} \ \cdots & \text{NN wretchedness} \\
\text{VB gladden} & \text{VB obey} & \text{NN despair} \\
\text{NN drink} & \text{RB loud} & \text{VB tie}
\end{bmatrix}
\times
\begin{bmatrix}
h_{1r_{11}} & h_{1r_{21}} & \cdots & h_{1r_{n1}} \\
\vdots & \vdots & \ddots & \vdots \\
0 & 0 & \cdots & 0 \\
\vdots & \vdots & \ddots & \vdots \\
h_{dr_{1d}} & h_{dr_{2d}} & \cdots & h_{dr_{nd}}
\end{bmatrix}
= (V')^T
$$

(columns headed F_1 reps., F_i reps., F_d reps.)

Figure 4: The least relevant features are removed by zeroing out their corresponding weights in matrix H. The updated H matrix is denoted by H'. The sentence vector model is then reconstructed by multiplying W by H' (Steps 3.3 & 3.4). The updated sentence vector model is represented by matrix V'.

$$W = [F_1 F_2 F_3 \ldots F_d] \text{ where } F_j = \begin{pmatrix} w_{1j} \\ w_{2j} \\ \vdots \\ w_{mj} \end{pmatrix} \qquad (5)$$

Each of the d rows of H matrix represents weights of the d features in F. This decomposition is shown in Figure 3.

Step 3.2: Term Selection

For every feature F_j, we identify a fraction r of terms with the highest weights as its representatives, where r is a hyper-parameter that can be fine-tuned during system optimization (r is usually less than 1%).

Step 3.3: Feature Removal

In this phase we remove the ρ features that have little or no emotional relevance, where ρ is a non-negative integer hyper-parameter that can be tuned. We will call a feature "emotionally irrelevant" if all of its representative terms (as selected in the previous step) are labeled as neutral by the lexicon. These features will always be removed first. If ρ is less than the number of emotionally irrelevant features, we choose at random. On the other hand, if the number of emotionally irrelevant features is less than ρ, we eliminate features F_j in order of their overall emotional relevance, which is computed by estimating the standard deviation of cosine similarity ratios between emotion vectors Y_e's obtained in

Step 2 and $F_j \circ R_j$ (element-wise product of F_j and R_j) where R_j is the binary identifier of whether a term is a representative for F_j and is constructed based on the outcome of Step 3.2. Symbolically, to quantify how emotionally relevant feature F_j is, we calculate the following standard-deviation:

$$\sigma_j = \text{StdDev}_{e \in E \backslash \text{neutral}} \left\{ \text{sim}_{\cos}(Y_e, F_j \circ R_j) \right\} \qquad (6)$$

Step 3.4: Vector Space Reconstruction

In this step, the vector space model is reconstructed (V') after eliminating the irrelevant features. Let I denote the set of indices whose corresponding features are identified as least relevant in previous step. Then the reconstructed vector space is:

$$V' = [v'_{ij}]_{m \times n} \text{ s.t. } v'_{ij} = \sum_{\substack{1 \le k \le d \\ k \notin I}} w_{ik} h_{kj} \qquad (7)$$

Figure 4 illustrates the vector space reconstruction.

Step 4: Labeling

Finally the emotion recognition process takes place by measuring the similarity between sentence vectors V_s and standard emotion vectors Y_e which are taken from the previous step with the help of NMF, PCA, or LDA. Label of each sentence s is calculated by the following formula:

$$\text{predicted label of } s = \arg\max_{e \in E} \ \text{sim}(V_s, Y_e) \qquad (8)$$

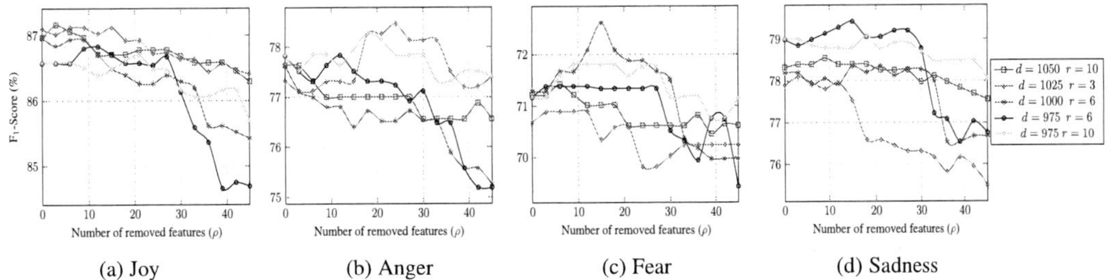

(a) Joy   (b) Anger   (c) Fear   (d) Sadness

Figure 5: Exploration of the hyper-parameter space for NMF. Each combination of hyper-parameters d, r, and ρ (dimensions, representatives, and removed features) results in a specific F_1 score for each emotion label. The model with $(d, r) = (975, 10)$, highlighted with green color, results in the highest overall F_1 score when $\rho = 18$. For each individual emotion, the best F_1 score is found at (a) Joy: $(d, r, \rho) = (1050, 10, 3)$, (b) Anger: $(d, r, \rho) = (1025, 3, 24)$, (c) Fear: $(d, r, \rho) = (1000, 6, 15)$, (d) Sadness: $(d, r, \rho) = (975, 6, 15)$.

where similarity function can be measured by the cosine of angle made by the two given vectors:

$$\text{sim}_{\cos}(V_s, Y_e) = \frac{V_s \cdot Y_e}{||V_s|| \times ||Y_e||} \qquad (9)$$

4 Performance on Fairy Tale Data

We tuned and tested our system using the manually annotated dataset of fairy tales constructed by Alm (2008), which comprises 176 children's fairy tales (80 from Brothers Grimm, 77 from Hans Andersen, and 19 from Beatrix Potter) with 15,087 unique sentences (15,302 sentences), 7,522 unique words and 320,521 total words. These fairy tales were annotated by two annotators labeling the emotion and mood of each sentence as one of joy, anger, fear, sadness, or neutral which resulted in four labels per sentence. Across the sentences, only 1,090 of them agreed on *all four non-neutral labels*. Kim et al. (2010) used only these sentence to train and test their system[3], and we followed the same procedure. There were 2,405 unique term-POS pairs. Also, the distribution of labels in the dataset is specified in the pie-chart depicted in Figure 6.

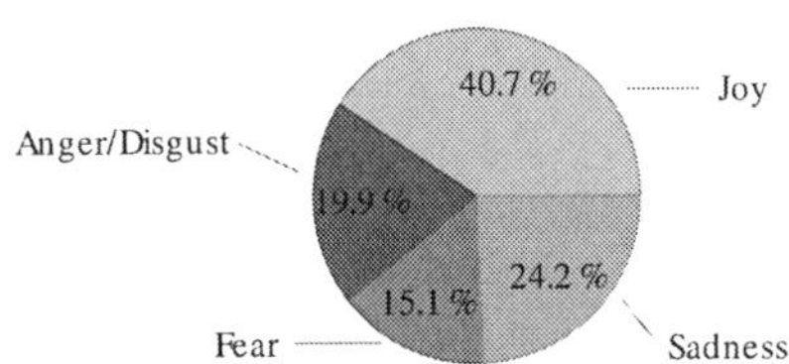

Figure 6: Fairy tales label distribution of sentences with unanimous inter-annotator agreement.

We measured the performance of our system on Alm's data. Without augmenting WNA, using

the original 1,471 synsets of WNA, the F_1 score is 0.625. The performance metrics presented in Table 4 were obtained by the model using the augmented WNA. The plots depicted in Figure 5 show the F_1 scores of various setups of the proposed model using NMF technique for noise cancellation. Also, Table 4 summarizes the precision, recall and F_1 score of our system for each of the four emotion classes as well as its overall F_1 score when using NMF, PCA, or LDA with different setups (values of hyper-parameters). As observed in this table, the highest overall F_1 score is obtained when using NMF with $(d, r, \rho) = (975, 10, 18)$. In this model, 209 sentences were labeled incorrectly. Among them, some challenging examples are in Table 3.

5 Unsolved Challenges and Future Work

As already discussed, one challenge regarding automatic emotion recognition is the context dependency of emotional semantics. For instance, *I'm over the moon!* is an expression of extreme happiness but does not use any explicitly happy or joyful words (or, indeed, any emotion word at all). Another obstacle is polysemous words, when words have both an emotional and non-emotional senses; recognizing which sense of the word is being used is challenging and remains an open problem. Aside from these fundamental issues, there is a serious lack of high-quality annotated data, not just for narrative text but for all discourse types. Annotated corpora use a wide variety of sometimes incompatible emotion theories and are often poorly annotated, with low inter-annotator agreements and many errors.

Given these considerations, there are many possible directions for future work, for example:

- Reconciling emotion lexicons and context de-

---

[3]Kim et al. (2010) reported 1,093 sentences, but we found and removed three sentences that were repeated in the data.

Sentence	Predicted	Gold Label
They told him that their father was very ill, and that they were afraid nothing could save him.	Fear	Sadness
And in sight of the bridge! Said poor pigling, nearly crying.	Sadness	Fear
She smiled once more, and then people said she was dead.	Sadness	Joy
Then he aimed a great blow, and struck the wolf on the head, and killed him on the spot! *. . . and when he was dead they cut open his body, and set Tommy free.*	Anger	Joy

Table 3: Challenging examples of sentences incorrectly labeled by the model with the most accurate settings.

Method	Setup	Joy			Anger			Fear			Sadness			Overall	
		P	R	F_1	P	R	F_1	P	R	F_1	P	R	F_1	F_1	Acc.
NMF	1050,10,3	0.872	0.872	**0.872**	0.878	0.696	0.776	0.672	0.758	0.712	0.753	0.818	0.784	0.807	0.806
	1025,3,24	0.859	0.876	0.867	0.884	0.705	**0.785**	0.682	0.715	0.698	0.733	0.799	0.764	0.800	0.799
	1000,6,15	0.872	0.858	0.865	0.861	0.687	0.764	0.692	0.764	**0.726**	0.742	0.830	0.784	0.804	0.803
	975,6,15	0.860	0.874	0.867	0.882	0.691	0.775	0.689	0.739	0.713	0.759	0.833	**0.794**	0.808	0.807
	975,10,18	0.858	0.874	0.866	0.879	0.705	0.783	0.703	0.733	0.718	0.755	0.830	0.791	**0.809**	**0.808**
PCA	1050	0.884	0.775	**0.826**	0.760	0.700	0.729	0.552	0.770	0.643	0.756	0.777	0.766	**0.760**	**0.689**
	1150	0.885	0.764	0.820	0.743	0.719	**0.731**	0.542	0.745	0.628	0.748	0.765	0.757	0.752	0.683
	950	0.883	0.766	0.820	0.722	0.696	0.709	0.571	0.782	**0.660**	0.759	0.777	0.768	0.757	0.686
	1100	0.888	0.768	0.824	0.744	0.710	0.726	0.542	0.745	0.628	0.765	0.788	**0.776**	0.758	0.684
LDA	1650	0.636	0.768	**0.696**	0.597	0.498	0.543	0.414	0.424	0.419	0.603	0.466	0.526	0.589	0.589
	1350	0.598	0.791	0.681	0.651	0.558	**0.600**	0.482	0.333	0.394	0.522	0.402	0.454	0.581	0.581
	1300	0.584	0.809	0.678	0.566	0.475	0.516	0.594	0.461	**0.519**	0.570	0.356	0.438	0.580	0.580
	2350	0.671	0.640	0.655	0.524	0.498	0.511	0.456	0.497	0.475	0.584	0.621	**0.602**	0.585	0.585
	1700	0.652	0.696	0.673	0.622	0.516	0.564	0.454	0.533	0.490	0.603	0.553	0.577	**0.601**	**0.601**

Table 4: Comparison of accuracy quantifiers of different models for detecting different emotions. The upper part of the table shows performance of the proposed model using NMF technique with different values of (d, r, ρ); while the middle and bottom parts determine the model accuracy when PCA and LDA techniques are used respectively. The highest F_1 scores of each noise cancellation technique are highlighted.

pendency of emotion detection models using learning techniques;

- Evaluating the performance of a bag-of-words multi-layer perceptron applied to the dataset to extract emotions;

- Applying multi-label prediction to the dataset and comparing the results with this work,

- Evaluating the effect of text unit size (sentence, paragraph, story) on the accuracy of sentiment labels; i.e., would there be an advantage in grouping sentences into longer units (e.g. paragraphs) and assigning a single label to this longer unit? It seems that a sentence by itself might not always carry sufficient cues to disambiguate its emotion, but its surrounding sentences might give this context.

6 Contributions

We identified a high performing approach to emotion recognition in narrative text (Kim et al., 2010) and carefully reimplemented and characterized the technique, exploring a design space of three different noise cancellation or dimension reduction techniques (NMF, PCA, or LDA), exploring various hyper-parameter settings. Our experiments indicated that NMF performed best, with an overall F_1 of 0.809. In the course of our investigation we clarified numerous implementational issues of the work reported by Kim et al. (2010), as well as made some improvements to WordNet Affect (WNA), one of the language resources used in the system, by adding new terms manually and using Wordnet similarity relations. This work suggests several promising future directions for improving the work, including careful annotation of a larger corpus, and augmenting WNA or similar lexicons to provide improved coverage of emotion terms. We release our code and data to enable future work[4].

Acknowledgments

This material is based upon work supported by the U.S. Department of Homeland Security under Grant Award Number, 2017-ST-062-000002. The views and conclusions contained in this document are those of the authors and should not be interpreted as necessarily representing the official policies, either expressed or implied, of the U.S. Department of Homeland Security.

---

[4]Code and data can be downloaded from `https://doi.org/10.34703/gzx1-9v95/03RERQ`

References

Hervé Abdi and Lynne J. Williams. 2010. Principal component analysis. *Wiley Interdisciplinary Reviews: Computational Statistics*, 2:433–459.

Ebba Cecilia Ovesdotter Alm. 2008. *Affect in *Text and Speech*. Ph.D. thesis, University of Illinois at Urbana-Champaign, Urbana-Champaign, IL.

Saima Aman and Stan Szpakowicz. 2008. Using roget's thesaurus for fine-grained emotion recognition. In *Proceedings of the Third International Joint Conference on Natural Language Processing: Volume-I*, pages 312–318, Hyderabad, India.

Anil Bandhakavi, Nirmalie Wiratunga, P Deepak, and Stewart Massie. 2014. Generating a word-emotion lexicon from #emotional tweets. In *Proceedings of the Third Joint Conference on Lexical and Computational Semantics (*SEM 2014)*, pages 12–21, Dublin, Ireland.

Anil Bandhakavi, Nirmalie Wiratunga, Deepak Padmanabhan, and Stewart Massie. 2017. Lexicon based feature extraction for emotion text classification. *Pattern Recognition Letters*, 93:133–142.

David M Blei, Andrew Y Ng, and Michael I Jordan. 2003. Latent dirichlet allocation. *Journal of Machine Learning Research*, 3(Jan):993–1022.

Christos Boutsidis and Efstratios Gallopoulos. 2008. SVD based initialization: A head start for non-negative matrix factorization. *Pattern Recognition*, 41(4):1350–1362.

Margaret M Bradley and Peter J Lang. 1999. Affective Norms for English Words (ANEW): Instruction manual and affective ratings. Technical Report C-1, The Center for Research in Psychophysiology, Gainseville, FL.

Fabio Calefato, Filippo Lanubile, and Nicole Novielli. 2017. EmoTxt: a toolkit for emotion recognition from text. In *Proceedings of the Seventh International Conference on Affective Computing and Intelligent: Interaction Workshops and Demos (ACIIW 2017)*, pages 79–80, San Antonio, TX.

Rafael A Calvo and Sunghwan Mac Kim. 2013. Emotions in text: Dimensional and categorical models. *Computational Intelligence*, 29(3):527–543.

Erik Cambria. 2016. Affective computing and sentiment analysis. *IEEE Intelligent Systems*, 31(2):102–107.

Erik Cambria, Andrew Livingstone, and Amir Hussain. 2012. The hourglass of emotions. In Anna Esposito, Antonietta M. Esposito, Alessandro Vinciarelli, Rüdiger Hoffmann, and Vincent Müller, editors, *Cognitive Behavioural Systems*, pages 144–157. Springer, Berlin. Published as Volume 7403, Lecture Notes in Computer Science (LNCS).

Colin Cherry, Saif M Mohammad, and Berry de Bruijn. 2012. Binary classifiers and latent sequence models for emotion detection in suicide notes. *Biomedical Informatics Insights*, 5:BII–S8933.

Roddy Cowie, Ellen Douglas-Cowie, and Cate Cox. 2005. Beyond emotion archetypes: Databases for emotion modelling using neural networks. *Neural Networks*, 18(4):371–388.

Charles Darwin and Phillip Prodger. 1998. *The Expression of the Emotions in Man and Animals*. Oxford University Press, Oxford, UK.

Paul Ekman. 1992a. Are there basic emotions? *Psychological Review*, 99(3):550–553.

Paul Ekman. 1992b. An argument for basic emotions. *Cognition & Emotion*, 6(3-4):169–200.

Paul Ekman. 1993. Facial expression and emotion. *American psychologist*, 48(4):384.

Christiane Fellbaum, editor. 1998. *WordNet: an electronic lexical database*. MIT Press, Cambridge, MA.

Johnny RJ Fontaine, Klaus R Scherer, Etienne B Roesch, and Phoebe C Ellsworth. 2007. The world of emotions is not two-dimensional. *Psychological Science*, 18(12):1050–1057.

Carroll E Izard. 2007. Basic emotions, natural kinds, emotion schemas, and a new paradigm. *Perspectives on Psychological Science*, 2(3):260–280.

William James. 1890. *The Principles of Psychology*. Henry Holt and Company, New York.

Sunghwan Mac Kim, Alessandro Valitutti, and Rafael A Calvo. 2010. Evaluation of unsupervised emotion models to textual affect recognition. In *Proceedings of the NAACL HLT 2010 Workshop on Computational Approaches to Analysis and Generation of Emotion in Text*, pages 62–70, Los Angeles, CA.

Matthew W Kreuter, Melanie C Green, Joseph N Cappella, Michael D Slater, Meg E Wise, Doug Storey, Eddie M Clark, Daniel J O'Keefe, Deborah O Erwin, Kathleen Holmes, et al. 2007. Narrative communication in cancer prevention and control: a framework to guide research and application. *Annals of Behavioral Medicine*, 33(3):221–235.

George Langroudi, Anna Jourdanous, and Ling Li. 2018. Music emotion capture: Sonifying emotions in eeg data. In *Symposium on Emotion Modeling and Detection in Social Media and Online Interaction*, pages 1–4, Liverpool, UK.

Daniel D Lee and H Sebastian Seung. 1999. Learning the parts of objects by non-negative matrix factorization. *Nature*, 401(6755):788–791.

Hugo Lövheim. 2012. A new three-dimensional model for emotions and monoamine neurotransmitters. *Medical Hypotheses*, 78(2):341–348.

Julien Mairal, Francis Bach, Jean Ponce, and Guillermo Sapiro. 2009. Online dictionary learning for sparse coding. In *Proceedings of the 26th Annual International Conference on Machine Learning*, pages 689–696, Montreal, Canada.

Christopher D Manning, Mihai Surdeanu, John Bauer, Jenny Rose Finkel, Steven Bethard, and David Mc-Closky. 2014. The Stanford CoreNLP natural language processing toolkit. In *Proceedings of 52nd Annual Meeting of the Association for Computational Linguistics (ACL 2014): System Demonstrations*, pages 55–60, Baltimore, MD, U.S.

DA Medler, A Arnoldussen, JR Binder, and MS Seidenberg. 2005. The Wisconsin Perceptual Attribute Ratings (WPAR) database. Retrieved from `http://www.neuro.mcw.edu/ratings` on April 23, 2020.

Saif M Mohammad, Svetlana Kiritchenko, and Xiaodan Zhu. 2013. NRC-Canada: Building the state-of-the-art in sentiment analysis of tweets. *arXiv preprint arXiv:1308.6242*.

Saif M Mohammad and Peter D Turney. 2010. Emotions evoked by common words and phrases: Using mechanical turk to create an emotion lexicon. In *Proceedings of the NAACL HLT 2010 Workshop on Computational Approaches to Analysis and Generation of Emotion in Text*, pages 26–34, Los Angeles, CA.

Keith Oatley and Philip N Johnson-Laird. 1987. Towards a cognitive theory of emotions. *Cognition and Emotion*, 1(1):29–50.

Andrew Ortony, Gerald L Clore, and Allan Collins. 1990. *The Cognitive Structure of Emotions*. Cambridge University Press, Cambridge, UK.

Jaak Panksepp, Brian Knutson, and Douglas L Pruitt. 1998. Toward a neuroscience of emotion. In *What develops in emotional development?*, pages 53–84. Springer, Boston, MA.

W Gerrod Parrott. 2001. *Emotions in Social Psychology: Essential Readings*. Psychology Press, London.

Haoruo Peng, Daniel Khashabi, and Dan Roth. 2019. Solving hard coreference problems. *arXiv preprint arXiv:1907.05524*.

James W Pennebaker, Martha E Francis, and Roger J Booth. 2001. Linguistic Inquiry and Word Count (LIWC) Software.

Robert Plutchik. 1980. A general psychoevolutionary theory of emotion. In Robert Plutchik, editor, *Theories of Emotion*, pages 3–33. Elsevier, Amsterdam, Netherlands.

Robert Plutchik. 1984. Emotions and imagery. *Journal of Mental Imagery*, 8:105–111.

Robert Plutchik. 2001. The nature of emotions: Human emotions have deep evolutionary roots, a fact that may explain their complexity and provide tools for clinical practice. *American scientist*, 89(4):344–350.

James A Russell. 1980. A circumplex model of affect. *Journal of personality and social psychology*, 39(6):1161.

Klaus R Scherer. 2005. What are emotions? and how can they be measured? *Social Science Information*, 44(4):695–729.

Shadi Shaheen, Wassim El-Hajj, Hazem Hajj, and Shady Elbassuoni. 2014. Emotion recognition from text based on automatically generated rules. In *Proceedings of the 2014 IEEE International Conference on Data Mining Workshop*, pages 383–392, Shenzhen, China.

Phillip Shaver, Judith Schwartz, Donald Kirson, and Cary O'connor. 1987. Emotion knowledge: Further exploration of a prototype approach. *Journal of Personality and Social Psychology*, 52(6):1061–1086.

Carlo Strapparava and Rada Mihalcea. 2008. Learning to identify emotions in text. In *Proceedings of the 2008 ACM symposium on Applied computing*, pages 1556–1560, Fortaleza, Ceara, Brazil.

Carlo Strapparava and Alessandro Valitutti. 2004. WordNet Affect: an affective extension of wordnet. In *Proceedings of the Fourth International Conference on Language Resources and Evaluation (LREC'04)*, pages 1083–1086, Lisbon, Portugal.

Jared Suttles and Nancy Ide. 2013. Distant supervision for emotion classification with discrete binary values. In *Proceedings of the International Conference on Intelligent Text Processing and Computational Linguistics*, pages 121–136, Berlin, Germany.

Zhi Teng, Fuji Ren, and Shingo Kuroiwa. 2007. Emotion recognition from text based on the rough set theory and the support vector machines. In *Proceedings of the 2007 International Conference on Natural Language Processing and Knowledge Engineering*, pages 36–41, Beijing, China.

Ryoko Tokuhisa, Kentaro Inui, and Yuji Matsumoto. 2008. Emotion classification using massive examples extracted from the web. In *Proceedings of the 22nd International Conference on Computational Linguistics: Volume 1*, pages 881–888, Manchester, UK.

Ozlem Uzuner, Andreea Bodnari, Shuying Shen, Tyler Forbush, John Pestian, and Brett R South. 2012. Evaluating the state of the art in coreference resolution for electronic medical records. *Journal of the American Medical Informatics Association*, 19(5):786–791.

Xiao Zhang, Wenzhong Li, Xu Chen, and Sanglu Lu. 2018. Moodexplorer: Towards compound emotion detection via smartphone sensing. *Proceedings of the ACM on Interactive, Mobile, Wearable and Ubiquitous Technologies*, 1(4):1–30.

Extensively Matching for Few-shot Learning Event Detection

Viet Dac Lai[1], Franck Dernoncourt[2] and Thien Huu Nguyen[1]
[1]Department of Computer and Information Science,
University of Oregon, Eugene, Oregon, USA
[2]Adobe Research, San Jose, CA, USA
`{vietl, thien}@cs.uoregon.edu`
`franck.dernoncourt@adobe.com`

Abstract

Current event detection models under supervised learning settings fail to transfer to new event types. Few-shot learning has not been explored in event detection even though it allows a model to perform well with high generalization on new event types. In this work, we formulate event detection as a few-shot learning problem to enable to extend event detection to new event types. We propose two novel loss factors that matching examples in the support set to provide more training signals to the model. Moreover, these training signals can be applied in many metric-based few-shot learning models. Our extensive experiments on the ACE-2005 dataset (under a few-shot learning setting) show that the proposed method can improve the performance of few-shot learning.

1 Introduction

Event Detection (ED) is an important task in Information Extraction (IE) in Natural Language Processing (NLP). Event Detection is the task to detect event triggers from a given text (e.g. a sentence) and classify it into one of the event types of interest. The following sentence is an example of ED:

In 1997, the company **hired** *John D. Idol to take over as chief executive.*

In this example, an ideal event detection system should detect the word *hired* as an event, and classify it to class of *Personnel:Start-Position*, assuming that *Personnel:Start-Position* is in the set of interested classes.

The current works in ED typically employ traditional supervised learning based on feature engineering (Li et al., 2014; Chen et al., 2017) and neural networks (Nguyen et al., 2016a; Chen et al., 2018; Lu and Nguyen, 2018). The main problem with supervised learning models is that they can not perform well on unseen classes (e.g. training a model to classify daily events, then run this

model to classify laboratory operations). As a result, supervised learning ED can not extend to unseen event types. A trivial solution is to annotate more data for unseen event types, then retraining the model with newly annotated data. However, this method is usually impractical because of the extremely high cost of annotation (Liu et al., 2019).

A human can learn about a new concept with limited supervision e.g. one can detect and classify events with 3-5 examples (Grishman et al., 2005). This motivates the setting we aim for event detection: **few-shot learning** (FSL). In FSL, a trained model rapidly learns a new concept from a few examples while keeping great generalization from observed examples (Vinyals et al., 2016). Hence, if we need to extend event detection into a new domain, a few examples are needed to activate the system in the new domain without retraining the model. By formulating ED as FSL, we can significantly reduce the annotation cost and training cost while maintaining highly accurate results.

In a few shot learning iteration, the model is given a support set and a query instance. The support set consists of examples from a small set of classes. A model needs to predict the label of the query instance in accordance with the set of classes appeared in the support set. Typical methods employ a neural network to embed the samples into a low-dimension vector space (Vinyals et al., 2016; Snell et al., 2017), then, classification is done by matching those vectors based on vector distances (Vinyals et al., 2016; Snell et al., 2017; Sung et al., 2018). One potential problem of prior FSL methods is that the model relies solely on training signals between query instance and the support set (Vinyals et al., 2016; Snell et al., 2017; Sung et al., 2018). Thus, the matching information between samples in the support set has not been exploited yet. We believe that this is not an efficient use of training data because dataset in ED is very small

Proceedings of the 1st Joint Workshop on Narrative Understanding, Storylines, and Events, pages 38–45
July 9, 2020. ©2020 Association for Computational Linguistics

(Grishman et al., 2005). Therefore, in this study, we propose to train an ED model using matching information (1) between query instance and the support set and (2) between the samples in the support themselves. This is implemented by adding two auxiliary factors into the loss function to constrain the learning process.

We apply the proposed training signals to different FSL models on the benchmark event detection dataset (Grishman et al., 2005). The experiments show that the training signal can improve the performance of the examined FSL models. To summarize, our contributions to this work include:

- We formulate event detection as a few-shot learning problem to extend ED to new event types and provide a baseline for this new research direction. To our best knowledge, this is a new branch of research that has not been explored.

- We propose two novel training signals for FSL. These signals can remarkably improve the performance of existing FSL models. As these signals do not require any additional information (e.g. dependency tree or part-of-speech), they can be applied in any metric-based FSL models.

2 Related work

Early studies in event detection mainly address feature engineering for statistical models (Ahn, 2006; Ji and Grishman, 2008; Hong et al., 2011; Li et al., 2014, 2015) including semantic features and syntactic features. Recently, due to the advances with deep learning, many neural network architectures have been presented for ED, e.g. convolutional neural networks (CNN) (Chen et al., 2015; Nguyen and Grishman, 2015, 2016; Nguyen et al., 2016b), recurrent neural networks (RNN) (Liu et al., 2017; Chen et al., 2018; Nguyen et al., 2016a; Nguyen and Nguyen, 2018) and graph convolutional neural networks (GCN) (Nguyen and Grishman, 2018; Pouran Ben Veyseh et al., 2019). These methods formulate ED as a supervised learning problem which usually fails to predict the labels of new event types.

By transitioning the symbolic event types to descriptive event types in the form of bags of keywords (Bronstein et al., 2015; Peng et al., 2016; Lai and Nguyen, 2019), the adaptibility of event detection can be formed as a supervised-learning problem. However, these studies have not examined

FSL as we do in this work. One can also address this problem in zero-shot learning with data generated from abstract meaning representation (Huang et al., 2018) or two-stage pipeline (trigger identification and few-shot event classification) based on dynamic memory network (Deng et al., 2020). A recent study has employed few-shot learning for event classification (Lai et al., 2020). Our work is similar in terms of formulation, however, we consider it in a larger extent of event detection where the *NULL* event is also included.

Few-shot learning has been studied early in the literature (Thrun, 1996). Before the era of the deep neural network, FSL approaches focused on building generative models that can transfer priors across classes. However, these methods are hard to apply to real applications because they require a subject-dedicated design such as handwritten characters (Lake et al., 2013; Wong and Yuille, 2015). As a result, they cannot capture the nature of the distribution (Salimans et al., 2016). Later studies, based on deep neural network, proposed metric learning to model the distribution of distance among classes, (Koch et al., 2015) with many incremental improvements in distance functions such as cosine similarity (Vinyals et al., 2016), Euclidean distance (Snell et al., 2017) and learnable distance function (Sung et al., 2018). Metric-based FSL presents its advantages in two dimensions. First, it is based on the well-studied theory in distance functions. Second, the simplicity in architecture and training processes can encourage its application in practice. Recently, meta-learning with parameter update strategy is also proposed to enable the models to learn quickly in few training iterations (Santoro et al., 2016; Finn et al., 2017).

3 Methodology

Our goal in this work is to formulate ED as a FSL problem, which has not been done in prior work. In order to achieve this, this section is divided into three parts. In the section 3.1 we present the overall framework that formulate Event Detection as an Few-Shot Learning problem. Then, we present popular models for FSL in the prior work and common sentence encoders which have been widely used in ED in section 3.2. Finally, we present two novel reguarlization technique to further improve the FSL model for ED in section 3.3.

3.1 Event Detection as Few-shot Learning

In few-shot learning, models learn to predict the label of a query instance x given a support set S (a set of well-classified instances) and a set of classes C, which appears in the support set S. Prior studies in FSL employ N-way K-shot setting, in which there are N clusters, which represent N classes, each cluster contains K data points (i.e., examples).

However, this setting is designed for problems that do not involve the "NULL" class (e.g., image classification and event classification). In event detection, the systems need to predict whether a query instance is an event (positive event type) or not (negative event type – the "NULL" type) before it is further classified into one of the classes of interest. To this end, we propose to extend the N-way K-shot setting to be N+1-way K-shot setting. In this setting, the support set contains N clusters representing N positive event types and 1 cluster representing the NULL event type. The support set is denoted as follows:

$$S = \{(s_1^1, a_1^1, t_1), \ldots, (s_1^K, a_1^K, t_1),$$
$$\cdots$$
$$(s_N^1, a_N^1, t_N), \ldots, (s_N^K, a_N^K, t_N),$$
$$(s_{N+1}^1, a_{N+1}^1, t_{null}), \ldots, (s_1^K, a_{N+1}^K, t_{null})\}$$

where:

- $\{t_1, t_2, \cdots t_N\}$ is the set of positive labels, which indicate an event

- t_{null} a special label for non-event.

- (s_i^j, a_i^j, t_i) indicates that the a_i^j-th word in the sentence s_i^j is the trigger word of an event mention with the event type t_i

3.2 Framework

Follow prior studies in FSL (Gao et al., 2019), we employ the metric-based FSL framework with three components: instance encoder, prototype encoder, and classification module.

3.2.1 Instance Encoder

Given a sentence of L words $\{w_1, w_2, \cdots, w_L\}$ and the event mention w_a, which is the a-th word of the sentence, we first map discrete words to a continuous high dimensional vector space to facilitate neural network using both pre-trained word embedding and position embedding as follow:

- In order to capture the syntactic and semantic of the word itself, we map each word in the sentence to a single vector using pre-trained word embedding, following previous studies in ED (Nguyen and Grishman, 2015). After this step, we derive a sequence of vectors $\{e_1, e_2, \cdots, e_L\}$ where $e_i \in R^u$.

- To provide a sense of the relative position of a word regarding the position of the anchor word, we further provide position embedding. It is mapped from the relative distance, $i - a$, of the i-th word with respect to the anchor word, a-th word to a single vector $p_i \in R^v$. We randomly initialize this word embedding and update the embedding during the training process.

- Following previous work (Nguyen and Grishman, 2015), the final embedding of a word w_i is derived by concatenating word embedding and position embedding $m_i = [e_i, p_i] \in R^{u+v}$.

Once we get the embedding for the whole sentence $E(s) = \{m_1, m_2, \cdots, m_L\}$, we employ a neural network, denoted as f, to encode the information of an instance (s, a) of the anchor w_a under the context in the sentence s into a single vector $v = f(E(s), a)$. In this work, consider the three following neural network architectures for this encoding purpose:

- Convolution Neural Network (CNN) (Kim, 2014) encodes the sentence by convolution operation on k consecutive vectors representing k-gram. Follow (Nguyen and Grishman, 2015), we use multiple kernel sizes $k \in \{2, 3, 4, 5\}$ to cover the context with 150 filters for each kernel size. To squeeze the information of the sentence, we apply max pooling to the top convolution layer to get a pooled vector p. We also introduce local embedding $e_{[a-w, a+w]}$ with window size $w = 2$. We concatenate pooled vector and local embeddings, and feed them through multiple dense layer to get the final representation:

$$v = W[p, e_{[a-w, a+w]}]$$

- Long Short-Term Memory (LSTM) (Hochreiter and Schmidhuber, 1997), at each step i, computes a hidden vector h_i from the hidden vector of the previous step h_{i-1} and the current input vector e_i. To capture the context from both sides a word in the sentence, we employ two separate LSTMs running on forward and backward directions. Eventually, we can obtain two sequence of hidden vector $\{h_i^{forward}, \cdots, h_L^{forward}\}$ and $\{h_i^{backward}, \cdots, h_L^{backward}\}$. Finally, we concatenate the a-th vectors, at the position of the anchor, to form the representation of the instance:

$$v = \text{concat}(h_a^{forward}, h_a^{backward})$$

- Graph Convolutional Neural Network features graph convolution (Kipf and Welling, 2017) on syntactic dependency graph, which allows the model to access to the nonconsecutive words based on the connection on the syntactic dependency tree. Following (Nguyen and Grishman, 2018), we transform the dependency tree into a syntactic graph by making it an undirected graph and adding node loops. The hidden vectors h_i^l of the l-th vector is obtained by feeding hidden vectors of the $l-1$-th layer through a GCN layer (Kipf and Welling, 2017). The final representation is the hidden vector in the top layer at the position of the trigger h_a^L where $L = 2$ is the number of GCN layers.

3.2.2 Prototype Encoder

This module computes a representative vector, called **prototype**, for each class $t \in T$ in the support set S from its instances' vectors. We employ two variants of prototype computation.

The first version, proposed in the original Prototypical Network (Snell et al., 2017), considers all representation vectors are equally important. To calculate the prototype for a class t_i, it aggregates all the representation vectors of the instance of class t_i, and then perform averaging over all vectors :

$$\mathbf{c}_i = \frac{1}{K} \sum_{(s_i^j, a_i^j, t_i) \in S} f(E(s_i^j), a_i^j) \qquad (1)$$

On the other hand, it was claimed that the supporting vectors are conditionally important with respect to the query (q, p). Thus, the second version computes the prototype as a weighted sum of the supporting vectors. The weights are obtained by attention mechanism according to the representational vector of the query as follow:

$$\mathbf{c}_i = \sum_{(s_i^j, a_i^j, t_i) \in S} \alpha_{ij} f(E(s_i^j), a_i^j)$$

$$\text{where } \alpha_{ij} = \frac{\exp(b_{ij})}{\sum_{(s_i^k, a_i^k, t_i) \in S} \exp(b_{ik})};$$

$$b_{ij} = \sum \left[\sigma(f(E(s_i^j), a_i^j) \odot f(E(q), p)) \right];$$

$\odot$ denotes the element-wise product.

$$(2)$$

3.2.3 Classification Module

This module computes the distribution on all the event types T of a query instance $x = (q, p)$ using a distance/similarity function $d : R \leftarrow R^d$.

$$P(y = t_i | x, S) = \frac{\exp(-d(f(q, p), \mathbf{c}^i))}{\sum_{j=1}^{N} \exp(-d(f(q, p), \mathbf{c}^j))}$$

$$(3)$$

where d is a distance/similarity function, and $\mathbf{c}^i$ and $\mathbf{c}^j$ are the prototype vectors obtained in either Equation (1) or Equation (2) from the support set S.

In this paper, we examine three kinds of distance/similarity function with prototype module to form 4 model as follow:

- Cosine similarity with averaging prototype as **Matching** network (Vinyals et al., 2016).

- Euclidean distance with averaging prototype as **Proto** network (Snell et al., 2017).

- Euclidean distance with weighted sum prototype as **Proto+Att** network (Gao et al., 2019).

- Learnable distance function with averaging prototype as **Relation** network (Sung et al., 2018).

3.3 Training Objectives

In the literature, a metric-based FSL model is typically trained by minimizing the negative log-likelihood as follow:

$$L_{query}(x, S) = -\log P(y = t | x, S) \qquad (4)$$

where x, t, S are query instance, ground truth label, and support set, respectively.

Model	5+1-way5-shot			10+1-way 10-shot		
Encoder	CNN	LSTM	GCNN	CNN	LSTM	GCNN
Proto	70.85	68.77	71.30	61.43	57.89	62.36
Proto+Att	71.23	69.32	72.76	63.50	59.56	65.08
Relation	54.36	68.33	58.37	41.37	62.85	44.43
Matching	34.71	49.40	32.49	23.05	33.84	21.51

Table 1: F1-score (micro) of models using CNN, LSTM and GCN encoders without proposed losses.

Encoder	Model	5+1-way 5-shot		10+1-way 10-shot	
		Original	$+ L_{inter} + L_{intra}$	Original	$+ L_{inter} + L_{intra}$
CNN	Proto	70.85	**72.07**	61.43	**62.84**
LSTM	Proto	68.77	**78.09**	57.89	**72.78**
GCN	Proto	71.30	**71.82**	62.36	**63.49**
CNN	Proto+Att	71.23	**72.46**	63.5	**64.38**
LSTM	Proto+Att	69.32	**78.44**	59.56	**72.94**
GCN	Proto+Att	72.76	**72.92**	65.08	**66.10**

Table 2: F1-score (micro) of models using CNN, LSTM, and GCN. *Original* columns show the models without additional training signal. $L_{inter} + L_{intra}$ columns demonstrate the models with additional inter and intra loss functions.

This loss function exploits the signal of matching information between the query instance and the supporting instances. It can work efficiently in computer vision because the number of samples in computer vision datasets are typically huge. However, in NLP tasks, the dataset is commonly relatively much smaller (e.g. ACE 2005 contains 4000 positive examples). So using this loss function is not enough to deliver a good system.

Therefore, providing more training signals is crucial to the problem which involves a small dataset. Fortunately, the support set is a well-classified set of instances with K examples per class in a total of N classes. In this paper, we proposed two ways to exploit this resourceful set as follow:

- Intra-cluster matching: We argue that the representational vectors in the same class should be close to each other. Therefore, we minimize the distance between instance in the same class.

$$L_{intra} = \sum_{i=1}^{N} \sum_{k=1}^{K} \sum_{j=k+1}^{K} \text{mse}(v_i^j, v_i^k) \quad (5)$$

- Inter-cluster information: We also argue that the clusters should distribute far away from each other. Hence, their prototypes are also distant from the other. Hence, we maximize the distances between pairs of prototypes.

$$L_{inter} = 1 - \sum_{i=1}^{N} \sum_{j=i+1}^{N} \text{cosine}(c_i, c_j) \quad (6)$$

In this work, we train our model using a combination of the loss functions in equations 4, 5,6. We control the contribution of the additional losses by two hyperparameters β and γ as follow:

$$L = L_{query} + \beta \hat{L}_{intra} + \gamma \hat{L}_{inter} \quad (7)$$

where $\hat{L}_{intra}$ and $\hat{L}_{inter}$ are scaled losses with respect to L_{query}, and β and γ are the trade-off parameters.

4 Experiments

4.1 Data

We use the ACE-2005 dataset to evaluate all of the models in this study. ACE-2005 is a benchmark dataset in event detection with 33 positive event subtypes, which are grouped into 8 event types *Business, Contact, Conflict, Justice, Life, Movement, Personnel, and Transaction*. Although the dataset is split into training, development, and testing sets, we cannot use these splits directly because, in FSL, the set of event types in the training set and testing sets are disjoint. Therefore, we further split these datasets to satisfy three conditions for FSL:

- The set of event types in the training set T^{train} are disjoint to those in the development and the testing set:

$$T^{dev} \equiv T^{test}; T^{train} \cap T^{test} = \emptyset;$$

- In order to run FSL with the 10-way 10-shot setting, the set of event subtypes should contain at least 10 subtypes.

- The training set should contain as many samples as possible.

Based on these criteria, we use all samples belonging to 4 event types: *Business, Contact, Conflict* and *Justice* as the training set. While the rest (*Life, Movement, Personnel* and *Transaction*) are used for the development and testing sets. We split the sample by ratio 50:50 in every subtype to ensure the balance of the development and the testing set. Finally, since there are event types that have less than 15 examples, we eliminate all of these from the training, development, and testing set.

4.2 Hyper-parameters

We evaluate using 5+1-way 5-shot and 10+1-way 10-shot FSL settings. Although it was seen that the higher number of classes we have during the training time, the better performance on testing (Snell et al., 2017), we avoid feeding all event types in every iteration during training time. We manage to sample 20 positive classes (over 21 in the training set) in each training iteration.

We initialize the embedding vectors with 300-dimension GLoVe embedding, trained from 6 billion tokens. We use 50-dimension position embedding and initialize it randomly. These embedding vectors are updated during training time.

We train Proto, Proto+Att, and Matching using Stochastic Gradient Decent (SGD) optimizer while Relation is trained with AdaDelta optimizer because SGD hardly converges with Relation network. The learning rate is initialized to 0.03 and decays after every 500 iterations. We trained our models in 2500 iterations and evaluation at every 200 iterations.

In order to find the best set of β and γ, we do grid search with with $(\beta, \gamma) \in \{0.0, 0.1, 0.2, 0.3\}^2$.

4.3 Result

In this section, we perform our experiment in three steps:(1) find the best FSL models among Proto, Proto+Att, Matching, Relation models; (2) evaluate the proposed additional training factors and (3)

analyze the effectiveness of each training factor in an ablation study.

Table 1 shows the F-scores of four models using three kinds of sentence encoders on the ACE-2005 dataset under 5+1-way 5-shot and 10+1-way 10-shot FSL settings without our proposed losses. As can be seen from the Table 1, the performance of the models on 5+1-way 5-shot is always better than 10+1-way 10-shot because the number of classes needs to be classified in the 10+1-way setting is almost twice as much of in 5+1-way setting. Second, we can see that Prototypical-based (Proto and Proto+Att) models outperform the Matching network and the Relation network on both FSL settings. Among Prototypical network models, Proto+Att is slightly better than Proto with a 0.8% performance gap in the 10+1-way 10-shot setting.

Most importantly, Table 2 presents the F-scores of Proto and Proto+A with the proposed loss functions (i.e., L_{intra}, L_{inter}). As we can see from the table, the proposed loss functions can significantly improve the performance of Proto and Proto+Att models over different encoders (i.e., CNN, LSTM, and GCN), clearly demonstrating the benefits of the intra and inter-similarity constraints in this work.

4.4 Ablation Study

In this study, we introduce two penalization factors, presented in Equations 5 and 6.

Besides the FSL formulation for event detection, a major contribution in this work involves the two loss functions L_{intra} and L_{inter} to improve the representation vectors for the models. To evaluate the contribution of these terms, Table 3 shows the performance of the FSL models with different combinations of loss functions on the development set. In particular, we focus on the prototypical-based FSL model on the 5+1-way 5-shot setting in this analysis (although the similar trends of the performance are also observed for the other models and settings). The "*Original*" column corresponds to the models where both L_{inter} and L_{intra} are not applied. The other columns, on the other hand, report the performance of the models when the combinations L_{inter}, L_{intra}, and $L_{inter} + L_{intra}$ of the loss terms are introduced.

It is clear from the table that both loss terms are important for the FSL models for ED as eliminating any of them would significantly hurt the performance excepting the Proto+Att model with GCN encoder. The best performance is achieved with

Encoder	FSL Model	Original	+Inter	+Intra	+Intra+Inter
CNN	Proto	67.92	68.78	68.83	69.37
LSTM	Proto	65.94	65.28	72.07	77.56
GCN	Proto	69.28	70.05	69.49	70.11
CNN	Proto+Att	69.90	70.23	70.06	70.43
LSTM	Proto+Att	67.26	67.48	72.00	77.81
GCN	Proto+Att	71.65	71.75	71.56	71.18

Table 3: Ablation study: F1-score (micro) of Prototypical-based models on dev set with 5+1-way 5-shot FSL setting

both loss terms are applied, thus testifying to the benefits of the proposed regularization techniques in this work.

5 Conclusion

In this paper, we address the problem of extending event detection to unseen event types through few-shot learning. We investigate four metric-based few-shot learning models with different encoder types (CNN, LSTM, and GCN). Moreover, we propose two novel loss functions to provide more training signals to the model exploiting domain-matching information in the support set. Our extensive experiments show that our method increases the efficiency of using training data, resulting in better classification performance. Our ablation study shows that both intra-cluster matching and inter-cluster matching contributes to the improvement.

Acknowledgments

This research is based upon work supported in part by the Office of the Director of National Intelligence (ODNI), Intelligence Advanced Research Projects Activity (IARPA), via IARPA Contract No. 2019-19051600006 under the Better Extraction from Text Towards Enhanced Retrieval (BETTER) Program. The views and conclusions contained herein are those of the authors and should not be interpreted as necessarily representing the official policies, either expressed or implied, of ODNI, IARPA, the Department of Defense, or the U.S. Government. The U.S. Government is authorized to reproduce and distribute reprints for governmental purposes notwithstanding any copyright annotation therein. This document does not contain technology or technical data controlled under either the U.S. International Traffic in Arms Regulations or the U.S. Export Administration Regulations.

References

David Ahn. 2006. The stages of event extraction. In *Proceedings of the Workshop on Annotating and Reasoning about Time and Events*.

Ofer Bronstein, Ido Dagan, Qi Li, Heng Ji, and Anette Frank. 2015. Seed-based event trigger labeling: How far can event descriptions get us? In *ACL-IJCNLP*.

Yubo Chen, Shulin Liu, Xiang Zhang, Kang Liu, and Jun Zhao. 2017. Automatically labeled data generation for large scale event extraction. In *ACL*.

Yubo Chen, Liheng Xu, Kang Liu, Daojian Zeng, and Jun Zhao. 2015. Event extraction via dynamic multi-pooling convolutional neural networks. In *ACL-IJCNLP*.

Yubo Chen, Hang Yang, Kang Liu, Jun Zhao, and Yantao Jia. 2018. Collective event detection via a hierarchical and bias tagging networks with gated multi-level attention mechanisms. In *EMNLP*.

Shumin Deng, Ningyu Zhang, Jiaojian Kang, Yichi Zhang, Wei Zhang, and Huajun Chen. 2020. Meta-learning with dynamic-memory-based prototypical network for few-shot event detection. In *Proceedings of the 13th International Conference on Web Search and Data Mining*, pages 151–159.

Chelsea Finn, Pieter Abbeel, and Sergey Levine. 2017. Model-agnostic meta-learning for fast adaptation of deep networks. In *ICML*.

Tianyu Gao, Xu Han, Zhiyuan Liu, and Maosong Sun. 2019. Hybrid attention-based prototypical networks for noisy few-shot relation classification. In *AAAI*.

Ralph Grishman, David Westbrook, and Adam Meyers. 2005. Nyu's english ace 2005 system description. In *ACE 2005 Evaluation Workshop*.

Sepp Hochreiter and Jurgen Schmidhuber. 1997. Long short-term memory. In *Neural Computation*.

Yu Hong, Jianfeng Zhang, Bin Ma, Jianmin Yao, Guodong Zhou, and Qiaoming Zhu. 2011. Using cross-entity inference to improve event extraction. In *ACL*.

Lifu Huang, Heng Ji, Kyunghyun Cho, and Clare R Voss. 2018. Zero-shot transfer learning for event extraction. In *ACL*, pages 2160–2170.

Heng Ji and Ralph Grishman. 2008. Refining event extraction through cross-document inference. In *ACL*.

Yoon Kim. 2014. Convolutional neural networks for sentence classification. In *EMNLP*.

Thomas N. Kipf and Max Welling. 2017. Semi-supervised classification with graph convolutional networks. In *ICLR*.

Gregory Koch, Richard Zemel, and Ruslan Salakhutdinov. 2015. Siamese neural networks for one-shot image recognition. In *ICML deep learning workshop*, volume 2.

Viet Dac Lai, Franck Dernoncourt, and Thien Huu Nguyen. 2020. Exploiting the matching information in the support set for few shot event classification. In *PAKDD*.

Viet Dac Lai and Thien Huu Nguyen. 2019. Extending event detection to new types with learning from keywords. In *Proceedings of the 5th Workshop on Noisy User-generated Text (W-NUT 2019)*.

Brenden M Lake, Ruslan R Salakhutdinov, and Josh Tenenbaum. 2013. One-shot learning by inverting a compositional causal process. In *NIPS*.

Qi Li, Heng Ji, Yu Hong, and Sujian Li. 2014. Constructing information networks using one single model. In *EMNLP*.

Xiang Li, Thien Huu Nguyen, Kai Cao, and Ralph Grishman. 2015. Improving event detection with Abstract Meaning Representation. In *Proceedings of the First Workshop on Computing News Storylines*.

Shulin Liu, Yubo Chen, Kang Liu, and Jun Zhao. 2017. Exploiting argument information to improve event detection via supervised attention mechanisms. In *ACL*.

Shulin Liu, Yang Li, Feng Zhang, Tao Yang, and Xinpeng Zhou. 2019. Event detection without triggers. In *NAACL:HLT*, pages 735–744.

Weiyi Lu and Thien Huu Nguyen. 2018. Similar but not the same: Word sense disambiguation improves event detection via neural representation matching. In *EMNLP*.

Thien Nguyen and Ralph Grishman. 2018. Graph convolutional networks with argument-aware pooling for event detection. In *AAAI*.

Thien Huu Nguyen, Kyunghyun Cho, and Ralph Grishman. 2016a. Joint event extraction via recurrent neural networks. In *NAACL*.

Thien Huu Nguyen, Lisheng Fu, Kyunghyun Cho, and Ralph Grishman. 2016b. A two-stage approach for extending event detection to new types via neural networks. In *Proceedings of the 1st ACL Workshop on Representation Learning for NLP (RepL4NLP)*.

Thien Huu Nguyen and Ralph Grishman. 2015. Event detection and domain adaptation with convolutional neural networks. In *ACL-IJCNLP*.

Thien Huu Nguyen and Ralph Grishman. 2016. Modeling skip-grams for event detection with convolutional neural networks. In *EMNLP*.

Trung Minh Nguyen and Thien Huu Nguyen. 2018. One for all: Neural joint modeling of entities and events. In *AAAI*.

Haoruo Peng, Yangqiu Song, and Dan Roth. 2016. Event detection and co-reference with minimal supervision. In *EMNLP*.

Amir Pouran Ben Veyseh, Thien Huu Nguyen, and Dejing Dou. 2019. Graph based neural networks for event factuality prediction using syntactic and semantic structures. In *ACL*.

Tim Salimans, Ian Goodfellow, Wojciech Zaremba, Vicki Cheung, Alec Radford, and Xi Chen. 2016. Improved techniques for training gans. In *NIPS*.

Adam Santoro, Sergey Bartunov, Matthew Botvinick, Daan Wierstra, and Timothy Lillicrap. 2016. Meta-learning with memory-augmented neural networks. In *ICML*.

Jake Snell, Kevin Swersky, and Richard Zemel. 2017. Prototypical networks for few-shot learning. In *NIPS*.

Flood Sung, Yongxin Yang, Li Zhang, Tao Xiang, Philip HS Torr, and Timothy M Hospedales. 2018. Learning to compare: Relation network for few-shot learning. In *CVPR*.

Sebastian Thrun. 1996. Is learning the n-th thing any easier than learning the first? In *NIPS*.

Oriol Vinyals, Charles Blundell, Timothy Lillicrap, Daan Wierstra, et al. 2016. Matching networks for one shot learning. In *NIPS*.

Alex Wong and Alan L Yuille. 2015. One shot learning via compositions of meaningful patches. In *ICCV*.

Exploring the Effect of Author and Reader Identity in Online Story Writing: the STORIESINTHEWILD Corpus

Tal August[†]   Maarten Sap[†]   Elizabeth Clark[†]
Katharina Reinecke[†]   Noah A. Smith[†◇]
[†]Paul G. Allen School of Computer Science & Engineering,
University of Washington, Seattle, WA, USA
[◇]Allen Institute for Artificial Intelligence, Seattle, WA, USA

Abstract

Current story writing or story editing systems rely on human judgments of story quality for evaluating performance, often ignoring the subjectivity in ratings. We analyze the effect of author and reader characteristics and story writing setup on the quality of stories in a short storytelling task. To study this effect, we create and release STORIESINTHEWILD, containing 1,630 stories collected on a volunteer-based crowdsourcing platform. Each story is rated by three different readers, and comes paired with the author's and reader's age, gender, and personality.

Our findings show significant effects of authors' and readers' identities, as well as writing setup, on story writing and ratings. Notably, compared to younger readers, readers age 45 and older consider stories significantly less creative and less entertaining. Readers also prefer stories written all at once, rather than in chunks, finding them more coherent and creative. We also observe linguistic differences associated with authors' demographics (e.g., older authors wrote more vivid and emotional stories). Our findings suggest that reader and writer demographics, as well as writing setup, should be accounted for in story writing evaluations.

1 Introduction

Reading or writing a story is an inherently subjective task that depends on the experiences and identity of the author, those of the reader, and the structure of the writing process itself (Morgan and Murray, 1935; Conway and Pleydell-Pearce, 2000; Clark et al., 2018). Despite this subjectivity, many natural language processing tasks treat human judgments of story quality as the gold standard for evaluating systems that generate or revise text. In creative applications, such as machine-in-the-loop story writing systems (Clark et al., 2018),

it is important to understand sources of variation in judgments if we hope to have reliable, reproducible estimates of quality.

In this work, we investigate how an author's and reader's identity, as well as overall writing setup, influence how stories are written and rated. We introduce and release STORIESINTHEWILD,[1] containing 1,630 short stories written on a volunteer-based crowdsourcing platform, paired with author demographics and personality information. For each story, we obtain three sets of ratings from third-party evaluators, along with their demographics and personality.

Our findings confirm that author identity, reader identity, and writing setup affect story writing and rating in STORIESINTHEWILD. Notably, people in general preferred stories written in one chunk rather than broken up into multiple stages. Raters age 45 and over generally rated stories as less creative, more confusing, and liked them less compared to raters under age 45. Additionally, we find that, in our corpus, men were more likely than women to write about female characters and their social interactions, and compared to younger authors, older authors wrote more vivid and emotional stories. We also find evidence of reader and author personality, and their interaction, influencing ratings of story creativity.

Our new dataset and results are first steps in analyzing how writing setup and author and reader traits can influence ratings of story quality, and suggest that these characteristics should be accounted for in human evaluations of story quality.

2 Background and Research Questions

To guide our study, we craft several research questions informed by existing literature on story writing and the relationship between author identity

---

[1]http://tinyurl.com/StoriesInTheWild

Proceedings of the 1st Joint Workshop on Narrative Understanding, Storylines, and Events, pages 46–54
July 9, 2020. ©2020 Association for Computational Linguistics

and language, outlined below.

RQ1 *How are author gender, age, and personality traits associated with language variation in stories?* A wealth of work has shown an association between an author's mental states and their language patterns. Variation in pronoun usage, topic choices, and narrative complexity correlates strongly with the author's age and gender (Nguyen et al., 2016) and moderately with their personality (Yarkoni, 2010). We aim to confirm these differences in a prompted storytelling setting, since most work has focused on self-narratives (e.g., diaries and social media posts; Pennebaker and Seagal, 1999; Hirsh and Peterson, 2009; Schwartz et al., 2013), with the exception of the essays studied by Pennebaker et al. (2014).

RQ2 *How are rater gender, age, and personality traits associated with variation in story quality ratings?* Ratings of stories are often only used to evaluate a story writing system's output (e.g., Fan et al., 2018; Yao et al., 2019) or to develop automatic evaluation metrics (e.g., Hashimoto et al., 2019; Purdy et al., 2018), ignoring the rater's identity. However, prior work has shown differences in crowdsourcing worker's behavior or annotations based on task framing (Levin et al., 2002; August et al., 2018; Sap et al., 2019) or the annotator's own identity or experiences (Breitfeller et al., 2019; Geva et al., 2019). We seek to confirm and characterize these differences in our story rating task. As a follow-up to **RQ2**, we also investigate the interaction between author and rater demographics on story ratings.

RQ3 *Is writing setup associated with different ratings of story quality?* Past work has investigated story writing as a turn-taking game (Clark et al., 2018) or as a distributed activity (Teevan et al., 2016) rather than a single event. We investigate whether writing setup (writing a story all at once or sentence-by-sentence) impacts overall story quality.

3 STORIESINTHEWILD Collection

We introduce and release STORIESINTHEWILD, containing 1,630 short stories (§3.1) paired with author demographics and personality information.[2] We pair these stories with third-party rat-

[2]Each stage of data collection was approved by the authors' institutional review board (IRB).

		total	written in...	
			full	*seq.*
stats	# stories	1630	792	838
	avg. # tokens	592	583	600
	avg. writing time (min.)	9.30	9.98	8.72
	avg. key press time (sec.)	0.96	1.09	0.83
ratings	coherent	4.52	4.78	4.27 **
	confusing	3.44	3.19	3.67 **
	creative	4.00	4.09	3.90 *
	entertaining	3.95	4.10	3.81 **
	grammatical	4.22	4.39	4.06 **
	liked	3.89	4.05	3.73 **

Table 1: Statistics in STORIESINTHEWILD for all stories, as well as broken down by writing setup (*full*: written in full, *seq.*: written sequentially). Discussed in §4.3, rating differences are significant after Holm-correcting for multiple comparisons (*: $p < 0.01$, **: $p < 0.001$), but story length (# tokens), writing time, and writing speed (key press time) are not.

ings (§3.2) to evaluate the effect of writing setup and author identity on story writing.

3.1 Crowdsourcing Stories

To construct STORIESINTHEWILD, we first collected 1,630 written stories using a volunteer-based online study platform, LabintheWild (Reinecke and Gajos, 2015).[3] Following best practices in recruiting on LabintheWild (August et al., 2018), we advertised our study as a way for participants to learn more about themselves by seeing how a simple pronoun-based classifier can predict their personality based on their story writing (described in Appendix A.1).

We first collected participants' identity and demographics (age, gender, race, and education level). Then, participants chose the *topic* of their story by selecting one of five preview thumbnails, each representing one of five image strips that participants subsequently used as prompts for their story. We selected the images from the Visual Storytelling dataset of Flickr images (Huang et al., 2016) and a cartoon dataset (Iyyer et al., 2017). All images are shown in Figure 1 in Appendix A.

Writing setup After choosing a topic, all authors are presented with a five image sequence corresponding to the topic they chose to write about. We then randomly assign authors to one of two writing setups: (1) *all at once* or (2) *se-*

[3]LabintheWild recruits study participants using intrinsic motivations (as opposed to monetary compensation, cf. Amazon Mechanical Turk), such as the the desire to compare oneself to others or to support science (Jun et al., 2017).

quential, both shown in Figure 2 in Appendix A. In (1), participants simply write a full 5–10 sentence story. In (2), participants are instructed to write five sets of 1–2 sentences in an accordion of text boxes, each box corresponding to an image in the strip. The second writing setup is inspired by machine-in-the-loop turn-taking for story writing (Clark et al., 2018). Once each text box is submitted, participants can no longer edit that text.

In both setups, participants are instructed to tell a story rather than just describe the images, to make sure their story has a clear beginning, middle, and end, and to use correct punctuation. The task took around 9 minutes in both conditions.

Following the story writing, participants can optionally fill out the Ten Item Personality Measure (TIPI; Gosling et al., 2003), a short personality questionnaire based on the Five Factor Model (FFM; Costa Jr and McCrae, 2008).[4]

Author demographics Of the authors in STORIESINTHEWILD, 57% were women and 40% men (3% declined to state their gender), with an average age of 25 ± 12 years and an average of 14.30 ± 4.20 years of education including primary school. Of the authors, 56% were white, 28% Asian, and 3% African-American (13% selected another ethnicity/race); we did not restrict participation to any specific country. 1,133 (70%) authors took the personality questionnaire.

3.2 Rating Stories

We create an Amazon Mechanical Turk task to obtain quality ratings for each of the stories collected in our previous task. For each story, we ask U.S.-based workers to rate stories on 6 dimensions (listed in Table 1), using a 7-point Likert scale.[5] Those dimensions include 5 fine-grained quality dimensions (e.g., grammaticality, coherence), as well as an overall impression of the story ("I liked this story"). Each worker also optionally filled out their demographics information (age, race, gender, education level). Additionally, as a measure of in-

tellect and creativity, workers filled out the four openness items from the Mini-IPIP Big 5 personality scale (Donnellan et al., 2006).

Rater demographics 56% of our raters were women and 42% were men. 79% identified as white, 6% as African-American, and 6% as Asian. On average, their age was 40 ± 12 years, and they had 15 ± 3 years of education, including primary school.

4 Analyses

We investigate the effects of author and rater characteristics on the story's language and ratings. Unless otherwise specified, we only consider the male and female gender labels[6] and use a continuous representation of age and personality. We also explore the impact the writing setup—whether authors wrote stories all at once or in sequential chunks—has on story ratings.[7]

Note that our findings are simply measuring associations between aggregate categories (e.g., number of pronouns used, authors over age 45) and should not be interpreted as applying to individual data points with specific contexts.

4.1 Author Identity (RQ1)

To analyze which types of words are associated with different demographic identities, we extract psychologically relevant linguistic categories from stories, using the Linguistic Inquiry Word Count (LIWC; Pennebaker et al., 2015). For each LIWC category, we compute a linear regression model on the z-scored features, controlling for writing setup and topic choice. We only report regression coefficients (βs) that are significant after Holm correction for multiple comparisons (Holm, 1979).

Gender, age We find that the author's age, gender, and personality correlate with differential usage of linguistic categories, controlling for image choice and writing setup.[8] Specifically, we find that men used more personal pronouns ($|\beta| = 0.30$, $p < 0.001$) and social words ($|\beta| = 0.28$,

---

[4]The FFM delineates five dimensions of personality (openness to experience, conscientiousness, extraversion, agreeableness, neuroticism), each represented as a continuous score. For more details, we refer the reader to `http://en.wikipedia.org/wiki/Big_Five_personality_traits`.

[5]To ensure the quality of responses, we restrict the task to workers with 99% or above approval rate and at least 1,000 HITs approved. Additionally, we ask that workers write out a short piece of feedback to improve the story, to encourage them to think critically while rating stories.

[6]Gender is a social construct that goes beyond the man-woman binary (Lorber et al., 1991); however, a more complex analysis is not possible given the limited number of individuals not identifying as male or female in our data.

[7]We exclude author and reader education from our findings, as we did not find any signification effects for those variables.

[8]See Appendix B.1 for associations between author demographics and image choice.

$p < 0.001$) to describe characters (specifically, female characters, $|\beta| = 0.33$, $p < 0.001$), compared to women. Controlling for gender effects, our findings show that older authors wrote more emotional and positive stories ($|\beta| = 0.05$ and $|\beta| = 0.04$, respectively, $p < 0.05$) that contained more visual descriptions ($|\beta| = 0.05$, $p < 0.001$), whereas younger authors used past tense more ($|\beta| = 0.04$, $p < 0.05$).

Personality We find significant correlations between LIWC categories and an author's personality traits, controlling for age and gender (see Appendix B.2 for the full set of results). Notably, highly conscientious authors focused on character motivations ($|\beta| = 0.12$, $p < 0.05$) and used a more positive tone ($|\beta| = 0.14$, $p < 0.01$), compared to low-conscientiousness authors who wrote stories that tended to be more negative ($|\beta| = 0.11$, $p < 0.1$). Finally, less agreeable authors used more swearing ($|\beta| = 0.15$, $p < 0.1$), and more differentiating words ($|\beta| = 0.10$, $p < 0.1$) compared to more agreeable authors.

4.2 Rater Identity (RQ2)

We examine the association between rater traits and their story ratings using linear regressions controlling for image type and writing setup (similar to §4.1). We also investigate interaction effects with author demographics, and show the full results of our regressions in Appendix B.3.

Gender, age For age, we first noticed that older workers rated stories noticeably more negatively than younger workers (e.g., $r = -.08$, $p < .001$ for both the like and entertaining ratings). When inspecting the data we noticed this trend was most defined for raters age 45 or older, and so we perform our analyses below using a binarized age variable, splitting raters as either 45 or older ($N = 921$) and younger than 45 ($N = 1916$).

Our findings indicate that, compared to younger raters, raters of age 45 and older liked the stories significantly less ($|\beta| = 0.42$, $p < 0.001$), and rated them as substantially less entertaining ($|\beta| = 0.39$, $p < 0.001$), less creative ($|\beta| = 0.25$, $p < 0.05$), more confusing ($|\beta| = 0.27$, $p < 0.05$), and less grammatical ($|\beta| = 0.30$, $p < 0.05$). Interestingly, there was no significant association between annotator gender and story ratings.

Personality Openness to experience is often linked to creativity (McCrae, 1987), so we ex-plore how ratings of creativity are associated with rater and author openness to experience personality scores. We find significant correlations between story ratings and rater openness to experience. Specifically, raters with higher openness to experience thought stories were generally more creative ($|\beta| = 0.38$, $p < 0.05$) and less confusing ($|\beta| = 0.64$, $p < 0.001$). Additionally, authors with higher openness scores wrote stories that were rated more creative ($|\beta| = 0.35$, $p < 0.1$)

Author-Rater Identity Interactions

We also investigate story ratings through the lens of author and rater demographics to see if any shared traits across raters and authors were associated with rater preferences.

While both reader and writer openness to experience were associated with significantly higher ratings of creativity, the interaction between the two was negative ($|\beta| = 0.50$, $p < 0.1$), meaning that as writer and reader openness to experience increased, the reader's rating of the story's creativity actually decreased. No other interactions (e.g., age, gender) were significant in our sample.

4.3 Differences in writing setup (RQ3)

We quantify the differences in ratings for our two writing setups. We average the ratings for each story, and report differences in Table 1 using Cohen's d. We find that stories written in full are rated to have higher quality across all dimensions, compared to stories written sequentially.

We also find that certain story topics were preferred over others ($F = 26.17$, $p < 0.001$). Specifically, stories written about the dog prompt were liked significantly more than others ($p < 0.001$), and those about the jail prompt significantly less ($p < 0.001$).

5 Conclusion

In this study we find that differences in author characteristics are associated with linguistic differences in stories and that rater characteristics are associated with differences in ratings. For authors, men were more likely than women to write about female characters and their social interactions, and compared to younger authors, older authors wrote more vivid and emotional stories. Raters preferred stories written all at once rather than broken up into multiple stages, and raters age

45 and older rate stories significantly lower than raters under age 45. We release our dataset, STO-RIESINTHEWILD, containing 1,630 stories with quality ratings and anonymized author and rater demographics.

Our results suggest that author and reader characteristics (e.g., demographics, personality) could explain variations in story writing evaluations. While work has shown that some study designs are more robust against this variation, (e.g., by ranking instead of rating Yannakakis and Martínez, 2015), rater differences could still lead to variation in annotations. We recommend that evaluations include some ability to collect characteristics, such as a short demographics and personality questionnaire, in order to assess any influence of these variables.

Furthermore, future work could explore alternative ways of collecting author and reader characteristics during evaluations. While demographic questionnaires are common and short (e.g., to collect gender and age would require two questions), full personality questionnaires are time consuming, asking multiple questions for each characteristic. Study designers could instead use reduced questionnaires, such as the ten item personality inventory (TIPI; Gosling et al., 2003). Alternatively, focusing on fewer, more highly trained raters—that represent a diverse set of demographics and personality—could reduce the cost of collecting many rater demographics. Finally, future work should investigate whether annotator variance might be better captured with psychological factors related to reading (e.g., propensity for liking long sentences or fiction) rather than stable traits such as personality or demographics.

Our results that author personality and gender were associated with topic selection and story writing also suggest that studies could leverage the behavior of participants to predict personality characteristics. While these results are not yet strong enough to provide robust measures of personality or demographics, future studies could explore how to leverage these associations to predict author characteristics in story writing or other writing evaluations rather than relying on questionnaires.

Acknowledgments

This work was partially funded by NSF award 1651487, an NSF graduate research fellowship, and the DARPA CwC program through ARO (W911NF-15-1-0543). We thank the anonymous reviewers and members of the UWNLP community for their helpful feedback. We would also like to thank the LabintheWild volunteers for writing stories and the Mechanical Turk workers for reading them.

References

Tal August, Nigini Oliveira, Chenhao Tan, Noah Smith, and Katharina Reinecke. 2018. Framing effects: Choice of slogans used to advertise online experiments can boost recruitment and lead to sample biases. *Proceedings of the ACM on Human-Computer Interaction*, (CSCW):1–19.

Luke Breitfeller, Emily Ahn, David Jurgens, and Yulia Tsvetkov. 2019. Finding microaggressions in the wild: A case for locating elusive phenomena in social media posts. In *Proceedings of the 2019 Conference on Empirical Methods in Natural Language Processing*.

Elizabeth Clark, Anne Spencer Ross, Chenhao Tan, Yangfeng Ji, and Noah A Smith. 2018. Creative writing with a machine in the loop: Case studies on slogans and stories. In *23rd International Conference on Intelligent User Interfaces*, pages 329–340.

Martin Conway and Christopher Pleydell-Pearce. 2000. The construction of autobiographical memories in the self-memory system. *Psychology Review*, 107(2):261–288.

Paul T Costa Jr and Robert R McCrae. 2008. *The Revised NEO Personality Inventory (NEO-PI-R)*. Sage Publications, Inc.

Brent Donnellan, Frederick Oswald, Brendan Baird, and Richard Lucas. 2006. The mini-IPIP scales: tiny-yet-effective measures of the big five factors of personality. *Psychological assessment*, 18(2):192.

Angela Fan, Mike Lewis, and Yann Dauphin. 2018. Hierarchical neural story generation. In *Association of Computational Linguistics*, pages 889–898.

Mor Geva, Yoav Goldberg, and Jonathan Berant. 2019. Are we modeling the task or the annotator? an investigation of annotator bias in natural language understanding datasets. In *Empirical Methods in Natural Language Processing*, pages 1161–1166.

Samuel D Gosling, Peter J Rentfrow, and William B Swann Jr. 2003. A very brief measure of the big-five personality domains. *Journal of Research in personality*, 37(6):504–528.

Tatsunori B. Hashimoto, Hugh Zhang, and Percy Liang. 2019. Unifying human and statistical evaluation for natural language generation. In *North American Chapter of the Association for Computational Linguistics: Human Language Technologies*.

Jacob B Hirsh and Jordan B Peterson. 2009. Personality and language use in self-narratives. *Journal of Research in Personality*, 43(3):524–527.

Sture Holm. 1979. A simple sequentially rejective multiple test procedure. *Scandinavian journal of statistics*, pages 65–70.

Ting-Hao K. Huang, Francis Ferraro, Nasrin Mostafazadeh, Ishan Misra, Jacob Devlin, Aishwarya Agrawal, Ross Girshick, Xiaodong He, Pushmeet Kohli, Dhruv Batra, et al. 2016. Visual storytelling. In *North American Chapter of the Association for Computational Linguistics: Human Language Technologies*.

Mohit Iyyer, Varun Manjunatha, Anupam Guha, Yogarshi Vyas, Jordan Boyd-Graber, Hal Daume, and Larry S Davis. 2017. The amazing mysteries of the gutter: Drawing inferences between panels in comic book narratives. In *Proceedings of the IEEE Conference on Computer Vision and Pattern Recognition*, pages 7186–7195.

Eunice Jun, Gary Hsieh, and Katharina Reinecke. 2017. Types of motivation affect study selection, attention, and dropouts in online experiments. *Proceedings of the ACM on Human-Computer Interaction*, 1(CSCW):1–15.

Irwin P Levin, Gary J Gaeth, Judy Schreiber, and Marco Lauriola. 2002. A new look at framing effects: Distribution of effect sizes, individual differences, and independence of types of effects. *Organizational behavior and human decision processes*, 88(1):411–429.

Judith Lorber, Susan A Farrell, et al. 1991. The social construction of gender. *Newbury Park*, 5.

Robert R McCrae. 1987. Creativity, divergent thinking, and openness to experience. *Journal of personality and social psychology*, 52(6):1258.

Christiana D Morgan and Henry A Murray. 1935. A method for investigating fantasies: The thematic apperception test. *Archives of Neurology & Psychiatry*, 34(2):289–306.

Dong Nguyen, A Seza Doğruöz, Carolyn P Rosé, and Franciska de Jong. 2016. Computational sociolinguistics: A survey. *Computational linguistics*, 42(3):537–593.

James W Pennebaker, Roger J Booth, Ryan L Boyd, and Martha E Francis. 2015. Linguistic inquiry and word count: LIWC 2015.

James W Pennebaker, Cindy K Chung, Joey Frazee, Gary M Lavergne, and David I Beaver. 2014. When small words foretell academic success: The case of college admissions essays. *Public Library of Science (PloS) one*, 9(12).

James W Pennebaker and Janel D Seagal. 1999. Forming a story: the health benefits of narrative. *Journal of Clinical Psychology*, 55(10):1243–1254.

Christopher Purdy, Xinyu Wang, Larry He, and Mark O. Riedl. 2018. Predicting generated story quality with quantitative measures. In *The Artificial Intelligence for Interactive Digital Entertainment Conference*.

Katharina Reinecke and Krzysztof Z Gajos. 2015. Labinthewild: Conducting large-scale online experiments with uncompensated samples. In *Proceedings of the ACM on Human-Computer Interaction*, pages 1364–1378. ACM.

Maarten Sap, Dallas Card, Saadia Gabriel, Yejin Choi, and Noah A Smith. 2019. The risk of racial bias in hate speech detection. In *Association of Computational Linguistics*.

Andrew Schwartz, Johannes Eichstaedt, Margaret Kern, Lukasz Dziurzynski, Stephanie Ramones, Megha Agrawal, Achal Shah, Michal Kosinski, David Stillwell, Martin EP Seligman, et al. 2013. Personality, gender, and age in the language of social media: The open-vocabulary approach. *Public Library of Science (PloS) one*, 8(9).

Jaime Teevan, Shamsi T Iqbal, and Curtis Von Veh. 2016. Supporting collaborative writing with microtasks. In *Proceedings of the 2016 CHI Conference on Human Factors in Computing Systems*, pages 2657–2668.

Georgios N Yannakakis and Héctor P Martínez. 2015. Ratings are overrated! *Frontiers in Information and communications technology*, 2:13.

Lili Yao, Nanyun Peng, Ralph Weischedel, Kevin Knight, Dongyan Zhao, and Rui Yan. 2019. Plan-and-write: Towards better automatic storytelling. In *Association for the Advancement of Artificial Intelligence*, volume 33, pages 7378–7385.

Tal Yarkoni. 2010. Personality in 100,000 words: A large-scale analysis of personality and word use among bloggers. *Journal of research in personality*, 44(3):363–373.

Figure 1: Prompts used in the story writing stage of our data collection.

A StoriesInTheWild Collection

We provide additional details about our data collection process, including the image prompts shown to authors (Figure 1) and the writing setups (Figure 2).

A.1 Motivating LabintheWild authors

Since LabintheWild is a volunteer-based crowd-sourcing platform, we design our task such that participants can learn about their personality through story writing as a motivation. The study was advertised on the front page of LabintheWild and posted on social media to recruit participants.

Once a participant finishes their story, we compute their personality estimate (using the Five Factor Model) based on their story language. Specifically, we extract their pronoun usage using the pronoun categories in LIWC (Pennebaker et al., 2015), and predict personality scores using the coefficients from Schwartz et al. (2013). At the end of the task, we display their personality predictions along with short descriptions of which trait is the most present in their writing (i.e., the trait whose score has the highest magnitude).

Optionally, participants could take a short personality questionnaire (TIPI; Gosling et al., 2003) before seeing their writing-based personality re-

sults. Those who answered these questions could then see their questionnaire-based and their writing-based personality estimates at the end of the task. The end of the task also debriefs participants, explaining the goal of the study and researcher contact information. The debriefing information also includes disclaimers about the personality scores computed from story writing and reiterates that the results should not be used for clinical or diagnostic purposes.

B Analyses

We present further details of our demographic analyses, both between the author demographics and their language use (§B.2) and between the author and reader demographics (§B.3).

B.1 Author demographics and topic choice

To ensure the validity of our other analyses, we examine whether an author's identity was associated with their choosing one of the five topics (Figure 1). We find that only an author's agreeableness affected their choice of image prompt, with highly agreeable authors preferring the dog story (Cohen's $d = 0.30$, $p < 0.001$; Figure 1a) and low agreeableness authors preferring the jail story ($d = 0.41$, $p < 0.001$; Figure 1b). Other demographic variables were comparable for every im-

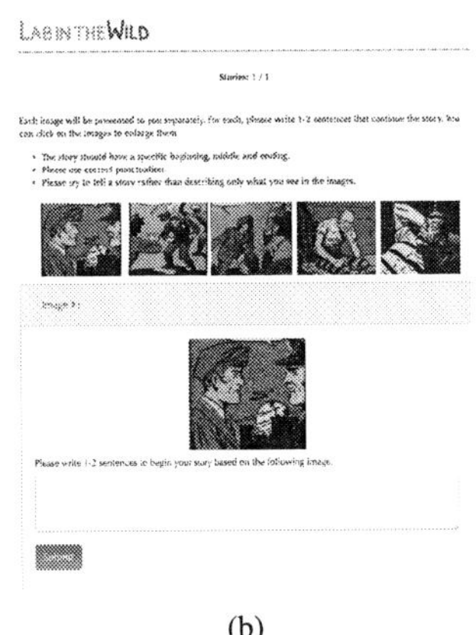

(a)

(b)

Figure 2: Writing interfaces for the crowdsourcing study using the jail cartoon. (a) is all-at-once interface and (b) is the accordion interface. For (b), participants could see all images at the top, but had to write 1-2 sentences about each image separately though an accordian of text boxes.

age prompt (as measured by one-way ANOVAs.)

B.2 Linguistic signal of author demographics

As described in §4.1, we first extract language categories from stories using the LIWC (Pennebaker et al., 2015) lexicon. Then, we use a linear regression model to compute the association between the category and the author's demographics, using z-scored LIWC features for easier interpretation of the regression coefficients (βs).

Our findings, outlined in Table 2, show that an author's identity and personality are somewhat associated with the types of stories they tell (controlling for the type of image prompt they used). Men focused on describing characters (pronoun, social), specifically female characters, whereas women displayed more hierarchical logical storytelling (Analytic; Pennebaker et al., 2014). Controlling for gender, we find that older authors wrote more vivid stories with more emotional tone (Tone, Exclam), more friendship words, and more visual descriptions (percept). In contrast, younger authors wrote in a more past-focused way.

Controlling for age and gender, we find effects of the author's agreeableness and conscientiousness personality traits on the types of language used in stories. We don't see significant effects on the extraversion, openness, or neuroticism scales, likely due to our small sample size of 1.6k (e.g., compared to the 75k users in Schwartz et al., 2013). Shown in Table 2, less conscientious authors wrote more negative stories, whereas more conscientious authors were more positive and fo-cused on character motivations (drives, reward). Less agreeable authors used more swear words.

B.3 Rater and author interaction

As explained in §4.2, we analyze how rater and author traits relate to story ratings. We run linear regression models using story ratings as dependent variables and rater demographics and personality traits as independent variables. We include author demographics and interaction features in these regression models to see if any shared traits across raters and authors were associated with rater preferences. As in all previous analyses, we include story and image type in each model as controlling variables. We report p-values and β coefficients for each regression feature. Full details on the regression results are in Table 3.

	gender β	age β	agreeableness β	conscientiousness β
Analytic	0.228**	n.s.	n.s.	n.s.
Tone	n.s.	0.047*	n.s.	0.144**
function	-0.192*	n.s.	n.s.	n.s.
pronoun	-0.224**	n.s.	n.s.	n.s.
ppron	-0.292***	n.s.	n.s.	n.s.
you	n.s.	0.037*	n.s.	n.s.
shehe	-0.191†	n.s.	n.s.	n.s.
conj	-0.263***	n.s.	n.s.	n.s.
verb	n.s.	-0.034†	n.s.	n.s.
number	n.s.	-0.033†	n.s.	n.s.
posemo	n.s.	0.04*	n.s.	n.s.
negemo	n.s.	n.s.	n.s.	-0.115†
sad	n.s.	-0.035†	n.s.	n.s.
social	-0.283***	n.s.	n.s.	n.s.
friend	n.s.	0.056***	n.s.	n.s.
female	-0.334***	n.s.	n.s.	n.s.
differ	-0.191*	n.s.	-0.097†	n.s.
percept	n.s.	0.051***	n.s.	n.s.
see	n.s.	0.04**	n.s.	n.s.
hear	n.s.	0.036*	n.s.	n.s.
drives	n.s.	n.s.	n.s.	0.116*
reward	n.s.	n.s.	n.s.	0.101†
focuspast	-0.184*	-0.038*	n.s.	n.s.
leisure	n.s.	0.036†	n.s.	n.s.
swear	n.s.	n.s.	-0.155†	n.s.
Exclam	n.s.	0.076***	n.s.	n.s.

Table 2: Results of our LIWC analyses, showing β coefficients between usage of each category with the author's gender, age (gender-controlled), personality (age- and gender-controlled). We additionally control for topic choice. Gender is coded 0 for men, 1 for women. Only results that are significant after applying Holm-correction are shown ($n.s.: p > 0.1$; †: $p < 0.1$; *: $p < 0.05$; **: $p < 0.01$; ***: $p < 0.001$). Extraversion, Opennness, and Neuroticism are omitted since there were no significant correlations for those traits (likely due dearth of data).

Traits	Like	Creative	Coherent	Confusing	Entertaining	Grammatical
Rater Age (45+)	-0.42***	-0.25*	-0.37***	0.27*	-0.39 ***	-0.30 *
Author Age (45+)	n.s.	n.s.	n.s.	n.s.	n.s.	n.s.
Rater Age:Author Age	n.s.	n.s.	n.s.	n.s.	n.s.	n.s.
Rater Gender (Woman)	n.s.	n.s.	n.s.	n.s.	n.s.	n.s.
Author Gender (Woman)	n.s.	n.s.	n.s.	n.s.	n.s.	n.s.
Rater Gender:Author Gender	n.s.	n.s.	n.s.	n.s.	n.s.	n.s.
Rater Openness	n.s.	0.38*	n.s.	-0.64***	n.s.	n.s.
Author Openness	n.s.	0.35†	n.s..	n.s.	n.s.	n.s.
Rater Openness:Author Openness	n.s.	-0.50†	n.s..	n.s.	n.s.	n.s.

Table 3: Table with regression results for associations between rater and author traits and story ratings. Corrected for multiple hypothesis testing. ($n.s.: p > 0.1$; †: $p < 0.1$; *: $p < 0.05$; **: $p < 0.01$; ***: $p < 0.001$).

Script Induction as Association Rule Mining

Anton Belyy and **Benjamin Van Durme**

Department of Computer Science
Johns Hopkins University
{abel,vandurme}@jhu.edu

Abstract

We show that the count-based Script Induction models of Chambers and Jurafsky (2008) and Jans et al. (2012) can be unified in a general framework of narrative chain likelihood maximization. We provide efficient algorithms based on Association Rule Mining (ARM) and weighted set cover that can discover interesting patterns in the training data and combine them in a reliable and explainable way to predict the missing event. The proposed method, unlike the prior work, does not assume full conditional independence and makes use of higher-order count statistics. We perform the ablation study and conclude that the inductive biases introduced by ARM are conducive to better performance on the narrative cloze test.

1 Introduction

The goal of this paper is to demonstrate how the efforts in Script Induction (SI), up until recently dominated by statistical approaches (Chambers and Jurafsky, 2008; Jans et al., 2012; Pichotta and Mooney, 2014; Rudinger et al., 2015a,b), can be productively framed and extended as a special case of Association Rule Mining (ARM), a well-established problem in Data Mining (Agrawal et al., 1993, 1994; Han et al., 2000).

We start by introducing SI and ARM and then demonstrate a unification under a general chain likelihood maximization framework. We discuss how the existing count-based SI models tackle this maximization problem using naïve Bayes assumptions. We provide an alternative: mining higher-order count statistics using ARM and picking the most reliable rules using the weighted set cover algorithm. We validate the proposed approach and demonstrate improved performance over other count-based approaches. We conclude with a discussion on the implications and potential extensions of the proposed framework.

ARM term	SI term
Transaction t	Narrative chain
Itemset I	Co-occurring events
$\sup(\{i_1, i_2\})$	$C(i_1, i_2)$
$\operatorname{int}(\{a\} \to \{e\})$	$P(a\|e) = \frac{C(a,e)}{C(*,e)}$
$\sup(I), \|I\| > 2$	**Eq. 5**
$\operatorname{int}(A \to \{e\}), \|A\| > 1$	**Eq. 12**

Table 1: Mapping between ARM and Count-based SI terminology. **Bolded** are contributions of this paper. Namely, we make use of *frequent itemsets* and *interesting rules*, or higher-order count statistics that can be efficiently mined and used in the narrative cloze test.

Our intent in this work is not to establish new state of the art results in the area of SI. Rather, our primary contribution is retrospective, drawing a connection between a sub-topic in Computational Linguistics (CL) with a major pre-existing area of Computer Science, i.e., Data Mining. In the case one approached SI through counting co-occurrence statistics, then the existing tools of ARM lead naturally to solutions that had not been previously considered within CL.

2 Background

2.1 Association Rule Mining

ARM is a prevalent problem in Data Mining, introduced by Agrawal et al. (1993). The task is often referred to as *market basket analysis* due to its widespread usage for discovering interesting patterns in consumer purchases. The applicability of ARM extends far beyond this specific scenario, where examples of ARM usage for NLP applications include detecting annotation inconsistencies (Novák and Razímová, 2009), discovering strongly-related events (Shibata and Kurohashi, 2011), adding missing knowledge to the KB

Proceedings of the 1st Joint Workshop on Narrative Understanding, Storylines, and Events, pages 55–62
July 9, 2020. ©2020 Association for Computational Linguistics

(Galárraga et al., 2013), as well as understanding clinical narratives (Boytcheva et al., 2017).

ARM aims to extract interesting patterns from a transactional database $\mathcal{D}$. A transaction is a set of *items*, and a non-empty subset of a transaction is called an *itemset*. We define *support* as the number of transactions we observe an itemset I in:

$$\text{sup}(I) = |\{t|t \in \mathcal{D}, I \subseteq t\}|. \quad (1)$$

We say that an itemset I is *frequent*, if its support (on a given database $\mathcal{D}$) exceeeds a user-defined threshold t_{sup}: $\text{sup}(I) \geq t_{sup}$.

A pair of itemsets A, B is called a *rule* if $A \cap B = \varnothing$ and is denoted as $A \rightarrow B$. We say that a rule $A \rightarrow B$ is *interesting* if 1) both A and B are frequent, 2) the *interestingess* of the rule exceeds a user-defined threshold t_{int}: $\text{int}(A \rightarrow B) \geq t_{int}$. The definition of the interestingness function $\text{int}(\cdot)$ is problem-specific.

ARM is thus concerned with:

1. mining frequent itemsets from a transactional database,

2. discovering interesting rules from frequent itemsets.

2.2 Script Induction

The concept of *script knowledge* in AI, along with early knowledge-based methods to learn scripts were introduced by Minsky (1974); Schank and Abelson (1977); Mooney and DeJong (1985).

With the rise of statistical methods, the next generation of algorithms made use of co-occurrence statistics and distributional semantics for script learning (Chambers and Jurafsky, 2008, 2009; Jans et al., 2012; Pichotta and Mooney, 2014). Our primary focus is on drawing connections between ARM and this body of work.

Following Chambers and Jurafsky (2008), we define a *narrative chain* as "a partially ordered set of narrative events that share a common actor", where the partial ordering typically represents temporal or causal order of events, and a *narrative event* is "a tuple of an event and its participants, represented as typed dependencies". Formally, we define a narrative event $e := (v, d)$, where v is a verb lemma, and d is a dependency arc between the verb and the common actor (dobj or nsubj). An example of a narrative chain is given in Figure 1.

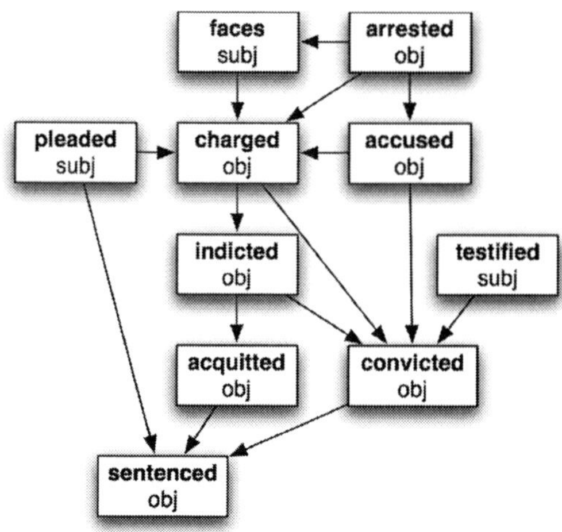

Figure 1: Graphical depiction of a Prosecution narrative chain learned by Chambers and Jurafsky (2008). Arrows indicate partial temporal ordering.

SI is thus concerned with:

1. automatic mining of commonly co-occurring sets of narrative events from text,

2. partially ordering those sets.

The *narrative cloze* test (Chambers and Jurafsky, 2008) is a standard extrinsic evaluation procedure for Task 1 of SI. In this test, a sequence of narrative events is automatically extracted from a document, and one event is removed; the goal is to predict the missing event. Formally, given an incomplete narrative chain $\{e_1, e_2, \ldots, e_L\}$ and an *insertion point* $k \in [L]$, we would like to predict the most likely missing event $\hat{e}$ to complete the chain:

$$\{e_1, e_2, \ldots, e_k, \hat{e}, e_{k+1}, \ldots e_L\}.$$

Although the recent work in SI (Rudinger et al., 2015b; Pichotta and Mooney, 2016; Peng and Roth, 2016; Weber et al., 2018) has focused on a Language Modeling (LM) approach for the narrative cloze test, it is fundamentally different from ARM in that it makes use of the total ordering of events and is thus incomparable to ARM, which does not assume any ordering of events within a chain.

In the next section, we survey two of the most influential count-based SI models, showing how each of them is related to ARM.

3 Count-based Script Induction

3.1 Unordered PMI model

The original model for this task by Chambers and Jurafsky (2008) is based on the pointwise mutual information (PMI) between events.

$$\text{pmi}(e_1, e_2) \propto \log \frac{C(e_1, e_2)}{C(e_1, *)C(*, e_2)}, \qquad (2)$$

where $C(e_1, e_2)$ is defined as the number of narrative chains where e_1 and e_2 both occurred and

$$C(e, *) := \sum_{e' \in E} C(e, e'),$$

where E is a fixed vocabulary of narrative events.

The model selects the missing event $\hat{e}$ in the narrative cloze test according to the score

$$\hat{e} = \arg\max_{e \in E} \sum_{i=1}^{L} \text{pmi}(e, e_i), \qquad (3)$$

assuming that the missing event $\hat{e}$ is inserted at the end of the existing chain ($k = L$).

From (2) and (3) we observe that

$$\begin{aligned}
\hat{e} &= \arg\max_{e \in E} \sum_{i=1}^{L} \text{pmi}(e, e_i) \\
&= \arg\max_{e \in E} \sum_{i=1}^{L} \log \frac{C(e, e_i)}{C(e, *)C(*, e_i)} \\
&= \arg\max_{e \in E} \log \prod_{i=1}^{L} \frac{C(e, e_i)}{C(e, *)} \\
&= \arg\max_{e \in E} \log \prod_{i=1}^{L} P(e_i|e) \\
&= \arg\max_{e \in E} \prod_{i=1}^{L} P(e_i|e). \qquad (4)
\end{aligned}$$

One way to interpret Eq. 4 is to say that it was obtained from the following model with the *naïve Bayes assumption*:

$$\hat{e} = \arg\max_{e \in E} P(e_1, e_2, \dots, e_L|e). \qquad (5)$$

Importantly, in the above equation, no assumptions are made about the order in which events $e_1, \dots, e_L$ happened and we treat the narrative chain as a document, where individual events are features (the "bag of events" assumption).

3.2 Bigram Probability model

The bigram probability model was proposed by Jans et al. (2012) and was also used by Pichotta and Mooney (2014). It utilizes positional information between co-occurring events. It selects the missing event $\hat{e}$ according to the score

$$\hat{e} = \arg\max_{e \in E} \left(\prod_{i=1}^{k} P(e|e_i) \right) \cdot \left(\prod_{i=k+1}^{L} P(e_i|e) \right),$$

where k is the insertion point of the missing event $\hat{e}$, $P(e_2|e_1) = \frac{C_{ord}(e_1, e_2)}{C_{ord}(e_1, *)}$, and counts $C_{ord}(e_1, e_2)$ are ordered, e.g. $C_{ord}(e_1, e_2) \neq C_{ord}(e_2, e_1)$.

Similarly to the Unordered PMI model, we can relax the conditional independence assumption. However, to apply Bayes' theorem, we would need (e_1, e_2) and (e_2, e_1) to be the same events in the outcome space, thus we have to assume unordered counts: $C(e_1, e_2) = C_{ord}(e_1, e_2) + C_{ord}(e_2, e_1)$. Proceeding with this, we get:

$$\begin{aligned}
\hat{e} &= \arg\max_{e \in E} \left(\prod_{i=1}^{k} P(e|e_i) \right) \cdot \left(\prod_{i=k+1}^{L} P(e_i|e) \right) \\
&= \arg\max_{e \in E} \left(\prod_{i=1}^{L} P(e_i|e) \right) \cdot (P(e))^k \\
&= \arg\max_{e \in E} \log \left(\left(\prod_{i=1}^{L} P(e_i|e) \right) \cdot (P(e))^k \right) \\
&= \arg\max_{e \in E} \log P(e_1, \dots, e_L|e) + k \cdot \log P(e),
\end{aligned}$$
$$(6)$$

where the last equality is obtained by relaxing the full conditional independence assumption (similar to Eq. 5). It follows that the Bigram Probability model with unordered counts is exactly the Unordered PMI model augmented with the prior probability of a missing event multiplied by its position in a chain. Additionally, note that if $k = 1$, this model is equivalent to maximizing the posterior probability of a missing event (rather than the likelihood of a narrative chain in Eq. 5):

$$\begin{aligned}
\hat{e} &= \arg\max_{e \in E} \log P(e_1, \dots, e_L|e) + \log P(e) \\
&= \arg\max_{e \in E} \log \left(P(e_1, \dots, e_L|e) \cdot P(e) \right) \\
&= \arg\max_{e \in E} \log P(e|e_1, \dots, e_L). \qquad (7)
\end{aligned}$$

Similar to Eq. 5, we view the narrative chain $e_1, \dots, e_n$ as a set, and thus Eq. 6 is not a language model in the traditional NLP sense.

4 SI as ARM

The models defined by Eqs. 5, 6, and 7 are hard to compute directly: without simplifying assumptions, they would require huge number of parameters and large training sets (Jurafsky and Martin, 2019). A common approach in the existing Count-based SI work is to assume full conditional independence. A viable and less restrictive alternative, as we show in this section, is estimating higher-order count statistics via mining association rules (Section 4.1) and combining the most confident rules to predict the missing event with a simple weighted set cover algorithm (Section 4.2).

More formally, during the training phase, we would like to populate the set of interesting rules $\mathbb{S} = \{S \to \{e\}\}$, whose antecedents are sub-sets of the event space $S \subset E$, and consequents are single events e, $e \notin S$. We denote as $\mathbb{S}_e$ all the rules with the same consequent event e.

During the test phase, where we have an incomplete narrative chain $\{e_1, e_2, \ldots, e_L\}$ and want to predict a missing event, we will use rules from $\mathbb{S}_e$ to efficiently decompose $P(e_1, e_2, \ldots, e_L | e)$ into $P(S_1 | e) \cdot P(S_2 | e) \cdot \ldots \cdot P(S_t | e)$ for each candidate event e. Naturally, this means selecting a set of rules whose antecedents $\{S_1, S_2, \ldots, S_t\}$ (we call this set a candidate cover) are pairwise disjoint $(S_i \cap S_j = \varnothing \ \forall i, j \in [t])$, and cover the event chain fully $(S_1 \cup S_2 \cup \ldots \cup S_t = \{e_1, e_2, \ldots, e_L\})$.

To quantify the goodness of the decomposition, we define a score function for a candidate cover $\{S_1, \ldots, S_t\}$ and a candidate event e as follows:

$$\text{score}(S_1, S_2, \ldots, S_t; e) = \prod_{i=1}^{t} P(S_i | e). \quad (8)$$

For each candidate event e, we select the best candidate cover $\hat{S}_e$ according to the score function:

$$\hat{S}_e = \underset{\{S_1', \ldots, S_{t'}'\} \in \mathbb{S}_e}{\arg\max} \ \text{score}(S_1', \ldots, S_{t'}'; e). \quad (9)$$

This allows to rewrite Eq. 5 as:

$$\hat{e} = \underset{e \in E}{\arg\max} \ \hat{S}_e. \quad (10)$$

In Section 4.1, we explain how the set of rules $\mathbb{S}$ is populated from the SI training corpus. In Section 4.2, we provide a randomized algorithm that solves problem 9 with a provably bounded error.

4.1 Mining interesting rules

As discussed in Section 2.1, in order to discover the set of interesting rules $\mathbb{S}$, we need to mine frequent itemsets first. This can be achieved by any frequent itemset mining algorithm, such as Apriori (Agrawal et al., 1994), Eclat (Zaki, 2000), or FP-growth (Han et al., 2000).

Next, for the rule mining step we define an interestingness function $\text{int}(S \to E)$ over a rule $S \to E$:

$$\text{int}(S \to E) = \frac{\sup(S \cup E)}{\sum_{S'} \sup(S' \cup E)}, \quad (11)$$

where S' ranges over all itemsets of size $|S|$ and is disjoint with E.

Note that $\text{int}(S \to E)$ provides a maximum likelihood estimate of $P(S|E)$ for the probability space defined over sets of events, and $\sup(\cdot)$ is a generalization of the previously defined $C(\cdot, \cdot)$ for event sets of size larger than two.

The denominator of (11) requires calculating the support over exponentially many itemsets. We can instead use the following simpler formula:

$$\text{wsup}_k(I) = \sum_{t \in \mathcal{D}} \binom{|t| - |I|}{k} \cdot \mathbf{1}_{I \subseteq t},$$

where $\mathcal{D}$ is a transactional database of narrative event chains.

Lemma 1. $\sum_{S'} \sup(S' \cup I) = \text{wsup}_k(I)$, where S' ranges over all itemsets of size k, disjoint with I.

Proof. By definition of support from Eq. 1,

$$\sum_{S'} \sup(S' \cup I)$$

$$= \sum_{S'} |\{t | t \in \mathcal{D}, S' \cup I \subseteq t\}|$$

$$= \sum_{S'} |\{t | t \in \mathcal{D}, (S' \subseteq t/I) \wedge (I \subseteq t)\}|$$

$$= \sum_{t \in \mathcal{D}} \mathbf{1}_{I \subseteq t} \cdot \sum_{S'} \mathbf{1}_{S' \subseteq t/I}$$

$$= \sum_{t \in \mathcal{D}} \mathbf{1}_{I \subseteq t} \cdot \binom{|t| - |I|}{k}$$

$$= \text{wsup}_k(I).$$

$\square$

Algorithm 1 Mining interesting rules

1: **Input:** A set of high-support itemsets $\mathbb{I}$,
2: **Output:** A set of interesting rules $\mathbb{S}$.
3: **Initialization:** $\mathbb{S} = \varnothing$
4: **for** $I \in \mathbb{I}$ **do**
5:    **for** $e \in I$ **do**
6:       $S = I \backslash \{e\}$
7:       **if** $\text{int}(S \to \{e\}) \geq t_{int}$ **then**
8:          $\mathbb{S} = \mathbb{S} \cup \{S \to \{e\}\}$
9:       **end if**
10:    **end for**
11: **end for**
12: Return $\mathbb{S}$.

Algorithm 2 Greedy weighted set cover

1: **Input:**
- A set of interesting rules $\mathbb{S}_e$,
- A narrative chain $e_1, e_2, \ldots, e_L$.

2: **Output:** An approximation (within a $O(\log L)$ factor) of the best cover $\{S_1, S_2, \ldots, S_t\}$.
3: **Initialization:**
4:    $U_0 = \{e_1, e_2, \ldots, e_L\}$
5:    $t = 0$
6: **while** $U_t \neq \varnothing$ **do**
7:    $t = t + 1$
8:    $S_t = \underset{S' \in \mathbb{S}_e}{\arg\max} \ \frac{|S' \cap U_{t-1}|}{w(S')}$
9:    $U_t = U_{t-1} \backslash S_t$
10: **end while**
11: Return $\{S_1, S_2, \ldots, S_t\}$.

Our intent is to use the above interestingness function to score rules from $\mathbb{S}$ that have a single event as a consequent, and thus Eq. 11 can be further simplified:

$$\text{int}(S \to \{e\}) = \frac{\sup(S \cup \{e\})}{\text{wsup}_{|S|}(\{e\})}. \qquad (12)$$

Assuming that for each rule $S \to \{e\}$ the antecedent is bounded in size and small, we can precompute $\text{wsup}_k(\{e\})$ for each $e \in E$ and each $k \in [|S|]$ in a single pass over the database. Note also that $\text{wsup}_0(I) = \sup(I)$ and thus $\text{wsup}_k(\cdot)$ is a generalization of support (1).

Given an interestingness function, we can now proceed to mine interesting rules over frequent event sets. The rule mining process is shown in Algorithm 1.

After a set of interesting rules $\mathbb{S}$ is populated, we can perform test-time inference on new narrative chains with Eqs. 9 and 10. To facilitate this, we frame the inference problem as the weighted set cover problem. The latter was known to be NP-complete by Karp (1972), but there is a simple greedy algorithm by Chvatal (1979) that provides an approximate solution. To make it applicable to the search problem 9, we will run it (for each candidate event e) on the set $\mathbb{S}$, mined by Algorithm 1, with the following weight function:

$$\begin{aligned} w(S) &= -\ln \text{int}(S \to \{e\}) \\ &= -\ln P(S|e). \end{aligned}$$

The following lemma provides a lower bound on the score of the candidate cover obtained by Algorithm 2.

4.2 Score estimation via weighted set cover

Lemma 2. *Algorithm 2 finds a candidate cover* $\{S_1, \ldots, S_t\}$ *for a narrative chain* $\{e_1, \ldots, e_L\}$ *and a candidate event e, such that* $\text{score}(S_1, \ldots, S_t; e) \geq OPT^{\ln L + 1}$, *where OPT is the score of the best candidate cover $\hat{S}_e$.*

Proof. Chvatal (1979) showed that Algorithm 2 finds a weighted set cover $\{S_1, \ldots, S_t\}$, such that

$$OPT_{cover} \leq \sum_{i=1}^{t} w(S_i) \leq (\ln L + 1)OPT_{cover}.$$

Since the weight $w(\cdot)$ is a negative log probability:

$$\begin{aligned} \sum_{i=1}^{t} w(S_i) &= -\sum_{i=1}^{t} \ln P(S_i|e) \\ &= -\ln \text{score}(S_1, \ldots, S_t; e) \\ &\leq (\ln L + 1)OPT_{cover}. \end{aligned}$$

By exponentiating left and right-hand sides and noting that $OPT = e^{-OPT_{cover}}$ (by definition of the weight and score functions), we get:

$$\begin{aligned} \text{score}(S_1, \ldots, S_t; e) &\geq e^{-(\ln L + 1)OPT_{cover}} \\ &\geq OPT^{\ln L + 1}. \end{aligned}$$

$\square$

If we group the rules $S \to \{e\}$ by the consequent event and order by $\frac{|S|}{w(S)}$ within each group, then step 8 in Algorithm 2 becomes equivalent to iterating over ordered rules in $\mathbb{S}_e$. The overall running time to score the candidate event e is $O(L + |\mathbb{S}_e|)$.

Additionally, $O(\sum_{e \in E} |\mathbb{S}_e| \log |\mathbb{S}_e|)$ preprocessing time is needed to group and order the rules in $\mathbb{S}$.

5 Experiments

5.1 Dataset

We perform experiments on the New York Times part of the Annotated Gigaword dataset by (Napoles et al., 2012). Chains of narrative events are constructed from the (automatically generated) in-document coreference chains: from each document in the dataset, we extract all coreference chains and retain the longest one, with length two or greater. We also filter top-10 occurring events which are mostly reporting verbs such as "say" and "think" and convey little meaning for SI task.

Training is done on the 1994–2006 portion (1.3M chains with 8.7M narrative events), development set is a subset of 2007–2008 portion (10K chains with 62K narrative events), and test set is a subset of 2009–2010 portion (5K chains with 31K narrative events).

5.2 Model setup

We implement and compare models described in Sections 3 and 4, along with a strong baseline Unigram model by Pichotta and Mooney (2014), which ranks each event according to its unigram probability in the training corpus.

For testing the Unordered PMI and Bigram models, we use implementations from the Nachos software package (Rudinger et al., 2015a). Both models are tuned to use skip-grams (as defined by Jans et al. (2012)) of size up to the chain length, which allows to reduce data sparsity and is consistent with the set of rules (of size two) generated by ARM.

ARM consists of 1) mining frequent itemsets and 2) obtaining interesting rules from those itemsets. For frequent itemsets mining, we use the FP-growth algorithm by Han et al. (2000) with a $t_{sup} = 100$ threshold. For rule mining, we implement Algorithm 1. Since the rule mining step is much less computationally intensive than itemset mining, we can use a more permissive $t_{int} = 10^{-5}$ threshold. We use the same thresholds across all models by applying the following back-off strategy in the Unordered PMI and Bigram models:

$$P(e_i|e) = \begin{cases} \frac{C(e_i,e)}{C(*,e)} & \text{if } C(e_i, e) \geq t_{ARM}, \\ \frac{1}{|E|+1} & \text{otherwise,} \end{cases}$$

where $t_{ARM} = \max\left(t_{sup}, C(*, e) \cdot t_{int}\right)$.

Ablation	R@50
ARM (posterior, (7))	0.36
ARM (bigram, (6))	0.34
ARM (UOP, (5))	0.30
ARM (UOP, binary rules only, (4))	0.28
UOP (both t_{sup} & t_{int} pruning, (4))	0.28
UOP (only t_{sup} pruning, (4))	0.28
UOP (only t_{int} pruning, (4))	0.03
UOP (no t_{int} & t_{sup} pruning, (4))	0.03

Table 2: Ablation experiments on NYTimes dev set. R@50 stands for Recall@50.

6 Experimental Results

We perform two experiments, comparing existing count-based SI models with three variants of the proposed ARM model. The performance is measured using Recall@50 and Mean Reciprocal Rank.

In the first experiment, we establish that the count-based pruning, introduced by ARM support and interestingness thresholds (t_{sup} and t_{int}, respectively) for reducing the search space during rule mining, does contribute to better performance on the narrative cloze test. We also validate empirically that the ARM model with binary (of size two) rules is equivalent to the UOP model by Chambers and Jurafsky (2008). Finally, we compare variants of the ARM model, which vary in a way of incorporating a prior probability of the missing event. We conclude that the posterior ARM model, given by Eq. 7, achieves the best performance. The results of this experiment are outlined in Table 2.

In the second experiment, we compare the best-scoring ARM model and other baseline models on 5,000 test chains. We achieve 5% relative improvement for Mean Reciprocal Rank (MRR) and 10% for Recall@50, which can be attributed to using higher-order count statistics and the selection of the prior for the missing event. The scalability of both rule mining and inference algorithms suggests that the performance may be further improved as the training corpus size grows and more reliable higher-order statistics become available. The results of this experiment are shown in Table 3.

Similar to Rudinger et al. (2015b), we also note that all models tend to improve their performance on longer chains, which may be explained by the availability of additional contextual information.

Len	UNI	UOP	BG	ARM	Tests
1	0.050	0.034	0.047	**0.060**	642
2	0.044	0.040	0.060	**0.061**	764
3	0.045	0.046	0.058	**0.063**	659
4	0.053	0.047	0.065	**0.070**	568
5	0.068	0.059	**0.087**	0.076	423
6	0.067	0.048	**0.074**	**0.074**	324
7	0.051	0.050	0.056	**0.063**	288
8	0.074	0.054	**0.088**	0.075	205
9	0.048	0.048	**0.068**	0.066	179
10+	0.044	0.064	0.062	**0.068**	948
ALL	0.051	0.049	0.063	**0.066**	5000

(a) Mean Reciprocal Rank (MRR)

Len	UNI	UOP	BG	ARM	Tests
1	0.34	0.17	0.24	**0.36**	642
2	0.28	0.22	0.28	**0.32**	764
3	0.30	0.28	0.32	**0.34**	659
4	0.32	0.29	0.34	**0.36**	568
5	0.33	0.30	0.35	**0.36**	423
6	0.33	0.33	0.36	**0.37**	324
7	0.30	0.32	0.33	**0.35**	288
8	0.33	0.34	0.36	**0.39**	205
9	0.35	0.35	**0.37**	**0.37**	179
10+	0.32	0.36	0.35	**0.36**	948
ALL	0.32	0.29	0.32	**0.35**	5000

(b) Percent Recall at 50

Table 3: Narrative cloze results bucketed by incomplete narrative chain length for each model and scoring function with best results in bold. The models are Unigram Model (UNI), Unordered PMI (UOP), Bigram Probability Model (BG), and proposed ARM model (ARM).

7 Conclusion

Our decision to approach count-based SI as ARM was motivated by a previously under-explored similarity of these well-established areas, which we outlined in this paper. Drawing similarities from the existing work on Classification using Association Rules (CAR) (Liu et al., 1998; Thabtah et al., 2005), we proposed a scoring function that uses ARM-based count statistics to reliably predict the missing event in the narrative cloze test.

One downside of relying solely on count-based statistics is the low support of longer itemsets due to data sparsity. On the other hand, modern contextual encoders (Devlin et al., 2018) mitigate this via parameter sharing. Reliably mining rules whose support and interestingness are based on both counts and properties of dense embeddings can be a promising direction of future work.

Acknowledgments

This work was supported by DARPA KAIROS. The U.S. Government is authorized to reproduce and distribute reprints for governmental purposes. The views and conclusions contained in this publication are those of the authors and should not be interpreted as representing official policies or endorsement.

We would like to thank Suzanna Sia, Kenton Murray, Noah Weber, and three anonymous reviewers for their feedback.

References

Rakesh Agrawal, Tomasz Imieliński, and Arun Swami. 1993. Mining association rules between sets of items in large databases. In *Proceedings of the 1993 ACM SIGMOD international conference on Management of data*, pages 207–216.

Rakesh Agrawal, Ramakrishnan Srikant, et al. 1994. Fast algorithms for mining association rules. In *Proc. 20th int. conf. very large data bases, VLDB*, volume 1215, pages 487–499.

Svetla Boytcheva, Ivelina Nikolova, and Galia Angelova. 2017. Mining association rules from clinical narratives. In *RANLP*, pages 130–138.

Nathanael Chambers and Dan Jurafsky. 2008. Unsupervised learning of narrative event chains. In *Proceedings of ACL-08: HLT*, pages 789–797.

Nathanael Chambers and Dan Jurafsky. 2009. Unsupervised learning of narrative schemas and their participants. In *Proceedings of the Joint Conference of the 47th Annual Meeting of the ACL and the 4th International Joint Conference on Natural Language Processing of the AFNLP: Volume 2-Volume 2*, pages 602–610. Association for Computational Linguistics.

Vasek Chvatal. 1979. A greedy heuristic for the set-covering problem. *Mathematics of operations research*, 4(3):233–235.

Jacob Devlin, Ming-Wei Chang, Kenton Lee, and Kristina Toutanova. 2018. Bert: Pre-training of deep bidirectional transformers for language understanding. *arXiv preprint arXiv:1810.04805*.

Luis Antonio Galárraga, Christina Teflioudi, Katja Hose, and Fabian Suchanek. 2013. Amie: association rule mining under incomplete evidence in ontological knowledge bases. In *Proceedings of the 22nd international conference on World Wide Web*, pages 413–422.

Jiawei Han, Jian Pei, and Yiwen Yin. 2000. Mining frequent patterns without candidate generation. *ACM sigmod record*, 29(2):1–12.

Bram Jans, Steven Bethard, Ivan Vulić, and Marie Francine Moens. 2012. Skip n-grams and ranking functions for predicting script events. In *Proceedings of the 13th Conference of the European Chapter of the Association for Computational Linguistics*, pages 336–344. Association for Computational Linguistics.

Dan Jurafsky and James H Martin. 2019. Speech and language processing (draft). *Chapter 4: Naive Bayes and Sentiment Classification (Draft of October 2, 2019)*.

Richard M Karp. 1972. Reducibility among combinatorial problems. In *Complexity of computer computations*, pages 85–103. Springer.

Bing Liu, Wynne Hsu, Yiming Ma, et al. 1998. Integrating classification and association rule mining. In *KDD*, volume 98, pages 80–86.

Marvin Minsky. 1974. A framework for representing knowledge. mit-ai laboratory memo 306. *Massachusetts Institute of Technology*.

Raymond J Mooney and Gerald DeJong. 1985. Learning schemata for natural language processing. In *IJCAI*, pages 681–687.

Courtney Napoles, Matthew Gormley, and Benjamin Van Durme. 2012. Annotated gigaword. In *Proceedings of the Joint Workshop on Automatic Knowledge Base Construction and Web-scale Knowledge Extraction*, pages 95–100. Association for Computational Linguistics.

Václav Novák and Magda Razímová. 2009. Unsupervised detection of annotation inconsistencies using apriori algorithm. In *Proceedings of the Third Linguistic Annotation Workshop*, pages 138–141. Association for Computational Linguistics.

Haoruo Peng and Dan Roth. 2016. Two discourse driven language models for semantics. *arXiv preprint arXiv:1606.05679*.

Karl Pichotta and Raymond Mooney. 2014. Statistical script learning with multi-argument events. In *Proceedings of the 14th Conference of the European Chapter of the Association for Computational Linguistics*, pages 220–229.

Karl Pichotta and Raymond J Mooney. 2016. Learning statistical scripts with lstm recurrent neural networks. In *Thirtieth AAAI Conference on Artificial Intelligence*.

Rachel Rudinger, Vera Demberg, Ashutosh Modi, Benjamin Van Durme, and Manfred Pinkal. 2015a. Learning to predict script events from domain-specific text. In *Proceedings of the Fourth Joint Conference on Lexical and Computational Semantics*, pages 205–210.

Rachel Rudinger, Pushpendre Rastogi, Francis Ferraro, and Benjamin Van Durme. 2015b. Script induction as language modeling. In *Proceedings of the 2015 Conference on Empirical Methods in Natural Language Processing*, pages 1681–1686.

Roger Schank and Robert Abelson. 1977. Scripts, plans, goals and understanding: An inquiry into human knowledge structures.

Tomohide Shibata and Sadao Kurohashi. 2011. Acquiring strongly-related events using predicate-argument co-occurring statistics and case frames. In *Proceedings of 5th International Joint Conference on Natural Language Processing*, pages 1028–1036.

Fadi Thabtah, Peter Cowling, and Yonghong Peng. 2005. Mcar: multi-class classification based on association rule. In *The 3rd ACS/IEEE International Conference onComputer Systems and Applications, 2005.*, page 33. IEEE.

Noah Weber, Leena Shekhar, Niranjan Balasubramanian, and Nathanael Chambers. 2018. Hierarchical quantized representations for script generation. *arXiv preprint arXiv:1808.09542*.

Mohammed Javeed Zaki. 2000. Scalable algorithms for association mining. *IEEE transactions on knowledge and data engineering*, 12(3):372–390.

Automatic extraction of personal events from dialogue

Joshua D. Eisenberg
Artie, Inc.
601 W 5th St, Los Angeles, CA 90071
joshua.eisenberg@artie.com

Michael Sheriff
Florida International University
Department of Creative Writing
11101 S.W. 13 ST., Miami, FL 33199
msher043@fiu.edu

Abstract

In this paper we introduce the problem of extracting events from dialogue. Previous work on event extraction focused on newswire, however we are interested in extracting events from spoken dialogue. To ground this study, we annotated dialogue transcripts from fourteen episodes of the podcast *This American Life*. This corpus contains 1,038 utterances, made up of 16,962 tokens, of which 3,664 represent events. The agreement for this corpus has a Cohen's κ of 0.83. We have open sourced this corpus for the NLP community. With this corpus in hand, we trained support vector machines (SVM) to correctly classify these phenomena with 0.68 F1, when using episode-fold cross-validation. This is nearly 100% higher F1 than the baseline classifier. The SVM models achieved performance of over 0.75 F1 on some testing folds. We report the results for SVM classifiers trained with four different types of features (verb classes, part of speech tags, named entities, and semantic role labels), and different machine learning protocols (under-sampling and trigram context). This work is grounded in narratology and computational models of narrative. It is useful for extracting events, plot, and story content from spoken dialogue.

1 Motivation

People communicate using stories. A simple definition of *story* is a series of events arranged over time. A typical story has at least one plot and at least one character. When people speak to one another, we tell stories and reference events using unique discourse. The purpose of this research is to gain better understanding of the events people reference when they speak, effectively enabling further knowledge of how people tell stories and communicate.

There has been no work, to our knowledge, about event extraction from transcripts of spoken language. The most popular corpora annotated for events all come from the domain of newswire (Pustejovsky et al., 2003b; Minard et al., 2016). Our work begins to fill that gap. We have open sourced the gold-standard annotated corpus of events from dialogue.[1] For brevity, we will hearby refer to this corpus as the Personal Events in Dialogue Corpus (PEDC). We detailed the feature extraction pipelines, and the support vector machine (SVM) learning protocols for the automatic extraction of events from dialogue. Using this information, as well as the corpus we have released, anyone interested in extracting events from dialogue can proceed where we have left off.

One may ask: why is it important to annotate a corpus of dialogue for events? It is necessary because dialogue is distinct from other types of discourse. We claim that spoken dialogue, as a type of discourse, is especially different than newswire. We justify this claim by evaluating the distribution of narrative point of view (POV) and diegesis in the PEDC and a common newswire corpus. POV distinguishes whether a narrator tells a story in a personal or impersonal manner, and diegesis is whether the narrator is involved in the events of the story they tell. We use POV and diegesis to make our comparisions because they give information about the narrator, and their relationship to the story they tell.

We back our claim (that dialogue is different than newswire) by comparing the distributions of narrative point of view (POV) and diegesis of the narrators in PEDC with the Reuters-21578 newswire corpus.[2] Eisenberg and Finlayson (2016) found that narrators in newswire texts from the Reuters-21,578 corpus use the first-person POV less than 1% of the time, and are homodiegetic less than 1%

---

[1] http://www.artie.com/data/personaleventsindialogue/
[2] http://archive.ics.uci.edu/ml/datasets/Reuters-21578+Text+Categorization+Collection

Proceedings of the 1st Joint Workshop on Narrative Understanding, Storylines, and Events, pages 63–71
July 9, 2020. ©2020 Association for Computational Linguistics

of the time. However, in the 14 episodes (1,028 utterances) of *This American Life*, we found that 56% narrators were first-person, and 32% narrators were homodiegetic.

We found these distributions in PEDC by using the automatic POV and diegesis extractors from Eisenberg and Finlayson (2016), which were open sourced.[3] Comparing the distributions of POV and diegesis for the PEDC to that of newswire demonstrates how different spoken dialogue is. This shows why building an annotated corpus specifically for event extraction of dialogue was necessary.

It is substantial that so many of the utterances in the PEDC are first-person narrators and homodiegetic. This means that people are speaking about their lives. They are retelling stories. They are speaking in more personal ways than narrators do in newswire. This is where the *Personal* in the Personal Events in Dialogue Corpus comes from. Additionally, using the modifier *personal* aligns this work with Gordon and Swanson (2009) who extracted personal stories from blog posts. We want our work to help researchers studying computation models of narrative.

1.1 What are *personal events*?

We define event as: an action or state of being depicted in text span. Actions are things that happen, most typically processes that can be observed visually. A state of being portrays the details of a situation, like the emotional and physical states of a character. For our work, we are only concerned with the state of being for animate objects. We use the concept of *animacy* from Jahan et al. (2018), which is defined as:

> Animacy is the characteristic of being able to independently carry out actions (e.g., movement, communication, etc.). For example, a person or a bird is animate because they move or communicate under their own power. On the other hand, a chair or a book is inanimate because they do not perform any kind of independent action.

We only annotated states of being for animate objects (i.e. *beings*) because we are interested in extracting the information most closely coupled with people or characters. We were less concerned

with extracting details about inanimate objects, like the states of being in this example,"The mountain was covered with trees," and more concerned with extracting states of being describing people, like in this example, "I was so excited when the dough rose," where *excited* is a state of being describing the speaker.

In the prior section we showed the PEDC contains a significant amount of personal events by running the POV and diegesis extractors from Eisenberg and Finlayson (2016). We found that the PEDC contains 56% first-person narrators, and 32% homodiegetic narrators. Our corpus has a significant amount of narrators telling personal stories.

1.2 Outline

First, in §2 we discuss the annotation study we conducted on fourteen episodes of *This American Life*. Next, in §3 we discuss the design of the event extractor. In §3.2 we discuss the different sets of features extracted from utterances. In §3.2 we talk about the protocols followed for training of support vector machine (SVM) models to extract events from utterances. In §4 we discuss the types of experiments we ran, and present a table containing the results of 57 experiments. The goal of these experiments is to determine the best set of features and learning protocols for training a SVM to extract events from dialogue. In §5 we discuss the results. In §6 we sumarize our contributions.

2 Personal events in dialogue annotation study

When beginning to think about extracting events from dialogue, we realized there is no corpus of transcribed dialogue annotated for events. There are many corpora of other text types with event annotations. TimeBank contains newswire text (Pustejovsky et al., 2003b). MEANTIME is made up of Wikinews articles (Minard et al., 2016).

Additionally there are many event annotation schema; one of the more prominent ones is TimeML (Pustejovsky et al., 2003a). We decided to develop our own annotation scheme due to the complexity of TimeML; it's an extremly fine-grained annotation scheme, with specific tags for different types of events, temporal expressions and links. We decided it would be too difficult to use TimeML while maintaining a high inter-annotator agreement and finishing the annotation study in a short amount

---

[3] https://dspace.mit.edu/handle/1721.1/105279

Episode Number	Episode Name	Utterances	Event tokens	Nonevent tokens	Cohen's Kappa
608	The Revolution Starts at Noon	50	130	630	0.8900
610	Grand Gesture	151	494	2032	0.7982
617	Fermi's Paradox	82	271	1204	0.8258
620	To Be Real	75	156	756	0.8258
621	Who You Gonna Call	49	104	435	0.8486
625	Essay B	54	130	417	0.8446
627	Suitable for Children	28	80	322	0.8362
629	Expect Delays	44	125	391	0.8320
639	In Dog We Trust	43	183	651	0.8777
647	LaDonna	51	143	477	0.8600
650	Change You Can Maybe Believe In	87	420	1629	0.8193
651	If You Build It Will They Come	64	264	880	0.8344
655	The Not So Great Unknown	89	400	1164	0.8256
691	Gardens of Branching Paths	171	764	2310	0.8302
Totals		1,038	3,664	13,298	
Average Kappa					0.8320

Table 1: Statistics for event annotations in dialogue corpus

of time (three months), and within a modest budget.

Given that our goal was to understand spoken conversational dialogue, we decided to create a corpus from transcribed audio. This matches the nature of the data we intend to use for our event extractor: audio recordings of dialogue that have been transcribed as a text file.

We weighed a number of different sources for the text transcripts, but we ultimately decided to use transcripts from the podcast *This American Life*[4]. We chose this podcast because: 1) The transcripts are freely available online. 2) A significant portion of these podcasts are made up of conversations, as opposed to narration. Additionally, *This American Life* formats their transcripts so that the conversations are indented as block quotations. This made it easy to separate conversations from typical podcast narration. 3) The subject matter of *This American Life* are typically stories from people's lives. We wanted our corpus to be made up of unscripted conversations; contemporary everyday conversations, so that the extractors we train from this data are better suited to understanding people talking about their lives.

2.1 Annotation study procedures

The two authors of this paper were the annotators for this study. The first author wrote the annotation guide[5]. We trained by reading the first version of the guide, discussing short-comings, and then compiling a new version of the guide. Next, we both annotated episode 685[6]. Since we were training, we were allowed to discuss questions regarding annotation decisions. After we both finished, we ran the annotations through a program that found all the utterances with disagreements, and we discussed the mistakes.

After adjudicating the training episode, the first author updated the annotation guide to address inconsistencies we found during adjudication. Next, we began the actual annotation study. While annotating each episode, we could not discuss specifics about the utterances. We independently annotated each episode.

Once both annotators finished their annotations for an episode, we used a program we made that compared the annotations for each utterance. If there was any disagreement between the two annotators, both sets of markings from the annotators were added to an adjudication list. Then, we went through each utterance with disagreements, and discussed how the markings should be corrected for the gold-standard. We adjudicated each episode before annotating the next so that we, as annotators, could learn from each other's mistakes. Once

[4]https://www.thisamericanlife.org/

[5]http://www.artie.com/data/personaleventsindialogue/
[6]https://www.thisamericanlife.org/685/transcript

the correction lists were created, they were used along with the original markings to create the gold-standard.

2.2 Annotation syntax

Before we discuss the annotation syntax, please take a look at an annotated utterance from episode 650[7]:

```
Alan:  Due to safety
{concerns}, safety
{purposes}.  But I mean,
I can {type out} a little
bit of, like, whatever
you {want} to {tell} them,
{tell} the shelter, and I
can {make sure} they {get}
the {message} if that'll
{work} for you.
```

The annotations were marked in text files. Each text file contains an episode transcript formated so that each utterance was on its own line. The spans of text that an annotator considered events were surrounded with brackets. Usually events were single words, but occasiaonally events were multi-word expressions, like the phrase *type out* above. For more information about what we considered an event, and which state-of-beings were considered events, please refer to our annotation guide[8].

2.3 Inter-annotator agreement

We used the Cohen's Kappa metric (κ) to compute the inter-annotator agreement Landis and Koch (1977). According to Viera et al. (2005) κ values above 0.81 are considered *almost perfect agreement*. The average κ for our annotations is 0.83 so our inter-annotator agreement is *almost perfect*. This average κ is a weighted average, where the κ for each episode is multiplied by the number of utterances in the episode. Once the sum of weighted averages is obtained, we divide by the total number of utterances in the corpus.

The κ for event extraction measures inter-annotator agreement for a binary classification task for each token across each utterance. If both annotators marked a token as an event, this counted as a true positive, and if both annotators marked a token as a non-event, this is counted as a true negative. All other cases are disagreements; these

were adjudicated by both authors. A token can be annotated as an *event*, or a *non-event*.

3 Developing the extractor

Our extractor was implemented in Java. This is due to the availability of high-quality open-sourced NLP libraries. There are two aspects of the extractor's design that we will cover: 1) feature engineering and 2) protocols for training SVM models.

3.1 Feature engineering

First, we will discuss the different types of features that we extracted from each utterance in the corpus.

3.1.1 Part of speech tags

We used the part of speech (POS) tagger (Toutanova and Manning, 2000; Toutanova et al., 2003) from Stanford CoreNLP (Manning et al., 2014) to extract part of speech tags for each word in each utterance of our corpus. We used the `english-bidirectional-distsim` model. This model was chosen since it has the most accurate performance, even though it has a slower run-time. For the purpose of these experiments run-time wasn't a limiting factor.

Each POS tag was assigned a unqiue integer value between 1 and 36. If a token has no POS tag, then it is assigned the value of -1. The following is the procedure for mapping POS tags into feature vectors: First, use Stanford CoreNLP to find the POS tags for each token in an utterance. Second, produce a vector of length 37 for each token, and fill each element with a -1. Third, for the vector representing each token, change the value of the element with the index cooresponding to the particular POS of the current token to 1. If the token has no POS tag, then the vector is unchanged.

3.1.2 Named entity tags

We used the Named Enitity Recognizer (NER) (Finkel et al., 2005) from Stanford CoreNLP (Manning et al., 2014) to extract named entity types from utterances. We included named entity tag as a feature type for event extraction because we hypothesized that some named entity types should never be considered as events, like PERSON, ORGANIZATION, and MONEY. However, the DATE and DURATION classes were often classified as events.

The NER tag feature was encoded into a vector of length nine. The first eight elements of this vector each represents one of the eight NER classes

---

[7]https://www.thisamericanlife.org/650/transcript
[8]http://www.artie.com/data/personaleventsindialogue/

in Stanford's NER. The vector's final element represents whether the current token is not a named entity. This is the procedure for extracting NER tag features from an utterance: First use Stanford CoreNLP to find the NER tags for each token in an utterance. Second, produce a vector of length nine for each token, and fill each element with a -1. Third, for the vector representing each token in an utterance, change the value of the element with the index corresponding to a particular NER tag of the current token to 1. If there is no NER tag for a given token, then set the final element of the vector to 1.

3.1.3 Verb classes

We use a similar pipeline as Eisenberg and Finlayson (2017) for verb class extraction. This pipeline determines which VerbNet (Schuler, 2005) verb classes each token in an utterance is represented by. A verb class is a set of verbs with the same semantics. For example, the verbs *slurp*, *chomp*, and *crunch* all belong to the verb class *chew*. We hypothesize that knowledge of what verb classes are instantiated by specific words is essential to extracting events from dialogue.

The features for verb classes are encoded into a vector of length 279. The first 278 elements represent which of the 278 verb classes is invoked by the current token. The final element represents if no verb classes are instantiated by the token. For the first 278 elements we use the following bipolar encoding: 1 if the verb class is instantiated in the token, or -1 if not. Note that any token can instantiate more than one verb class. The final element in the vector is assigned a 1 if no verb classes are represented by the current token, or -1 if verb classes are used (which means at least one of the first 278 elements has the value of 1).

Here is a quick overview of the pipeline for verb class extraction: first, we use *It Makes Sense* to perform word sense disambiguation on an utterance (Zhong and Ng, 2010). This produces WordNet sense keys (Fellbaum, 1998) for each token in an utterance. Next we use JVerbnet[9] to map WordNet sense keys to VerbNet classes. This produces a list of VerbNet classes for each token. Finally, each list is mapped to a bipolar feature vector of length 279, as explained in the paragraph above.

---

[9]http://projects.csail.mit.edu/jverbnet/

3.1.4 Semantic role labels

We use the *Path LSTM* Semantic Role Labeler (SRL) to extract a set of features from utterances (Roth and Lapata, 2016). We extract two features for each token in an utterance: 1) is the token a predicate? and 2) is the token an argument of a predicate? These features fill a vector of length two, and once again we use bipolar encoding as all the previous features discussed in this section.

There are many more features in Path LSTM, however we didn't have the time to find an intelligent way to use them. One of those features is the ability to parse into semantic frames from FrameNet (Baker and Sato, 2003). Path LSTM can parse into the over 1,200 semantic frames in FrameNet. We hypothesize that knowing which tokens represent different frame elements for each frame would be a useful feature extracting events from dialogue. This feature would provide even more fine-grained information than the verb class features.

Here is the way we extracted SRL features from utterances: first, for each utterance use Path LSTM to extract an SRL parse. Second, produce a feature vector of length two for each token in the utterance, and initialize both elements to -1. Third, get the list of predicates from the SRL parse. For each token, if it is a predicate, set the first element of the feature vector to 1. Otherwise, do nothing. Fourth, for each predicate, get the argument map. For each token, if it is a member of any argument map, set the second element of the feature vector to 1. Otherwise, do nothing.

3.2 Learning protocols

Second, we discuss the details about how the SVM models were trained.

3.2.1 Cross-validation

We used 14-fold cross-validation, or colloquially speaking *episode-fold cross-validation*. There are 14 episodes in our corpus. For each fold of cross-validation, one episode is reserved for testing, and the remaining 13 folds are used for training. This procedure is performed 14 times, so that each of the 14 episodes has the chance to be used as testing data.

3.2.2 Under-sampling

We incorporated under-sampling into our SVM based experiments. Undersampling is a technique for boosting performance of models when training

POS	NER	Verb Classes	SRL	Under-sampling	Trigrams	F1	Precision	Recall	F1	Precision	Recall
						Events			Nonevents		
X						0.5763	0.7364	0.4791	0.9095	0.8705	0.9529
X				X		0.6185	0.4777	0.8848	0.8347	0.9595	0.7390
X					X	0.5786	0.7435	0.4791	0.9104	0.8706	0.9545
X				X	X	0.6262	0.4890	0.8783	0.8420	0.9579	0.7516
	X					NaN	0	NaN	0.8805	0.7871	1.0
X	X					0.5800	0.7366	0.4840	0.9098	0.8715	0.9523
X	X			X		0.6205	0.4837	0.8768	0.8381	0.9572	0.7463
X	X				X	0.5823	0.7435	0.4841	0.9107	0.8717	0.9539
X	X			X	X	0.6252	0.4870	0.8818	0.8406	0.9588	0.7489
		X				0.5609	0.9281	0.4039	0.9206	0.8594	0.9918
		X		X		0.5637	0.9225	0.4079	0.9207	0.8601	0.9910
		X			X	0.5608	0.9044	0.4087	0.9195	0.8599	0.9886
		X		X	X	0.5658	0.6457	0.5074	0.8979	0.8729	0.9249
X		X				0.6698	0.8593	0.5530	0.9298	0.8886	0.9756
X		X		X		0.6763	0.5555	0.8712	0.8792	0.9586	0.8123
X		X			X	0.6755	0.8475	0.5654	0.9299	0.8911	0.9727
X		**X**		**X**	**X**	**0.6794**	**0.5593**	**0.8736**	**0.8805**	**0.9594**	**0.8141**
	X	X				0.5648	0.4088	0.4088	0.9209	0.8604	0.9912
	X	X		X		0.5675	0.9188	0.4126	0.9209	0.8611	0.9903
	X	X			X	0.5676	0.9188	0.4126	0.9210	0.8611	0.9903
	X	X		X	X	0.5666	0.6411	0.5116	0.8972	0.8738	0.9226
X	X	X				0.6732	0.8580	0.5579	0.9301	0.8896	0.9750
X	X	X		X		0.6736	0.5513	0.8731	0.8768	0.9589	0.8082
X	X	X			X	0.6769	0.8460	0.5679	0.9300	0.8917	0.9722
X	X	X		X	X	0.6750	0.5510	0.8792	0.8764	0.9606	0.8062
			X			0.4687	0.6751	0.3613	0.8959	0.8458	0.9530
			X	X		0.5287	0.4764	0.6000	0.8509	0.8826	0.8220
			X		X	0.4687	0.6751	0.3613	0.8959	0.8458	0.9530
			X	X	X	0.5287	0.4764	0.6000	0.8509	0.8826	0.8220
X			X			0.5763	0.7364	0.4791	0.9095	0.8705	0.9529
X			X	X		0.6239	0.4892	0.8726	0.8416	0.9559	0.7526
X			X		X	0.6564	0.7667	0.5826	0.9207	0.8923	0.9519
X			X	X	X	0.6257	0.4868	0.8833	0.8408	0.9595	0.7487
	X		X			0.4717	0.6786	0.3636	0.8965	0.8463	0.9535
	X		X	X		0.5359	0.4872	0.6017	0.8552	0.8839	0.8289
	X		X		X	0.4714	0.6784	0.3633	0.8965	0.8463	0.9535
	X		X	X	X	0.5358	0.4872	0.6015	0.8552	0.8839	0.8290
X	X		X			0.5800	0.7366	0.4840	0.9098	0.8715	0.9523
X	X		X	X		0.6150	0.4752	0.8824	0.8319	0.9587	0.7358
X	X		X		X	0.6631	0.7739	0.5897	0.9221	0.8942	0.9529
X	X		X	X	X	0.6254	0.4862	0.8847	0.8402	0.9598	0.7475
		X	X			0.5609	0.9281	0.4039	0.9206	0.8594	0.9918
		X	X	X		0.5769	0.5037	0.6812	0.8588	0.9036	0.8187
		X	X		X	0.5608	0.9044	0.4087	0.9195	0.8599	0.9886
		X	X	X	X	0.5753	0.4937	0.6977	0.8528	0.9068	0.8058
X		X	X			0.6698	0.8593	0.5530	0.9298	0.8886	0.9756
X		X	X	X		0.6759	0.5566	0.8679	0.8795	0.9575	0.8138
X		X	X		X	0.6760	0.8477	0.5660	0.9300	0.8912	0.9727
X		X	X	X	X	0.6769	0.5535	0.8780	0.8780	0.9605	0.8089
	X	X	X			0.5648	0.9244	0.4088	0.9209	0.8604	0.9912
	X	X	X	X		0.5841	0.5132	0.6845	0.8628	0.9051	0.8248
	X	X	X		X	0.5648	0.9011	0.4137	0.9198	0.8610	0.9879
	X	X	X	X	X	0.5824	0.4900	0.7243	0.8499	0.9131	0.7955
X	X	X	X			0.6732	0.8580	0.5579	0.9301	0.8896	0.9750
X	X	X	X	X		0.6732	0.5502	0.8748	0.8765	0.9595	0.8072
X	X	X	X		X	0.6769	0.8460	0.5679	0.9300	0.8917	0.9722
X	X	X	X	X	X	0.6729	0.5491	0.8764	0.8758	0.9601	0.8006

Table 2: Classification results across different feature sets and machine learning protocols

on unbalanced datasets (Japkowicz et al., 2000). Our event corpus has about four nonevents for every one event. To mitigate this, during training a SVM model on an episode we add the feature vectors for every event to the training set. Next, we count the number of feature vectors for events in the training set. Then, we randomly select nonevent feature vectors, and add the same number of vectors to the training set as there are event vectors. Hence, for every event feature vector in the training set, there is only one nonevent feature vector. In our experiments (§4) we saw that undersampling raised the F1 for most feature sets. Our implementation of under-sampling allows us to toggle it on and off for different experiments. Hence, under-sampling could be parameterized, along with the types of features used, and other variations on the SVM learning discussed below.

Since there is an element of randomness in our implementation of undersampling, we ran each undersampling experiment 100 times. We report the result for the experiment that had the highest F1 relative to the event class. This is a somewhat crude approach. In the future, we would like to employ an entropy based approach, where we select which majority class feature vectors to use based on the entropy of the set of vectors.

3.2.3 Simulating context through trigrams

We simulate context by appending feature vectors for neighboring words to the current word's feature vector. Specifically, for each token, get the feature vector for the preceding token and the feature vector for the proceeding token, and append these two vectors to the original vector. If there is no preceding token make a feature vector where each element is -1. The length of this negative vector is that of the original feature vector. Similarly, follow the same procedure if there is no proceeding token. Using trigram context vectors slightly raised the F1 for many SVM models, but it did not have a significant effect. This leads us to hypothesize that there is probably a better way to encode context for this task.

Our implementation of trigram context is modular, along with the other learning protocols: context can be toggled for any experiment. Furthermore, experiments that make use of trigram context, can also take advantage of under-sampling. Each set of features can have four seperate experiments: 1) training with no augmentations, 2) training with under-sampling, 3) training with trigram context vectors, and 4) training with both under-sampling and trigram context vectors.

3.2.4 SVM hyperparameters

All our SVM models used a linear kernel. We chose a linear kernel because of bipolar encoding of the feature values, and it produced the best F1 during early experiments. The hyperparameters for all the SVMs were as follows: $\gamma = 0.5$, $\nu = 0.5$, $C = 20$, and $\epsilon = 0.01$.

4 Results

We report our results in Table 2. The table is organized in four vertical columns, from left to right:

1) *Features*: this section contains the features used for an experiment. The possible types of features are POS, NER, Verb Classes, and SRL. The combination of features used for an experiment are indicated by X's in the column of the corresponding features. There are four possible experiments (for each of the four possible machine learning protocols chosen) run for a given feature type. In rare cases (like for experiments with only NER features) only the basic experiment results are reported because the SVM classifier could not adequately learn and classify everything as a nonevent.

2) *ML Protocols*: this section contains the machine learning (ML) protocols used for an experiment. The possible protocols are: undersampling and trigrams. The combination of ML protocols used for an experiment are indicated by X's in the column of the coresponding protocols. For each combination of features, four experiments are run. Each of the four experiments, for a feature set, represent a unique combination of the two ML protocols.

3) *Events*: in this section we report the results (F1, precision, and recall) for all tokens that were marked as events in the gold-standard.

4) *Nonevents*: similarly, in this section we report the results for all tokens that were marked as nonevents in the gold-standard.

Table 2 contains all combinations of features and ML protocols. We report all the results to show the fluctuations of performance for different combinations of features and protocols.

We will compare the results in Table 2 to a minority class baseline. For our experiments, the minority class is the event class. We are interested in maximizing the F1 of the event class as opposed to the nonevent class, because we want to accurately extract events. Events are more rare than nonevents, hence this is the phenomena we are exploring. Our baseline, relative to the event class is: F1 = 0.3553, precision = 0.2160, and recall = 1.

5 Discussion

Our best performing event extractor uses POS and verb class features, and the ML protocols used were undersampling and trigrams, however, the performance is not significantly better than the extractors that only use either one of the two protocols. Our best peforming event extractor with no extra ML protocols was the extractor with POS, NER, and verb class features. The performance of the extractor that had all four features had the same performance as the former, so we can say that the addition of SRL features adds no extra information to the classification process.

It is interesting to see the affect of undersampling on performance. It boosted the event F1 for most feature sets. Not only did it boost the F1, but it flipped the values of precision and recall with respect to the original experiment. Without undersampling, the precision is always higher than the recall. Once undersampling is toggled, the recall becomes larger than the precision. Also, the undersampled recall is typically higher than the nonundersampled precision. This flippage is important to note for situations when the event extractor is actually used in real-world systems.

If the situation requires a minimal number of false positives, than precision should be maximized, therefore no undersampling should be used when training the model. However, if minimal false negatives is a bigger priority, then recall should be maximized, hence undersampling should be used in training. Whether undersampling is used, or not, depends on the actual context the event extractor is being deployed.

In general, undersampling helped boost performance of event classification in most experiments. Trigrams gave an even smaller boost to event classification in most experiments. Experiments that had both undersampling and trigrams had the largest boost when compared to the experiment with no extra ML protocols.

There were two feature sets that trigram context had a significant affect, both POS + SRL and POS + VERB + SRL. These are the only experiments where the trigram context protocol led to the greatest performance for the feature set, and by a significant margin. Overall, trigrams had a much smaller affect on overall performance. We hypothesize that there are better ways to implement this form of context. Either a classifier that's better suited for sequential data should be used, or a different form of encoding the context feature should be explored. Another note about a negative result: the impact of the SRL features was much less influential than we hypothesized. Going forward, we think that the actual semantic frames instantiated should be used as features, as well as different frame elements, and not just occurence of predicates and arguments.

6   Contributions

In this paper we presented two sets of contributions: First, we have open sourced the first corpus of dialogue annotated for events.[10] This corpus can be used by researchers interested in the automatic understanding of dialogue, specifically dialogue that is rich with the personal stories of people. Second, we share the design and evaluate the performance of 57 unique event classifiers for dialogue. These results can be used by researchers to decide which features and machine learning protocols should be implemented for their own event extractors. Our best performing extractor has a 0.68 F1, which is over 100% higher than baseline. We hope that this work can be used by the community to better understand how people reference events from stories in dialogue.

Acknowledgments

A huge thanks to *This American Life* for giving us permission to distribute their transcripts for the open sourced PEDC. Thanks to Frances Swanson for coordinating the permissions. Thanks to Ryan Horrigan and Armando Kirwin, from Artie, Inc., for giving me the time and resources to pursue this research. Thanks to Aimee Rubensteen for being an amazing editor.

References

Collin F. Baker and Hiroaki Sato. 2003. The FrameNet data and software. In *The Companion Volume to the Proceedings of 41st Annual Meeting of the Association for Computational Linguistics*, pages 161–164, Sapporo, Japan. Association for Computational Linguistics.

Nathanael Chambers, Taylor Cassidy, Bill McDowell, and Steven Bethard. 2014. Dense event ordering with a multi-pass architecture. *Transactions of the Association for Computational Linguistics*, 2:273–284.

Joshua Eisenberg and Mark Finlayson. 2016. Automatic identification of narrative diegesis and point of view. In *Proceedings of the 2nd Workshop on Computing News Storylines (CNS 2016)*, pages 36–46, Austin, Texas. Association for Computational Linguistics.

Joshua Eisenberg and Mark Finlayson. 2017. A simpler and more generalizable story detector using verb and character features. In *Proceedings of the 2017 Conference on Empirical Methods in Natural Language Processing*, pages 2708–2715, Copenhagen, Denmark. Association for Computational Linguistics.

Christiane Fellbaum. 1998. *WordNet: An electronic lexical database*. MIT Press.

Jenny Rose Finkel, Trond Grenager, and Christopher Manning. 2005. Incorporating non-local information into information extraction systems by gibbs sampling. In *Proceedings of the 43rd Annual Meeting on Association for Computational Linguistics*, ACL '05, page 363–370, USA. Association for Computational Linguistics.

Andrew Gordon and Reid Swanson. 2009. Identifying personal stories in millions of weblog entries. In *Third International Conference on Weblogs and Social Media, Data Challenge Workshop, San Jose, CA*, volume 46, pages 16–23, San Jose, CA.

---

[10]http://www.artie.com/data/personaleventsindialogue/

Labiba Jahan, Geeticka Chauhan, and Mark Finlayson. 2018. A new approach to Animacy detection. In *Proceedings of the 27th International Conference on Computational Linguistics*, pages 1–12, Santa Fe, New Mexico, USA. Association for Computational Linguistics.

Nathalie Japkowicz et al. 2000. Learning from imbalanced data sets: a comparison of various strategies. In *AAAI workshop on learning from imbalanced data sets*, volume 68, pages 10–15. Menlo Park, CA.

J Richard Landis and Gary G Koch. 1977. The measurement of observer agreement for categorical data. *biometrics*, pages 159–174.

Christopher Manning, Mihai Surdeanu, John Bauer, Jenny Finkel, Steven Bethard, and David McClosky. 2014. The Stanford CoreNLP natural language processing toolkit. In *Proceedings of 52nd Annual Meeting of the Association for Computational Linguistics: System Demonstrations*, pages 55–60, Baltimore, Maryland. Association for Computational Linguistics.

Anne-Lyse Minard, Manuela Speranza, Ruben Urizar, Begoña Altuna, Marieke van Erp, Anneleen Schoen, and Chantal van Son. 2016. MEANTIME, the NewsReader multilingual event and time corpus. In *Proceedings of the Tenth International Conference on Language Resources and Evaluation (LREC'16)*, pages 4417–4422, Portorož, Slovenia. European Language Resources Association (ELRA).

James Pustejovsky, José M Castano, Robert Ingria, Roser Sauri, Robert J Gaizauskas, Andrea Setzer, Graham Katz, and Dragomir R Radev. 2003a. Timeml: Robust specification of event and temporal expressions in text. *New directions in question answering*, 3:28–34.

James Pustejovsky, Patrick Hanks, Roser Sauri, Andrew See, Robert Gaizauskas, Andrea Setzer, Dragomir Radev, Beth Sundheim, David Day, Lisa Ferro, et al. 2003b. The timebank corpus. In *Corpus linguistics*, volume 2003, page 40. Lancaster, UK.

Michael Roth and Mirella Lapata. 2016. Neural semantic role labeling with dependency path embeddings. In *Proceedings of the 54th Annual Meeting of the Association for Computational Linguistics (Volume 1: Long Papers)*, pages 1192–1202, Berlin, Germany. Association for Computational Linguistics.

Karin Kipper Schuler. 2005. *VerbNet: A broadcoverage, comprehensive verb lexicon*. PhD dissertation, University of Pennsylvania.

Kristina Toutanova, Dan Klein, Christopher D. Manning, and Yoram Singer. 2003. Feature-rich part-of-speech tagging with a cyclic dependency network. In *Proceedings of the 2003 Human Language Technology Conference of the North American Chapter of the Association for Computational Linguistics*, pages 252–259.

Kristina Toutanova and Christopher D. Manning. 2000. Enriching the knowledge sources used in a maximum entropy part-of-speech tagger. In *Proceedings of the 2000 Joint SIGDAT Conference on Empirical Methods in Natural Language Processing and Very Large Corpora: Held in Conjunction with the 38th Annual Meeting of the Association for Computational Linguistics - Volume 13*, EMNLP '00, page 63–70, USA. Association for Computational Linguistics.

Anthony J Viera, Joanne M Garrett, et al. 2005. Understanding interobserver agreement: the kappa statistic. *Fam med*, 37(5):360–363.

Zhi Zhong and Hwee Tou Ng. 2010. It makes sense: A wide-coverage word sense disambiguation system for free text. In *Proceedings of the ACL 2010 System Demonstrations*, pages 78–83, Uppsala, Sweden. Association for Computational Linguistics.

Annotating and quantifying narrative time disruptions in modernist and hypertext fiction

Edward Kearns

National University of Ireland, Galway

`edward.kearns@nuigalway.ie`

Abstract

This paper outlines work in progress on a new method of annotating and quantitatively discussing narrative techniques related to time in fiction. Specifically those techniques are analepsis, prolepsis, narrative level changes, and stream-of-consciousness and free-indirect-discourse narration. By counting the frequency and extent of the usage of these techniques, the narrative characteristics of different works from different time periods and genres can be compared. This project uses modernist fiction and hypertext fiction as its case studies.

1 Introduction

This project annotates and analyses a specific combination of narrative techniques that have not been treated in this way before. Its understanding of narrative emanates from English literary studies, but is applied using a methodology that combines the methods of that field with digital humanities methods, specifically annotation. There has been work on annotating narrative features, but not featuring the combination of narrative levels, time disruptions, and subjective narration. This paper shows a new way for this to be done using a custom XML schema and analysis of preliminary data gleaned from the application of that schema. This process can be used to compare fiction from any genre or time period because most of the techniques involved in the annotation scheme have been used in fiction for centuries. This project applies the process to modernist fiction (experimental novels from the early 20th century) and hypertext fiction (texts from the last four decades which are designed specifically to be read on a computer) because comparing them quantitatively can help to trace the relationship between the two genres which has been proposed in literary theory. This is work in progress, and this paper's analysis will mainly focus on the use of analepsis, which is one of the techniques of disrupting narrative time.

2 Description of project and research question

This project seeks to determine whether a valid and useful system of encoding narrative characteristics related to time in fiction can be developed. It then asks how the narratives thus encoded can be quantitatively analysed, using modernist and hypertext fiction as case studies. The narrative techniques which this project addresses are analepsis, prolepsis (flashbacks and flashes forward in story time, respectively, and collectively referred to as anachronies), changes in narrative level (stories within stories), and two kinds of subjective narration: stream of consciousness (prose that reports a character's thoughts directly and continuously, often ignoring rules of grammar in order to do so) and free indirect discourse (prose that still uses a separate narrator and third-person sentences, but in which the words are affected by the biases and perspective of a particular character). If one is comparing transitions in narrative time, then one must determine to what extent those things are happening, and how frequently. The workflow consists of annotating the novels and hypertexts; counting the encoded instances of anachrony, subjective narration, and changes in narrative level; determining where these phenomena appear in each text; comparing those patterns between the texts; and then going back to the texts themselves to read what is going on at particular points of activity, to see why these changes in the narration are occurring. Works are regularly compared in literary studies, and narrative theory is often used to compare the portrayal of time in fiction works of different kinds. What this project adds to that is a more measurable

Proceedings of the 1st Joint Workshop on Narrative Understanding, Storylines, and Events, pages 72–77
July 9, 2020. ©2020 Association for Computational Linguistics

way of describing the structural positioning and role of of narrative time disruptions in fiction.

3 Related quantitative work

Several annotation schemes and digital humanities literary studies have influenced this project. Pre-existing annotation schemes have shown how some similar narrative aspects can be encoded. NarrativeML is intended for encoding the goals of characters and narrators, aspects of pacing in narrative, and embedded narratives (Mani, 2013). Its tagset has a small number of elements, but a large amount of attributes and values that can be added to those elements. This makes NarrativeML good for its intended use, but its complexity is not necessary for the goals of this project, and it does not address the combination of narrative time, subjective narration, and changes in level. ProppML is useful as another example of a system for manually encoding some narrative features in fiction (Yarlott and Finlayson, 2016), but it is intended for folk tales with formulaic plots and it is also quite complex with many attributes for each element. Narrative time is the primary focus of TimeML (Saurí et al., 2006). Its Timex3 and Tlink tags allow numbers to be assigned in their values for recording the relative order of events, but there are no specific tags for analepsis or prolepsis, and the annotation scheme is not concerned with subjective narration or narrative levels so there are no tags for them either. These kinds of schemes have shown that narrative characteristics can be encoded, but have not addressed the specific ones that this project addresses.

The Narrelations tool represents annotated narratives as a diagram consisting of concentric rings (Schwan et al., 2019). It is excellent for showing how many narrative levels a story has, and the proportion of story length spent in each level. However, it does not show the degree to which narrative level changes and anachronies are happening - how many words are being encompassed by these techniques. It cannot show relative peaks or troughs in the usage of those techniques over the course of a text, only binary information on whether they are happening or not. It does not feature stream-of-consciousness or free indirect discourse, or display word counts. As such, it too does not address the specific pieces of information that this project requires.

Some digital humanities projects have shown how quantitative methods can be useful for comparing fiction works individually and in corpora. Ramsay (2011) compared sections of *The Waves* by Virginia Woolf against each other, noting the difference in the vocabulary used in sections narrated by the different characters, and what that can tell us about those characters. Jockers (2014) has shown how to visually represent the relative similarities and differences in prose style of a corpus of nineteenth- and twentieth-century novels using cluster dendrograms. Clement (2012) uses visualisations of the frequency of usage of the word "one" increasing dramatically in the second half of Gertrude Stein's *The Making of Americans*, just as the usage of the word "I" becomes far less frequent. Using this graph Clement shows definite and deliberate structural change in the second half of the novel, driven by its syntax. This illustrates how quantitative measures can help to interrogate the structure of fiction texts, as well as the style of their prose. Text-mining does not work for this project because the narrative concepts being addressed require too much critical interpretation for a computer program to detect, but these practices show the insights that can be gained from comparing data gleaned from fiction works, and then applying those insights to further literary study of those novels.

4 Data

The corpus of this project contains six modernist novels and seven pieces of hypertext fiction. The modernist novels are *To the Lighthouse* by Virginia Woolf, *Tender is the Night* by F. Scott Fitzgerald, *Pointed Roofs* by Dorothy Richardson, *The Sound and the Fury* by William Faulkner, *Three Lives* by Gertrude Stein, and *The House in Paris* by Elizabeth Bowen. They have been selected because their publication dates span from 1909 to 1935, and because they feature a wide range of prose and narrative styles. The hypertext fictions chosen are *Uncle Roger* by Judy Malloy, *Twelve Blue* by Michael Joyce, *my body - a Wunderkammer* by Shelley Jackson, *Seed* by Joanna Walsh, *Voyage Into the Unknown* by Roderick Coover, *Victory Garden* by Stuart Moulthrop, *The Jew's Daughter* by Judd Morrissey and Lori Talley. Similarly, these texts span from 1986 to 2017 and have a variety of different writing styles and narrative structures. Modernist and hypertext fiction often share characteristics such as narrative fragmentation, the effort to make a "significant formal break with the traditions that preceded" them (Rettberg, 2018), while still seeking "inspiration and validation in a literary past" (Pressman, 2014). They also share a certain "narrative complexity, and an aesthetic of difficulty" (Pressman, 2014).

5 Methodology

In order to compare narrative features in a structured way across different texts, it is necessary to count how much and how frequently those features were occurring. Annotating each occurrence of those features was the way to do this, and this project's combination of tags is necessary so that they can be interwoven in a way that mimics how the narrative techniques are interwoven in the fiction. XML has been used for the annotation.

The elements in the annotation scheme are: Analepsis, Prolepsis, Level (with the attribute 'degree', to which integers can be assigned for each narrative level), SOC (for stream-of-consciousness), and FID (for free indirect discourse). Each tag can be used on its own, or nested inside one another. Due to the modular structure of this system, the annotation routine does not have to follow a particular order, and not every tag needs to be used. The tags can be applied as necessary. The criteria for beginning and ending annotation spans is the same for all tags. The annotation should begin at the point in the text where the narrative transitions either to a higher or lower level, a different point in time, or into or out of stream-of-consciousness or free-indirect-discourse narration. This can occur in the middle of a sentence, and can continue into another sentence, paragraph, or chapter. The annotation is ended when the phenomenon ends and the narration changes to a different level, transitions to a different point in time, or changes back to omniscient narration after its spell in more subjective narration has ceased.

Once the texts have been encoded, a number of features are measured quantitatively. They are: (1) numbers of each of the analepsis, prolepsis, narrative level, stream-of-consciousness and free indirect discourse tags in each text, both as total numbers and as percentages relative to the total word counts of each text; (2) how frequently those tags are occurring relative to word counts; (3) numbers of words contained within all tags relative to the total word counts of whole texts, pages, lexias, chapters, and sections; (4) which tags are occurring inside other tags. The analyses in this paper use the

first two of those measures.

The scope and budget of the project does not allow for multiple annotators to be hired; as such all text encoding was completed by one annotator, the author. However, the project's schema has been tested for inter-annotator agreement using a separate, smaller corpus, and compared against other similar annotation guidelines that focus on narrative levels, as part of the Systematic Analysis of Narrative Texts through Annotation (SANTA) project. Gius et al. (2019) explain that SANTA "employed the metric γ (gamma)" so that they could "compare evaluation schemes with different complexities and to avoid favouring more simple schemes (if the scheme is simpler, chance agreement is higher)". The IAA result for my guidelines was 0.24 in gamma (Willand et al., 2019). By normal IAA measures, 0.24 is quite low (Mathet et al., 2015), but all of the scores in the SANTA project were similarly low. The IAA for my guidelines was the third-highest of the eight annotation guidelines, with results ranging from 0.05 to 0.30. Further rounds of evaluation are pending in that project.

Recording and analysing number and frequency of narrative features related to time allows direct comparisons of the narrative strategies and structures of literary texts from different genres and time periods. We can see how different or similar these texts are in their treatment of narrative time, in a way that is different to what can be achieved with traditional literary analysis alone. However, that literary analysis is more important, and these quantitative measures do not replace that; rather they are used in concert with it, as can be seen in the next section of this paper. The data only ever serves to lead us back to reading the texts.

6 Preliminary results and discussion

These examples are small parts of the overall project, and work is ongoing to develop further comparisons, but for now we can look at all of the texts in the corpus using a basic measure, and then do some more detailed analysis of a select few texts which have characteristics in common. One of the first things to consider across the corpus - and the quantitative measure numbered (1) in the methodology - is how frequently each tag is occurring in each text, relative to the word counts of those texts. To achieve a relative comparison across texts of different lengths, normalised frequency has been used, which is simply the number of a times a particular tag occurs in a text, divided by the total word count of that text, with that result multiplied by 10,000. This calculation comes from McEnery and Hardie (2011), and the base of normalisation of 10,000 is essentially arbitrary, but is somewhat similar to the length of the texts in this corpus, most of which are in the tens of thousands of words. Figure 1 in this paper shows the normalised frequency for the analepsis tag across all texts in the corpus. Analepsis is used in all of these examples because it is the most significant tag for the themes of the project, but these measures can be made with all of the tags in the schema.

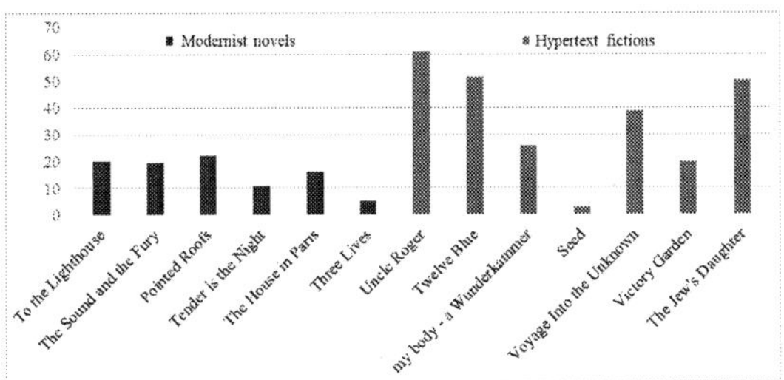

Figure 1: Normalised frequency of analepsis tags, for all texts ((Total no. of analepsis tags / Total no. of words in a text) x 10,000)

As we can see, the modernist novels tend to have comparable frequency of analepsis tags occurring; four of the six novels have normalised frequencies close to 20. The other two, *Tender is the Night* and *Three Lives*, both have long sections that are wholly encompassed by one analepsis tag, so their less frequent occurrence of tags does not reflect the large proportion of their narratives that occurs inside analepsis.

For a clearer analysis of these narratives, we need to examine the numbers of words contained within analepsis tags and their placement in the text. *Tender is the Night* and *The House in Paris* are useful as an example for this comparison because both novels are divided into three long sections, beginning in the present, then flashing back about ten years in their middle sections, then returning to the present in their final portion. Those long middle analepses in turn contain analepses of their own.

In both of these novels, there are fewer words in analepsis tags at the beginning and end, while the large amount of words within analepsis in their middle sections is clearly evident. The difference is with the analepsis within analepsis. In *The House in Paris*, the long flashback in the middle has sev-

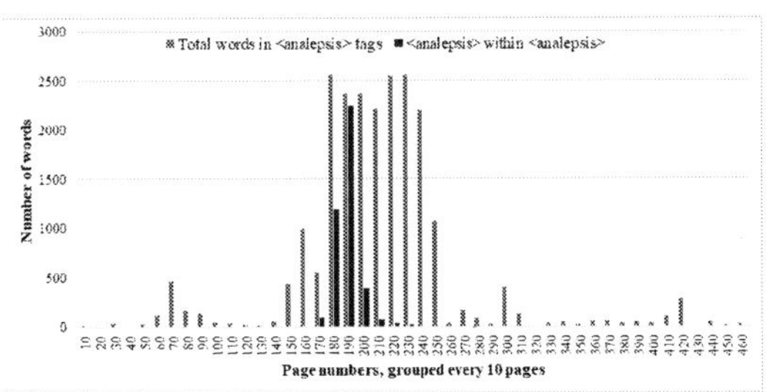

Figure 2: Words in analepsis in *Tender is the Night*

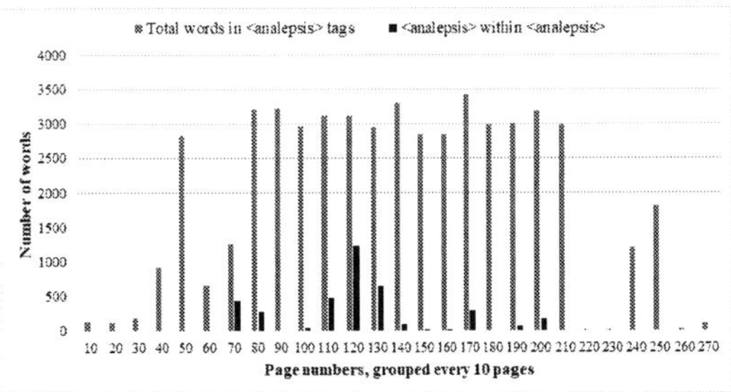

Figure 3: Words in analepsis in *The House in Paris*

eral small clusters at various points throughout it, rather than the large cluster of analepsis-within-analepsis that we see at the beginning of the long flashback in *Tender is the Night*. The dispersed analepses in Bowen's novel mimic the natural references to the past that occur in memory (or story-telling), while Fitzgerald's novel shows a more deliberate construction of particular flashbacks, like a Freudian psychoanalyst imposing a narrative on a patient, a subject with which the novel is concerned in its content.

A linear comparison works for linear texts, but hypertexts are usually nonlinear. They can be analysed on the level of individual lexias, but for overall comparisons between hypertexts and modernist novels, one can compare how frequently tags are occurring, and how the two texts compare in terms of words within analepsis tags as percentages of their overall length. *To the Lighthouse* and *Twelve Blue* are useful texts to compare because they both use free-indirect discourse narration from the perspectives of many characters, mostly families and groups of friends. Along with those changing narrative perspectives, both texts also often transition backwards and forwards through time and memory. So, their similar content invites one to ask whether they have similarities in narrative form, despite their different genres. As such, Figures 4 and 5 compare the usage of analepsis in these two texts.

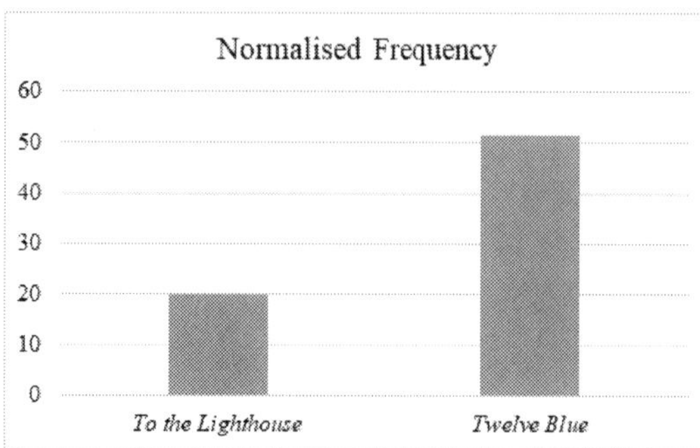

Figure 4: Analepsis tags occur 2.5 times more frequently in *Twelve Blue* than in *To the Lighthouse*.

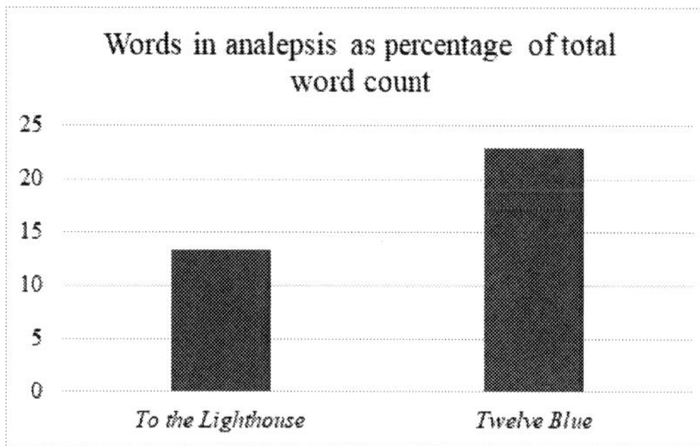

Figure 5: Relative to their total word counts, *Twelve Blue* only has 1.7 times as many words in analepsis tags than *To the Lighthouse*

At first it would appear that analepsis is happening overwhelmingly more in *Twelve Blue* than in *To the Lighthouse*, but one can see in Figure 5 that the difference is not as great as it initially seems, when word counts are taken into consideration. Still, proportionally, more of *Twelve Blue* occurs in analepsis than *To the Lighthouse*. Both texts are concerned with memory and the intersecting lives of groups of people over spans of years. That thematic similarity stands in contrast with their structural differences. The first part of *To the Lighthouse* is its longest section, setting up most of the significant relationships and story themes; it is the part that the characters spend the shorter final part of the book remembering. *Twelve Blue* does not work like this; its interweaving-thread structure diverts the reader to different times and places with each click rather than following one story from start to finish. It is more fragmented, with analepses occurring throughout rather than at the end. This invites the question of whether

hypertext narratives generally are even more temporally fragmented than those found in modernism, whether hypertext has taken the aesthetics of modernism and experimented with them even further. That is one of the questions that the rest of this project will address.

7 Conclusion

Annotation and quantitative analysis allows temporal narrative features to be assessed in a different way than with traditional literary methods. The quantitative perspective enables aspects of literary structure to be measured as well as compared. This methodology can show exactly where spans of narrative disruptions begin and end, and what their length and frequency can tell us about the narrative strategies of a text. In turn this helps us to unpack the "incessant shower of innumerable atoms" with their "sudden lightning flashes of significance" that are the temporally fragmented narratives of modernist and hypertext fiction (Woolf, 1984).

References

Tanya Clement. 2012. The Story of one: Narrative and Composition in Gertrude Stein's The Making of Americans. *Texas Studies in Literature and Language*, 54(3):426–448.

Evelyn Gius, Nils Reiter, and Marcus Wielland. 2019. A Shared Task for the Digital Humanities Chapter 2: Evaluating Annotation Guidelines. *Journal of Cultural Analytics*.

Matthew Jockers. 2014. *Text Analysis with R for Students of Literature*. Springer, New York. Google-Books-ID: K4_IAwAAQBAJ.

Inderjeet Mani. 2013. *Computational Modeling of Narrative*. Morgan & Claypool.

Yann Mathet, Antoine Widlcher, and Jean-Philippe Mtivier. 2015. The Unified and Holistic Method Gamma (γ) for Inter-Annotator Agreement Measure and Alignment. *Computational Linguistics*, 41(3):437–479.

Tony McEnery and Andrew Hardie. 2011. *Corpus Linguistics: Method, Theory and Practice*. Cambridge University Press. Google-Books-ID: 3j3Wn_ZT1qwC.

Jessica Pressman. 2014. *Digital Modernism: Making It New in New Media*. Oxford University Press, Oxford.

Stephen Ramsay. 2011. *Reading Machines: Toward and Algorithmic Criticism*. University of Illinois Press. Google-Books-ID: JxPgmAEACAAJ.

Scott Rettberg. 2018. *Electronic Literature*. Polity Press, Cambridge, UK ; Medford, MA, USA.

Roser Saurí, Jessica Littman, Bob Knippen, Robert Gaizauskas, Andrea Setzer, and James Pustejovsky. 2006. TimeML Annotation Guidelines Version 1.2.1.

Hannah Schwan, Janina Jacke, Rabea Kleymann, Jan-Erik Stange, and Marian Drk. 2019. Narrelations - Visualizing Narrative Levels and their Correlations with Temporal Phenomena. *Digital Humanities Quarterly*, 013(3).

Marcus Willand, Evelyn Gius, and Nils Reiter. 2019. A Shared Task for the Digital Humanities Chapter 3: Description of Submitted Guidelines and Final Evaluation Results. *Journal of Cultural Analytics*.

Virginia Woolf. 1984. Modern Fiction. In Andrew McNeille, editor, *The Essays of Virginia Woolf. Volume 4: 1925 to 1928*. The Hogarth Press, London.

W. Victor H. Yarlott and Mark A. Finlayson. 2016. ProppML: A Complete Annotation Scheme for Proppian Morphologies. In *7th Workshop on Computational Models of Narrative (CMN 2016)*, volume 53 of *OpenAccess Series in Informatics (OASIcs)*, pages 8:1–8:19, Dagstuhl, Germany. Schloss DagstuhlLeibniz-Zentrum fuer Informatik.

Exploring aspects of similarity between spoken personal narratives by disentangling them into narrative clause types

Belen Saldias
MIT Media Lab
Cambridge MA 02139, USA
belen@mit.edu ✉

Deb Roy
MIT Media Lab
Cambridge MA 02139, USA
dkroy@media.mit.edu

Abstract

Sharing personal narratives is a fundamental aspect of human social behavior as it helps share our life experiences. We can tell stories and rely on our background to understand their context, similarities, and differences. A substantial effort has been made towards developing storytelling machines or inferring characters' features. However, we don't usually find models that compare narratives. This task is remarkably challenging for machines since they, as sometimes we do, lack an understanding of what similarity means. To address this challenge, we first introduce a corpus of real-world spoken personal narratives comprising 10,296 narrative clauses from 594 video transcripts. Second, we ask non-narrative experts to annotate those clauses under Labov's sociolinguistic model of personal narratives (i.e., action, orientation, and evaluation clause types) and train a classifier that reaches 84.7% F-score for the highest-agreed clauses. Finally, we match stories and explore whether people implicitly rely on Labov's framework to compare narratives. We show that `actions` followed by the narrator's `evaluation` of these are the aspects non-experts consider the most. Our approach is intended to help inform machine learning methods aimed at studying or representing personal narratives.

1 Introduction

We can develop the ability to retrieve a story that we have experienced or heard when someone else is telling a story. We find ourselves thinking about our story, and so we think that we know what is coming next in our friend's story. However, in order for computers to match stories automatically, we need to understand what "matching" implies and what aspect of a story should be attended to.

There have been some attempts to match stories (Nguyen et al., 2014; Chaturvedi et al., 2018)

and to understand human judgment about matched stories (Nguyen et al., 2014; Reagan et al., 2016). Nevertheless, these efforts have been mostly developed in supervised scenarios that already have a set of matched stories in hand, and they are mostly focused on non-personal narratives (e.g., fictional). From these insightful works, however, we want to explore the understanding that when we consider stories to be similar, we attend to some aspects more than others, stressing the need for comparison of different aspects rather than at a global level.

As a first effort towards our purpose, we collect the largest annotated corpus of spoken personal narratives to our knowledge, comprising 10,296 narrative clauses from 594 stories. We use transcripts of Roadtrip Nation (RTN) videos[1], where professionals share stories about their lives and career pathways. As for the annotation task, we ask Mechanical Turkers to annotate each clause under Labov's sociolinguistic model of personal narratives (Labov et al., 1967), where a narrative is defined by a structural component, which includes a temporal organization (action clauses) and contextual orientation (orientation clauses), and an evaluation component (evaluation clauses), which represents storytellers'/characters' needs and desires (explained in more depth in section 3).

Next, aiming to automatically tag stories, we develop a model to classify these clauses that reaches 84.7% F-score for the highest-agreed clauses. Once we can automatically differentiate among clause types, we would like to use them to compare stories, but, do ordinary people rely on these clause types to compare narratives? To approach that question, we pair stories and run experiments to understand to what extent ordinary people (as opposed to literary experts) rely on Labov's model to think about similarities among these stories.

---

[1] https://roadtripnation.com/

Proceedings of the 1st Joint Workshop on Narrative Understanding, Storylines, and Events, pages 78–86
July 9, 2020. ©2020 Association for Computational Linguistics

Our approach is intended to help inform machine learning methods aimed at studying personal narratives and at modeling abstract information extraction. To the best of our knowledge, this work is the first to propose and develop an approach to understand whether ordinary people rely on Labov's framework to compare personal narratives and what they perceive as similarities among those narratives. We show that actions followed by the narrator's evaluation of these are the aspects non-experts consider the most when they compare stories. Our main contributions can be summarized as follows:

- We acquire annotations to comprehensively label real-world spoken personal narratives, amounting to 10,296 clauses under Labov's clause types, and develop a straightforward strategy to classify those clauses.

- We explore to what extent people rely on Labov's framework to compare stories and show that people tend to recognize better similarities in action and evaluation clauses.

The rest of the paper is organized as follows. In section 2, we present some main related work. In section 3, we specify the story aspects to be used in our experiments. In section 4, we describe the uniqueness of our introduced narrative corpus. In section 5 and 6 we describe results, and we end with conclusion and future directions in section 7.

2   Related Work

Our work is preceded by substantial efforts toward document (Blei et al., 2003; Dai et al., 2015; Yang et al., 2016) and story (Mostafazadeh et al., 2016; Chaturvedi et al., 2018; Iyyer et al., 2016; Antoniak et al., 2019; Fu et al., 2019) representation. We find that most approaches to text similarity focus on non-narrative corpora (vor der Brück and Pouly, 2019; Lin et al., 2013; Cer et al., 2017). We also observe that most works in stories have been developed for non-personal narratives.

An specific approach to story matching was proposed by Chaturvedi et al. (2018), who used movie remakes from Wikipedia as paired stories and showed that even in that scenario it was challenging to match the remakes. Additionally, their method does not generalize well to other story types (or even movie plots) since they include specific movie parameters, like characters' name and gender, as the basis of their solution, which does not apply to our case since we do not attempt to match stories based on these surface-level indicators. The closest work to ours was done by Nguyen et al. (2014), who proposed a set of crowdsourcing tasks to analyze perception of similarity in folk narratives. They tried various approaches to retrieve these narratives. Nevertheless, they had in hand a set of metadata labels that allowed them to match narratives prior to any experiment.

How we narrate our stories was initially studied by Labov et al. (1967). More recently, Swanson et al. (2014) proposed the first mechanism to automatically classify Labov's clauses (action, orientation, and evaluation-type clauses) in personal narratives based on clauses' syntactical structure, namely part-of-speech (POS). By using 50 short stories from online mini-blogs, of diverse topics and structures, they developed a well-defined set of instructions to properly annotate Labov's clause types (referred to as *baseline* method and dataset onward). However, personal narratives from spoken stories set a more challenging context for both annotation and collection (see section 4). We get inspiration from these works to approach clause types classification using newer techniques like word embeddings (Pennington et al., 2014) and neural networks (Kim, 2014).

Furthermore, as we learn to disentangle narrative dimensions or aspects (namely, action, orientation, and evaluation-type clauses), we can use them for other story representation tasks. For instance, identifying the clauses within a story that tell people's intents/desires, reactions, and evaluation of the events (e.g., emotions) can help train and evaluate models aimed at detecting, or planning plots conditioned on, those underlying intentions and reactions (Rashkin et al., 2018; Guan et al., 2019).

3   Story aspects of comparison

Stories can be thought to be similar in a variety of dimensions; unlike most non-narrative texts, stories have "meta" dimensions that go beyond what is said (context of a story, actions that happen, emotional content, speaker's backgrounds, among others). In this work, we explore to what extent Labov's model for personal narratives underlies how non-expert people perceive story similarities. We focus on the following three aspects:

Temporal organization (action clauses): These clauses express a series of events. The narrator might play with the story's chronology, causing differences between narrative structures of one narrator and another.

Contextual world (orientation clauses): These clauses describe information about the context in which actions occur; they serve to orient the audience about people, places, time, and behavioral situations.

Human needs and desires (evaluation clauses): These clauses give significance and tell about the purpose of telling that story; they express the narrator's needs and desires.

See figure 1 for an example of a narrative annotated under Labov's model for personal narratives.

4 Narrative corpus

We introduce the largest dataset of annotated spoken personal narratives to our knowledge, from now on referenced as Roadtrip Nation or RTN corpus. These narratives were obtained from transcripts of stories video-recorded by Roadtrip Nation (RTN). In those videos, people from many backgrounds share stories about their lives and career pathways. The corpus comprises 10,296 narrative clauses from 594 stories (each one told by a different person), which account for more than 10 hours of people telling stories, each one averaging 17.1 clauses or 62 seconds long, where each clause has on average 11 tokens.

To split narratives into clauses, we proceed as follows. For every sentence in the story, we take every independent clause along with its dependent clause, which account for one narrative clause. To determine clauses, we rely on top-level S* (S, SINV, SBAR, SBARQ, SQ) tags from Penn Treebank II (Bies et al., 1995). For each top-level S* tag, we take its subtree along with hanging prepositions, conjunctions, and adverbs.

While we propose to automatically split our data, Swanson et al. (2014)'s data (our *baseline* dataset) was split by trained humans. We compared our strategy implemented using NLTK with their strategy by spliting their stories as well; we found that our method differs at most in one clause from their manually split stories.

4.1 Uniqueness of this narrative corpus

This corpus is particularly well-suited to study oral personal narratives for a few reasons. First of all, these stories were all video-recorded and manually transcribed (by Roadtrip Nation (RTN)[2]). These

[2]https://roadtripnation.com/

Story clause	Clause type
I had no photography experience	Orientation
, so I started from scratch.	Action
I was an older student and didn't have any bad habits.	Orientation
So I became obsessed with that and became a double major with a specialization in photojournalism, minor in art.	Action
And, uh, worked very hard at that then.	Action
If I could wish upon you one thing, it would be that whatever you find to earn a living, you find something that you love to do.	Evaluation

Figure 1: A fragment of a personal narrative in the RTN corpus annotated by Turkers using Labov's model.

stories are raised from spontaneous questions during real-world interviews to adults conducted by high school or college students, which produces a fluid and constantly changing dynamic.

Additionally, we recognize the storytellers' awareness of the listeners due to the presence of oral discourse markers that are prominent in oral narratives, such as "you know," "right," "anyway," "like," "ah," "uh," among others. Particularly, "you know" is the most frequent bigram in our dataset (0.5% of all bigrams, 437 appearances) compared to the baseline dataset to study Labov's model, which has "you know" mentioned only 3 times throughout all stories (Swanson et al., 2014). Furthermore, we find that the word "you" appears in the RTN stories an average of 5.3 times per story vs. 1.4 times in the baseline stories.

Besides giving a background (orientation clauses) and telling events (action clauses), RTN stories are specifically produced to display meaningful life experiences or pathway decisions to make the listener reflect or engage with the stories. These purposes emphasize Labov's evaluative function (evaluation clauses) of describing the storyteller's motivation in telling their story.

Here are two randomly sampled full transcripts (i.e., RTN stories), where we can see some of the spectrum of the stories in this corpus:

1. *"In college, I was figuring my life out. I didn't have an exact plan in terms of what I wanted to do. Everybody that acted in the capacity of a guidance counselor to me helped mold me into where I am today. For instance, when I was in high school, my guidance counselor told me , Chris, based on what I know about you, I know you love to be in big cities. I know you love to study human behavior and psychology. We discussed where I might end up in college , so I chose to go to NYU based on that feedback. And when I got my first job in marketing analytics, it's when I realized that hey, this is really cool, I actually really like this. Don't feel like you have to know all the answers right now. The more*

strict you are in terms of what you think you want to do, the less options you'll have. So think outside the box and keep an open mind."

2. *"And slowly and slowly, I started doing small jobs, you know, like, you know, I think one of my first jobs was doing, like, you know, ironing Peter Gabriel's suit and giving him powder for Good Morning America. Like, you know, kind of little things like that. But already, working with musicians , I was like, 'This is is where I belong.' So, a magical thing happened at this time. I got introduced to Lenny Kravitz , and Lenny Kravitz, at the time, ah, was, uh, a poor, starving musician. Eventually, after working with Lenny for a long time, my work started to grow , and I was working with more and more people and doing other things. So, I realized that ... the next step for me... would be to work on a movie."*

Note that in written stories (such us the ones in the baseline dataset), all the oral discourse markers present in this last story can be proofread and extracted. However, these are inherent to spontaneous oral narratives.

Finally, even though we ran our experiments prompting Turkers to "focus on the content and not the speakers' characteristics such as accent or gender" (first note in full instructions), the released dataset[3] includes speakers' gender to encourage further analysis across people with different backgrounds but similar stories. From results in section 6.2, we estimate that Turkers were rarely biased in their assessment of similarity towards gender because when they were asked to explain why two stories were similar, not one reason related to gender (out of 180 explained reasons).

4.2 Annotation process

We followed the annotation guidelines, for Labov's model extended label set, constructed by trained researchers in Swanson et al. (2014) to explain to Mechanical Turkers how to annotate our clauses. Since both domains of stories (RTN vs. baseline data from Swanson et al. (2014)'s) are different, we ran earlier small quality-control experiments to understand whether workers could reach an agreement and, if so, generate labeled stories to add as examples to the task description. Turkers were also invited to provide feedback during these early experiments; after two iterations, we converged to a

detailed task description. Finally, each story was assigned to three different workers, and an average of 2.23 workers agreed on every clause.

Aiming for clean annotations, along with injecting gold examples to reduce randomness, workers were rewarded $1.35 per story, were restricted to living in a English-speaking country, had a HIT Approval Rate $\geq$ 99 and Number of HITs Approved $\geq$ 500, and had been granted Masters status on the platform. We made annotation tasks full description, some audible stories, and collected data for this task available at `https://github.com/social-machines/acl-nuse-personal-narratives`. Gold labels were assigned by simple majority, and for those clauses without agreement, we randomly selected one of the assigned labels by annotators. Find the label distribution in table 1. Overall, we have 9,234 clauses with at least 2 Turkers agreed on them, and 3,495 clauses with 3 Turkers agreed on them.

5 Narrative clauses classification

Learning to classify narrative clauses can help us disentangle personal narratives' dimensions. Our specific intention is to understand how this decomposition helps compare stories in different aspects (clause types are assumed to be aspects or dimensions within stories for this work). Additionally, each of these clause types can be used independently for various objectives. For instance, action-type clauses could guide events extraction where, even though the narrator might play with the story's chronology, having these clauses apart can help find causal or temporal orders. Also, identifying orientation-type clause can help create a grounded understanding of the story, where actions and emotions depend on the story's environment described in these clauses. Finally, evaluation-type clauses could bring to surface narrators' mental states,

Clause type	RTN	*baseline*
Action	26.7% (2.15)	24.2%
Evaluation	40.0% (2.29)	50.0%
Orientation	29.7% (2.24)	24.2%
Not story	3.6% (2.13)	1.6%
Total clauses	10,296	1,602

Table 1: Label distribution. Find between parentheses the average agreement for each clause type. Note that the evaluation clause type is the most common clause type in both datasets.

---

[3] `https://github.com/social-machines/acl-nuse-personal-narratives`

which could push forward research on language models conditioned on mental states (Rashkin et al., 2018).

We propose to use a convolutional neural network (CNN) with max-over-time pooling to classify clauses (Zhang and Wallace, 2015). More specifically, our model consists of a non-static CNN as in Kim (2014), where we initialize embeddings using $d = 300$-dimensional GloVe pre-trained vectors (Pennington et al., 2014) and concatenate to each vector a one-hot vector (45-dimensional) that encodes POS tags associated with every token. We perform 1-max pooling with ReLU activations over each map generated by filters of sizes 2, 3, and 4; we use 30 filters per size. Then, we use two linear ((90, 45), (45, 3)) layers with dropout of 0.3 before the final softmax layer. We also explored fine-tuning BERT (Devlin et al., 2018) and found that, in most tried scenarios, this simple word-based CNN-based model outperformed BERT in accuracy, maybe due to the small fine-tuning dataset.

We randomly split the RTN dataset into 86% for training, 7% for validation, and 7% for testing, removing the "not story"-clause type. This gives 7,698 training, 619 test, and 634 validation clauses with agreement ≥ 2. Our vocabulary has around 6,000 tokens, including an unknown word token we use for uncommon words (≤ 2 appearances).

For training, we used 60 epochs and early stopping based on the validation error. We trained with different number of filter, linear layer sizes, batch sizes and learning rates set through experimentation based on performance. We find our best results using Adam with a learning rate of 5e-5 and use batch sizes of 64.

5.1 Baseline

We compare our best architecture to the baseline approach proposed by Swanson et al. (2014). To reproduce this baseline, we follow the authors' feature engineering approach and use their data split. By running experiments, we observed correspondence with the top 5 feature-relevance ranking that the baseline model found (POS:IND-VBD being the top 1). This informed our decision of using POS in our proposed approach as well. Note that, originally, the baseline model also included relative clause position within a story (which we are not including here since we mostly care about the clause purpose given its language), lexical seman-

tic categories from LIWC (Pennebaker et al., 2001), dependency relations (DEP), and lexical unigrams (STEM). Using all these engineered features, Swanson et al. (2014) reached an F-score of 76.7% on the cases with the highest annotator agreement. We refrained from using all but part-of-speech (POS) engineered features and still achieved 72.7% F-score by replicating their approach (see table 2).

5.2 Results

We report results for models trained and tested with (disjoint) sets composed only of clauses where at least two annotators agreed on their corresponding clause types, and as described in section 4.2, gold truth labels were assigned by simple majority.

Results are shown in table 2. Our results demonstrate that a simple CNN with pre-trained embedding and no feature engineering reaches high performance in our RTN dataset. Furthermore, we can see that our proposed model (trained on RTN data) still achieved high performance while evaluated on the baseline test set, even though these datasets are from different domains. On the other hand, the baseline support vector machine (SVM, linear and l1-penalized) (Cortes and Vapnik, 1995) model performs poorly when evaluated in RTN data, likely because it only uses POS (syntactic) features to represent clauses, and both written (baseline) and spoken (RTN) clauses pose different challenges in syntactical structure. We address these challenges by taking advantage of word embeddings' representational power. *From this, we see that our approach (model and dataset) can be generalized to the baseline dataset better than the other way around.*

Model	RTN test	*baseline* test
CNN - RTN	84.7%	*62.9%
SVM - *baseline*	*37.1%	72.7%
RF - RTN	48.3%	*52.5%
Random (see table 1)	40%	50%

Table 2: F-scores of our model vs. the *baseline* for clauses of highest agreement (= 3) in test sets. "- RTN" (236 clauses) and "- *baseline*" (238 clauses) refer to what dataset was used for training and validation. "*" implies testing in a domain that was not part of the training set (RTN vs. baseline dataset), where we trained in one dataset and predicted on the other. Among the different feature-based models that we tried, a linear l1-penalized support vector machine (SVM) and a random forest (RF) reached highest performance. For clauses with agreement ≥ 2, we obtained 68.31% F-score (619 clauses).

Additionally, note that if a model always predicts the most common label (or randomly assigns them), the micro-F1-score (i.e., accuracy) for RTN would be 40% and for the baseline 50%. We found that when we used the feature-engineering approach proposed by Swanson et al. (2014) in the RTN corpus, the best trained and tested standard model, a random forest with 100 estimators (RF) (Breiman, 2001), does not perform well in this new corpus. Though, from table 2, we also see that it still does better than random (third vs. fourth row). This result suggests that sentence structure and part-of-speech (POS) do not generalize well to classify narrative clause types, as one would expect from POS being predominant in the top 10 most relevant features in this feature-engineering (original and baseline) approach. While the baseline model found POS features to be highly relevant, since our model uses word embeddings, POS information only contributed $2 - 3\%$ to the F-score. Furthermore, these results stress the difference between both story domains: video-recorded spoken narratives (RTN) vs. mini-blog written stories (baseline from Swanson et al. (2014)).

To sum up, the fact that a simple CNN performs well on this classification task, as illustrated in table 2, reflects the high disentangling power that Labov's model proposes for analyzing spoken personal narratives. Finally, since we can automatically annotate and thus disentangle narrative clauses under this framework, our approach shows to be plausible, so we now proceed to explore aspects of similarity.

6 People's perception of similarity

Aiming to understand the aspects (i.e., clause types) that ordinary people attend to the most when they think about similarities among stories, we proceeded as follows. We represent each story as a set of narrative clauses, where each clause is initially encoded into a high-dimensional vector by using the Universal Sentence Encoder (USE) introduced by Cer et al. (2018). Next, given stories s and s', for each clause in s we find the closest clause in cosine similarity in s' ($s \rightarrow s'$), and vice versa ($s' \rightarrow s$), and obtain an average similarity score. Using this mechanism, we match stories only at clause-type subsets (action, evaluation, or orientation-type only). Finally, we sample 60 story pairs with average cosine similarity ≥ 0.5 for one of the clause types matches. See appendix A for some sample matched stories.

For our experiments, we use these 60 stories, which are presented to Turkers in audio form only (as opposed to transcript text). While reading and listening might require different attention spans, since Labov's sociolinguistic model focuses on stories that are produced orally (just like these) and these are short stories – 62 seconds long on average – we rely on Turkers' auditory cognitive processing.

6.1 Annotation task: matching stories

We prompted: *"Which one of the following stories, A or B, was the most similar to the main story (and why)?"*. Each main story was annotated twice, switching order for A and B; one of these stories is matched at only one clause type level and the other is randomly selected. Table 3 shows these results.

Match only at	% of times detected
Action	67.8%
Evaluation	60.9%
Orientation	48.0%

Table 3: What aspects are paid attention. For those stories matched at the action-clause level, 67.8% of times Turkers recognized the matched story accurately, and selected the random story the remaining 32.2% of the times (these action-level matched stories were more than two times recognized correctly than incorrectly). Stories matched in evaluation-type clauses were also recognized accurately 60.9% of the times, which is 50% more than those stories that were wrongly recognized (60.9% vs. 39.1%). As for orientation-level matches, these were recognized somewhat randomly (48% of the times Turkers selected the matched stories and 52% of the times they selected a random story). Some reasons behind mismatches could be (1) that Turkers might be paying attention to other not covered aspects (further explored in section 6.2), (2) some randomness on annotations, and (3) the matching strategy.

From this experiment, we conclude that action and evaluation-type clauses were relevant for non-experts when they compared stories for similarity. Hence, our hypothesis on whether ordinary people rely on these Labov's aspects to compare narratives proved to be true for both action and evaluation aspects of a story but not for the orientation aspect.

6.2 Map of crowdsourced aspects to Labov's

Trying to understand how Turkers perceived the different aspects, and where mismatches could possibly come from, for the same 60 stories, we selected the story C that has score ≥ 0.5 at a given match and has the smallest matching score for the other clause types. We asked *"Explain in what aspects (at least three) are the following personal narratives similar"*, hoping that Turkers would give reasons related to the matched dimensions. Note that with this open-ended question, Turkers were invited to think about *any aspects* that came to mind, thus we did not impose aspects on them beforehand.

Next, we map their responses to Labov's aspects; for example, the explanation *"They both have pessimistic thoughts..."* refers to how a narrator feels or perceives the situation $\rightarrow$ `evaluation` clause type. Some results of this mapping strategy are illustrated in table 4, and results for this mapping process are summarized in table 5.

Explanation	Mapped aspects
"Both started out in one direction and switched to a different field."	`action`
"Both people spoke about intense passion for something."	`evaluation`
"Both were from small towns."	`orientation`
"Both speakers suggest [ac] *pursuing their career goals* [ev] *makes them a better person* in real life too."	`action,` `evaluation`

Table 4: Examples of mapped explanations. We analyzed every open-ended explanation given by Turkers and mapped them to Labov's model according to what aspects these explanations were mostly referring to. Note that not all explanations were granular, hence, for some of them we highlighted more than one aspect (see fourth row in this table).

We show that for action- and evaluation-type clauses, Turkers mentioned aspect of similarity related to these clauses at least twice as often (as relevant) as the less relevant aspect in the matched stories, which (again) proves that these Labov's clause types can work as aspects of similarity.

As for orientation-type clauses, while they are still identified as reasons for similarity as illustrated in table 5, these are not the main reason to match two stories. We argue that this is due to the nature of our prompts to Turkers, which specifically asked for "stories" (section 6.1) or "narratives" (section 6.2); in ordinary people's mind (i.e., non-narrative experts), both of these concepts might not relate to the physical space or context where events and emotions/intentions happen, causing Turkers to not pay as much attention to them. It might also be that since all RTN stories are within the pathways/inspiration/career domain, people get engaged with that part as opposed to if our domain were more diverse in topics, which would then have led people to recur to the orientation aspect (background/set-up/place) to match them in the absence of common feelings or similar actions/decisions among stories.

Match at	Action	Evaluation	Orientation
Action	**100%**	88%	44%
Evaluation	95%	**90%**	45%
Orientation	92%	96%	**58%**

Table 5: Aspects referenced in 180 explanations of similarity (3 for each of 60 stories). As expected from results in table 3, explanations related to action and evaluation aspects are highly present in detected reasons for similarity. We see that, for most story pairs, Turkers gave explanations regarding actions that happen within stories. In particular, for pairs matched at action-clause level, every pair was said to be similar due to similar actions. For evaluation-clause level matches, we find explanations mapped to that aspect twice as often as for the least present aspect (90% vs. 45%). Finally, while orientation-type clauses were not perceived as a main similarity aspect (see table 3), we find that for stories matched at orientation clauses, Turkers recognized this aspect to be a reason for similarity more often than for any other matches (58% / 45% = 1.28 times).

7 Conclusion

We introduce the largest corpus of annotated spoken personal narratives, to our knowledge, and develop a straightforward method to classify these narratives' clauses using Labov's sociolinguistic model. Our model's high performance in classification reflects the disentangling power that Labov's model offers for analyzing oral personal narratives. Only by being trained in our introduced corpus, our model performs well in an earlier proposed dataset of written stories. Furthermore, we propose the first attempt to understand whether ordinary people (i.e., non-narrative experts), such as Mechanical Turkers, rely on Labov's model to compare personal stories, and show that these people do rely on two out of three Labov's aspects of narrative. Namely, action-type and evaluation-type clauses are perceived as central aspects of comparison, but the same does not apply to, and remains unresolved for, orientation-type clauses. One natural next step would entail shedding light on how different questions' wording and emphasis, aimed at matching stories, affect what people think of as similarity aspects. We hope that these precursory findings about the aspects that proved to underlie story-matching could also be used in a broader set of tasks, such as finding causal or temporal relationships between events, inferring mental states, or grounding actions and emotions in a story's set-up.

Finally, we acknowledge that we have only scratched the surface of this wonderfully rich space of personal narrative representations and of what people focus on when they compare stories. Our overarching goal, of modeling human judgment of narrative similarity and building a machine capable of replicating that behavior, leaves untouched several questions that future research should explore. For example, what other aspects should be examined to represent personal narratives, how to decide the relative relevance of these aspects, and how to model similarity judgments within aspects.

Acknowledgments

The authors would like to thank Roadtrip Nation for collecting and sharing their data. We also thank Swanson et al. (2014) who shared their corpus with us, and the anonymous reviewers who provided valuable feedback. We were inspired by researchers at the Laboratory for Social Machines (LSM) at MIT who are passionate about storytelling. This project was funded by LSM Member companies McKinsey & Company and Twitter.

References

Maria Antoniak, David Mimno, and Karen Levy. 2019. Narrative paths and negotiation of power in birth stories. *Proceedings of the ACM on Human-Computer Interaction*, 3(CSCW):1–27.

Ann Bies, Mark Ferguson, Karen Katz, Robert MacIntyre, Victoria Tredinnick, Grace Kim, Mary Ann Marcinkiewicz, and Britta Schasberger. 1995. Bracketing guidelines for treebank ii style penn treebank project. *University of Pennsylvania*, 97:100.

David M Blei, Andrew Y Ng, and Michael I Jordan. 2003. Latent dirichlet allocation. *Journal of machine Learning research*, 3(Jan):993–1022.

Leo Breiman. 2001. Random forests. *Machine learning*, 45(1):5–32.

Tim vor der Brück and Marc Pouly. 2019. Text similarity estimation based on word embeddings and matrix norms for targeted marketing. In *Proceedings of the 2019 Conference of the North American Chapter of the Association for Computational Linguistics: Human Language Technologies, Volume 1 (Long and Short Papers)*, pages 1827–1836.

Daniel Cer, Mona Diab, Eneko Agirre, Inigo Lopez-Gazpio, and Lucia Specia. 2017. Semeval-2017 task 1: Semantic textual similarity multilingual and crosslingual focused evaluation. *Proceedings of the 11th International Workshop on Semantic Evaluation (SemEval-2017)*.

Daniel Cer, Yinfei Yang, Sheng-yi Kong, Nan Hua, Nicole Limtiaco, Rhomni St John, Noah Constant, Mario Guajardo-Cespedes, Steve Yuan, Chris Tar, et al. 2018. Universal sentence encoder. *arXiv preprint arXiv:1803.11175*.

Snigdha Chaturvedi, Shashank Srivastava, and Dan Roth. 2018. Where have i heard this story before? identifying narrative similarity in movie remakes. In *Proceedings of the 2018 Conference of the North American Chapter of the Association for Computational Linguistics: Human Language Technologies, Volume 2 (Short Papers)*, pages 673–678.

Corinna Cortes and Vladimir Vapnik. 1995. Support-vector networks. *Machine learning*, 20(3):273–297.

Andrew M Dai, Christopher Olah, and Quoc V Le. 2015. Document embedding with paragraph vectors. *arXiv preprint arXiv:1507.07998*.

Jacob Devlin, Ming-Wei Chang, Kenton Lee, and Kristina Toutanova. 2018. Bert: Pre-training of deep bidirectional transformers for language understanding. *arXiv preprint arXiv:1810.04805*.

Liye Fu, Jonathan P Chang, and Cristian Danescu-Niculescu-Mizil. 2019. Asking the right question: Inferring advice-seeking intentions from personal narratives. *arXiv preprint arXiv:1904.01587*.

Jian Guan, Yansen Wang, and Minlie Huang. 2019. Story ending generation with incremental encoding and commonsense knowledge. In *Proceedings of the AAAI Conference on Artificial Intelligence*, volume 33, pages 6473–6480.

Mohit Iyyer, Anupam Guha, Snigdha Chaturvedi, Jordan Boyd-Graber, and Hal Daumé III. 2016. Feuding families and former friends: Unsupervised learning for dynamic fictional relationships. In *Proceedings of the 2016 Conference of the North American Chapter of the Association for Computational Linguistics: Human Language Technologies*, pages 1534–1544.

Yoon Kim. 2014. Convolutional neural networks for sentence classification. *arXiv preprint arXiv:1408.5882*.

William Labov et al. 1967. Waletzky (1967). narrative analysis: Oral versions of personal experience. *Essays on the verbal and visual arts*, pages 12–44.

Yung-Shen Lin, Jung-Yi Jiang, and Shie-Jue Lee. 2013. A similarity measure for text classification and clustering. *IEEE transactions on knowledge and data engineering*, 26(7):1575–1590.

Nasrin Mostafazadeh, Nathanael Chambers, Xiaodong He, Devi Parikh, Dhruv Batra, Lucy Vanderwende, Pushmeet Kohli, and James Allen. 2016. A corpus and evaluation framework for deeper understanding of commonsense stories. *arXiv preprint arXiv:1604.01696*.

Dong Nguyen, Dolf Trieschnigg, and Mariët Theune. 2014. Using crowdsourcing to investigate perception of narrative similarity. In *Proceedings of the 23rd ACM International Conference on Conference on Information and Knowledge Management*, pages 321–330. ACM.

James W Pennebaker, Martha E Francis, and Roger J Booth. 2001. Linguistic inquiry and word count: Liwc 2001. *Mahway: Lawrence Erlbaum Associates*, 71(2001):2001.

Jeffrey Pennington, Richard Socher, and Christopher Manning. 2014. Glove: Global vectors for word representation. In *Proceedings of the 2014 conference on empirical methods in natural language processing (EMNLP)*, pages 1532–1543.

Hannah Rashkin, Maarten Sap, Emily Allaway, Noah A Smith, and Yejin Choi. 2018. Event2mind: Commonsense inference on events, intents, and reactions. *arXiv preprint arXiv:1805.06939*.

Andrew J Reagan, Lewis Mitchell, Dilan Kiley, Christopher M Danforth, and Peter Sheridan Dodds. 2016. The emotional arcs of stories are dominated by six basic shapes. *EPJ Data Science*, 5(1):31.

Reid Swanson, Elahe Rahimtoroghi, Thomas Corcoran, and Marilyn Walker. 2014. Identifying narrative clause types in personal stories. In *Proceedings of the 15th Annual Meeting of the Special Interest Group on Discourse and Dialogue (SIGDIAL)*, pages 171–180.

Zichao Yang, Diyi Yang, Chris Dyer, Xiaodong He, Alex Smola, and Eduard Hovy. 2016. Hierarchical attention networks for document classification. In *Proceedings of the 2016 Conference of the North American Chapter of the Association for Computational Linguistics: Human Language Technologies*, pages 1480–1489.

Ye Zhang and Byron Wallace. 2015. A sensitivity analysis of (and practitioners' guide to) convolutional neural networks for sentence classification. *arXiv preprint arXiv:1510.03820*.

A Sample matched stories

These stories were matched in the action-clause level (stories A and B, with a similarity score of 0.58), and in the orientation-clause level (stories B and C, score of 0.50). Note that some clauses are not displayed due to space limitations.

Narrative clause	Clause type
"Did I have the pathway figured out, by no means, no at that time, right?	evaluation
So I also got involved in a atmospheric chemistry lab	**action**
, so nothing to do with animals	orientation
, but a lot to do with the environment.	orientation
I loved that, but I was like, well	evaluation
, I really wanna still apply this to animals.	evaluation
So I went on to graduate school	**action**
, and I enjoyed teaching, cuz I also worked as a teaching assistant at CSU Long Beach."	**action**

Story A

Narrative clause	Clause type
"When I was in school, I wanted to be a doctor.	**orientation**
I went to college	**action**
and I realized I actually didn't wanna be a doctor.	evaluation
I wanted to do something more in public health.	**orientation**
And so I went to graduate school	**action**
and I ultimately got a PhD in international relations and global health cuz I'm interested in this question on sort of a global level.	**action**
So although I started off wanting to be a doctor and although I never became a doctor, except that I guess I do get to be called Dr. Clinton because I have a doctorate degree.	**orientation**
I've figured out what my passion is and how to do that in a way that feels right for me."	evaluation

Story B

Narrative clause	Clause type
"Up until the time I got to college	**orientation**
, I still had the aspiration to maybe go to medical school.	**orientation**
Until I started to really reality hit in that my family wasn't very financially well off	evaluation
, and the reality of the fact that medical school costs a lot of money , takes a long time.	evaluation
And then it kinda broad my horizons a little bit in that I could explore some other options."	action

Story C

Extracting Message Sequence Charts from Hindi Narrative Text

Swapnil Hingmire   Nitin Ramrakhiyani   Avinash Kumar Singh[*]
Sangameshwar Patil   Girish K. Palshikar
{swapnil.hingmire,nitin.ramrakhiyani,singh.avinash3}@tcs.com
{sangameshwar.patil,gk.palshikar}@tcs.com
TRDDC, TCS Research and Innovation, India

Pushpak Bhattacharyya
pb@cse.iitb.ac.in
IIT Patna, India

Vasudeva Varma
vv@iiit.ac.in
IIIT Hyderabad, India

Abstract

In this paper, we propose the use of Message Sequence Charts (MSC) as a representation for visualizing narrative text in Hindi. An MSC is a formal representation allowing the depiction of actors and interactions among these actors in a scenario, apart from supporting a rich framework for formal inference. We propose an approach to extract MSC actors and interactions from a Hindi narrative. As a part of the approach, we enrich an existing event annotation scheme where we provide guidelines for annotation of the mood of events (realis vs irrealis) and guidelines for annotation of event arguments. We report performance on multiple evaluation criteria by experimenting with Hindi narratives from Indian History. Though Hindi is the fourth most-spoken first language in the world, from the NLP perspective it has comparatively lesser resources than English. Moreover, there is relatively less work in the context of event processing in Hindi. Hence, we believe that this work is among the initial works for Hindi event processing.

1 Introduction

Narratives are used to communicate complex ideas, detailed accounts of complex events or arguments about one's beliefs (Valls Vargas, 2017). Moreover, a narrative is a powerful tool not just from entertainment perspective but is one of the core component of human memory, knowledge and intelligence (Schank and Morson, 1995). Narrative texts are common in History where they mostly describe events that have happened in the past. Narrative text can also be routinely seen in news articles reporting events that have happened (or about to happen) in various political, corporate and social walks of a country. For multiple applications in text analysis, it becomes important to

किसानों ने अंग्रेज सरकार से भारी कर में छूट की मांग की । (The farmers demanded a waiver in the heavy taxes from the British Government.)
जब यह स्वीकार नहीं किया गया तो सरदार पटेल और गांधीजी ने किसानों का नेतऋत्व किया और उन्हे कर न देने के लिये प्रेरित किया । (When the British government didn't agree, Sardar Patel and Gandhi led them and motivated them to not pay the taxes.)
अन्त में सरकार झुकी और उस वर्ष करों में राहत दी गयी ।
(In the end, the government agreed and that year, waivers were provided in the tax.)

Table 1: Example Text Narrative

understand and analyse such narratives. A narrative has two key aspects, *plot* also referred to as *story* and *discourse*, the way in which the plot is described (Chatman, 1975). In this paper we focus on visualization of the plot aspect of a Hindi narrative.

Hindi is an Indo-Aryan language spoken by around 300 million people in India. Additionally, Hindi is the fourth most-spoken first language in the world[1]. In comparison to English, Hindi has different linguistic characteristics leading to a different set of NLP challenges. First of all, Hindi is a Subject-Object-Verb (SOV) language with relatively free word order, as against the SVO order in English. Secondly, Hindi does not have high accuracy NLP toolkits such as Stanford CoreNLP (Manning et al., 2014). In this paper, we make one of the first attempts to facilitate event processing in Hindi by proposing annotation guidelines for events as well as *their arguments*.

We propose to represent a Hindi narrative using Message Sequence Charts (MSC) (Rudolph

---

[*]Work done during internship at TCS Pune.

[1]https://en.wikipedia.org/wiki/Hindi

Proceedings of the 1st Joint Workshop on Narrative Understanding, Storylines, and Events, pages 87–96
July 9, 2020. ©2020 Association for Computational Linguistics

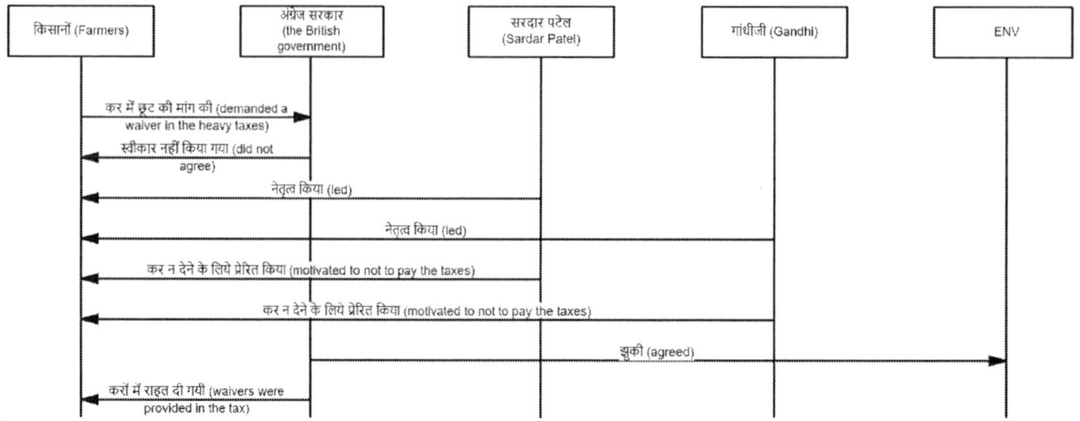

Figure 1: MSC of example text narrative described in Table 1

et al., 1996). MSC is a widely used notation to depict interactions among components of communicating devices. In an MSC, a vertical line represents a component and horizontal arrows indicate message from one component to another. We assume actors (or entities) in a narrative as components and message among the components as interactions among the corresponding actors. As an example, consider the text narrative from the Indian Independence Movement in Table 1 and the corresponding MSC in Figure 1.

We also address the problem of automatically extracting the MSC representation from a given narrative text. MSC extends the notion of a single event-timeline (Bedi et al., 2017) for a narrative by providing a timeline per actor (entity of interest). MSC representation captures all the actors and interactions in an easy to visualize manner and hence make the text more comprehensible. Further, the representation's support for inference mechanisms opens up possibilities of tackling natural language understanding problems like text comprehension and question answering. Our work is similar to (Palshikar et al., 2019) to represent a English narrative using MSC. However, due to intricacies of events in Hindi language, their approach cannot be used for construction of MSC of a Hindi narrative.

The key contributions of the paper are (i) we extend an existing scheme of annotation of events (Goud et al., 2019); we provide guidelines for annotation of mood of events (realis vs irrealis) and guidelines for annotation of event arguments, (ii) we propose an approach to identify event predicates and their arguments, (iii) MSC based visualization of actors and interactions, (iv) we report performance on multiple evaluation criteria by experimenting with four Hindi narratives from Indian History.

2 Key Annotation and Extraction Challenges for Events in Hindi

Annotation and extraction of events and their arguments from English texts is a challenging task (Mitamura et al., 2015). In case of Hindi there are more challenges as compared to English. Following are the key challenges we observed while processing Hindi narratives.

I. Absence of annotation guidelines and labelled data similar to ACE: Only few attempts have been made to define comprehensive event annotation guidelines for Hindi. (Goud et al., 2019; Goel et al., 2020) propose a set of guidelines for annotation of event mentions in Hindi. However, they do not consider arguments of events, which are vital for narrative processing.

II. Annotation of events with Light Verb Constructs (LVCs): LVCs are formed from a commonly used verb and usually a noun phrase (NP) in its direct object position, such as *have a look* or *take an action*. For example, in the sentence राम ने किताब दी ('Ram ne Kitab di'; Ram gave the book), दी (di;*give*) is the event, however in the sentence राम ने किताब खो दी ('Ram ne Kitab kho di'; *Ram lost the book.*), खो दी('kho di'; *lost*) is the event. Similarly, in the sentence राम से किताब गुम हो गई ('Ram se kitab gum ho gayee'; *Ram lost the book*), गुम हो गई ('gum ho gayee'; *lost*) is the event. As compared to English, LVCs are more common in Hindi, have different characteristics and are used as a preferred method for introducing new predicates into the language (Vaidya et al., 2016). A state-of-the-art approach (Chen et al., 2015) propose a supervised approach to identify LVCs in English using resources like PropBank, the OntoNotes sense groupings, WordNet and the British National Corpus. However, it is difficult to extend this approach for Hindi as it would require extensive efforts to create labelled data based on such resources for Hindi.

III. Annotation of nominal events: An event is a nominal event if it is described by a noun. Annotation of nominal events is a challenging task, as eventiveness of a noun depends on the context in which it is used. In this paper, we restrict our focus to events pivoted around verbs in the past tense as interactions. We plan to explore nominal events in the future.

3 Proposed Annotation Guidelines and Approach

As highlighted earlier, an MSC consists of a set of actors and interactions among them. The proposed approach is accordingly divided into two major stages: (1) Extraction of actors and their coreference resolution; (2) Extraction of interactions with their sender and receiver arguments.

3.1 Actor Extraction and Coreference Resolution

Since we are focusing on narratives of historical events, we assume the actors to be entities of type PERSON, LOCATION and ORGANIZATION. Further, we are interested in identifying all types of actor mentions - proper nouns, common nouns and pronouns. To extract proper noun mentions, we perform Named Entity Recognition of the text and mark all noun phrases of type PERSON, LOCATION and ORGANIZATION as actors. Since Hindi is a relatively resource-poor language and it is very costly to generate necessary labeled data to train a supervised model, we propose an unsupervised technique to identify actors based on Wordnet. Given a noun which is the head of a noun phrase, we query its hypernym hierarchy to check if specific senses of स्थान (sthaan; *place*), क्षेत्र (kshetra; *region*), भू-भाग (bhu-bhaag; *geographical area*), व्यक्ति (vyakti; *person*), मानव (maanav; *person*) and समुदाय (samudaay; *group*) are found. If so, we tag the type of the respective noun phrase corresponding to the hypernym

found. As pronouns are a closed set of words, we use a manually prepared list of pronouns and corresponding types to identify all pronoun mentions of the actors. It is ensured that the list does not include any demonstrative pronouns (such as यह, वह, उन, उस). Each pronoun in the text is checked against the list and marked as an actor, if found.

As the actor mentions are to be visualized on a MSC, it is not sufficient to depict only head words of actor phrases. For example, सरदार पटेल (*Sardar Patel* is more informative as well as describes the complete entity than just the headword पटेल (*Patel*). Hence, we propose a simple dependency parse based approach to identify the complete noun phrase given the head word. We append to the head word all nouns which are dependent on it through the *compound* dependency. For example, the word महात्मा (*Mahatma*) is dependent on the head word गांधी (*Gandhi*) through the *compound* dependency and hence, the complete phrase becomes महात्मा गांधी (*Mahatma Gandhi*). We also append any adjectives/quantifiers which modify the head word using the *amod* dependency. For example, प्रथम प्रधानमंत्री (pratham pradhanmantri; *first prime minister*) is formed as a complete phrase where प्रथम (pratham; *first*) modifies प्रधानमंत्री (pradhanmantri; *prime minister*) using the *amod* dependency. A complex construct observed is a noun dependent on the head word with a *nmod* dependency with no verbs or prepositions occurring between the two. Such nouns are also considered part of the complete phrase and are handled through this approach. For example, in the phrase स्वतंत्रता संग्राम सेनानी (swatantrata sangram senani; *freedom fighter*), the word स्वतंत्रता (swatantrata; *independence*) is dependent on the head word सेनानी (senani; *soldier*) through the *nmod* dependency with only a noun संग्राम (sangram; *struggle*) appearing in between.

For coreference resolution, we employ the technique proposed in (Ramrakhiyani et al., 2018). The authors assume gold actor mentions as input and predict coreferences between the actor mentions. They apply a set of linguistically motivated rules coded in a Markov Logic Network (MLN) based framework to perform the coreference resolution. In this paper, we develop an MLN with the stated rules and input it the extracted actor mentions to perform the coreference resolution. We also annotate the first observed mention in each mention cluster as the canonical actor mention for that coreference group. The canonical actor mention is used for its depiction on the output MSC.

3.2 Interaction Extraction

An interaction in the MSC notation is composed of the central event and its sender and receiver actor arguments. To extract interactions it hence becomes important to identify the meaningful events and their actor arguments. In this paper, we focus on events which are primarily described by verbs. We define such verbal events based on linguistic properties of Hindi verbs (Vaidya, 2015). We also propose a set of annotation guidelines to mark such verbal events and their arguments.

3.2.1 Verbal Events

A verbal event can be of two types: 1) simple predicate where a verb triggers the event. For example, in the sentence, राम ने आम **खाया** (Ram ne aam khaya; *Ram ate a mango.*), the verb **खाया** is a simple predicate, 2) complex predicate where an event is triggered by a verb and an additional element of type *verb* or *adjective* or *adverb* or borrowed English verb or *noun* (Vaidya, 2015). A complex predicate further has two important types: 1) *conjunct predicate* where the additional element is of type *noun*. For example, in the sentence, २०१७ में राम का जन्म हुआ (2017 me Ram ka janma hua; *Ram was born in 2017.*) the verbal predicate हुआ triggers an event with the additional noun element जन्म, 2) *compound predicate* where the additional element is of type *verb*. For example, in the sentence, राम ने किताब **खो दी** (Ram ne kitab kho di; *Ram lost the book.*), the verbal predicate दी triggers an event with the additional verb element खो.

3.2.2 Annotation of Events

The proposed annotation guidelines for marking verbal events are described as follows:

I. In this paper, we restrict our scope to events represented using verbs. For example, in the following sentence महोत्सव (mahotsav; *festival*) is not annotated as an event: फिल्म महोत्सव के दौरान पुराने अभिनेता पधारे (film mahotsav ke dauran purane abhineta padhare; *senior actors arrived during the film festival*)

II. The head verb of an event predicate is tagged as PIVOT. If an event predicate is a *conjunct predicate*, its *noun* element is tagged as P-CONJ. In case of a *compound predicate*, the *verb* element of the head verb is tagged

as P-COMP. Following are the examples of *conjunct predicate* and *compound predicate* annotated as per this guideline:

Conjunct predicate:
उनकी शिक्षा मुख्यत: स्वाध्याय से ही हुई
P-CONJ   PIVOT
(unki shiksha mukhtah swadhyay se hui;*His education happened mainly through self-learning*)

Compound predicate:
उन्हे ग्रह मंत्री का कार्य सौंपा गया
                    PIVOT P-COMP
(unhe grha mantri ka karya saupa gaya;*He was made in-charge of the home ministry*)

III. Based on the guidelines in (Mitamura et al., 2015), events with realis mood are considered valid events. An event is in realis mood, if it has explicitly happened in the past. On the other hand, if an event has irrealis mood then we can not say whether the event has actually happened or not. Following are examples of sentences with realis and irrealis mood events:

- Realis: लंदन जाकर उन्होंने बैरिस्टरी की पढाई की
  (landan jakar unhone baristari ki padhai ki; *He went to London and studied law*)
- Irrealis: यदि सरदार कुछ वर्ष और जीवित रहते तो भारत का कायाकल्प हो जाता
  (yadi sardar kuch varsh aur jeewit rehte to pure bharat ka kayakalp ho jata; *If Sardar remained alive for a few more years, India would have been transformed.*)

IV. Only punctual events are annotated as events. An event is punctual if it "does not have a transitional phase between its start and end point" (Kay and Aylett, 1996). This implies that a process in continuation is not punctual and hence not marked as a valid event.

- Punctual event: किसानों ने अंग्रेज सरकार से भारी कर में छूट की मांग की
  (kisano ne angrejh sarkar se bhari kar me chut ki mang ki; *The farmers demanded the British government, a waiver in the heavy taxes*)
- Non-punctual event: गुजरात का खेडा खंड उन दिनों सूखे की चपेट में था
  (gujrat ka kheda khand un dino sukhe ki

Algorithm 1: Identification of Event Predicates

Input: Sentence s
Result: E : List of event predicate tuples:
$< PIVOT, P\text{-}CONJ, P\text{-}COMP >$ in sentence s

```
1  E := ∅ // list of event predicates
2  S_d := GetDependencyTree(s);
3  root := S_d.root // get the root of the
      dependency tree
4  if root is a past tense verb then
5      e :=<>; e.PIVOT = root;
6      E := E ∪ e;
7      foreach child c ∈ S_d.root.children do
8          if
             dep_rel(c, root) ∈ [advcl, conj, acl : relcl]
             then
9              e :=<>; e.PIVOT = c;
10             E := E ∪ e

11 foreach event predicate e ∈ E do
12     foreach child c ∈ S_d.e.children do
13         if dep_rel(c, e) == compound and c is a
            noun then
14             e.P-CONJ = c
15         else if dep_rel(c, e) ∈ [aux, auxpass] and c
            is an auxiliary verb then
16             e.P-COMP = c

17 return E
```

Algorithm 2: Identification of Interactions

Input: Sentence s, E = List of event predicate tuples:
$< PIVOT, P - CONJ, P - COMP >$ in sentence s, A = List of actors in s
Result: I = List of tuples:
$< SENDER, PIVOT, RECEIVER >$

```
1  I := ∅ // list of interactions
2  S_d := GetDependencyTree(s);
3  root := S_d.root // get the root of the
      dependency tree
4  rootSender := NULL;
5  rootCONJ := NULL;
6  foreach Event e ∈ E do
7      p := e.PIVOT  n := e.P-CONJ
       i :=< NULL, p, NULL >;
8      foreach child c ∈ S_d.p.children do
9          if dep_rel(c, p) == nsubj and c ∈ A then
10             i.SENDER := c;
11             if p is root then
12                 rootSender := c;
13                 rootCONJ := n
14         else if dep_rel(c, p) ∈ [dobj, nmod] and
            c ∈ A then
15             i.RECEIVER := c
16     if i.SENDER is NULL or i.RECEIVER is
       NULL then
17         foreach child c ∈ S_d.n.children do
18             if i.SENDER is NULL and
                dep_rel(c, n) == nsubj and c ∈ A
                then
19                 i.SENDER := c;
20                 if n == rootCONJ then
21                     rootSender := c
22             else if i.RECEIVER is NULL and
                dep_rel(c, n) ∈ [dobj, nmod] and
                c ∈ A then
23                 i.RECEIVER := c
24     if i.SENDER is NULL and e is not root then
25         i.SENDER := rootSender
26     I := I ∪ i

27 return I
```

chapet me tha; *Those days Gujarat's Kheda district was affected by drought.*)

- Verbs appearing in the authors' opinions are not considered valid events. For example, the verbs in the quoted part जाएंगे (jayenge;will go) and है (hai) of the following sentence are ignored:
  सरदार पटेल ने केवल इतना कहा "क्या हम गोवा जाएंगे, केवल दो घंटे की बात है"
  (sardar patel ne kewal itna kaha "kya hum goa jayenge, kewal do ghante ki baat hai"; *Sardar Patel only said "Will we go to Goa, its a matter of only two hours".*)

3.2.3 Annotation of Event Arguments

We consider an actor who initiates or triggers an event as the sender of the event. All other actors that participate in the event are considered as receivers of the event. For example, in the sentence राम ने राजू को लन्दन भेजा (ram ne raju ko london bheja; *Ram sent Raju to London*), राम is the sender of the event भेजा, while राजू and लन्दन are its receivers.

3.3 Approach to Identify Verbal Events

In this paper, we propose an approach to identify the above described verbal events and their arguments. Our proposed approach makes use of POS tagging and dependency parsing.

Algorithm 1 shows our approach to identify event predicates and their compound and conjunct predicates (if available) from a sentence.

Figure 2 shows an illustration of our approach on an example sentence. The verb हुए (hue; *became*) is the root of the dependency tree of the sentence. We can determine the tense of हुए based on its child थे (thhe) with the dependency relation *aux*. As हुए is the root of the sentence with past tense, we identify it as the PIVOT of an event.

In the dependency tree of this sentence, the word नाराज (naraj; *unhappy*) is a *noun* child of हुए with dependency relation *compound* and hence, we identify नाराज as P-CONJ of हुए. Similarly, we identify थे as its P-COMP.

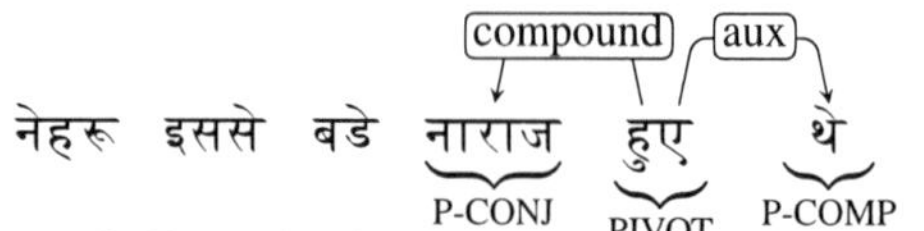

Figure 2: Example of event identification from a sentence (only relevant dependencies are shown for the sake of brevity)

In order to filter out an irrealis or non-punctual event, we check its respective P-COMP against a manually curated list of verbs such as जाता ,जाया, रही, रहे, चाहे, चाहती, होना, होती indicating either continuity or uncertainty of events. We also ignore events appearing in quotes as they are likely to be authors' opinions.

3.4 Approach to Identify Event Arguments

Algorithm 2 discusses our event argument identification approach leading to formation of the interactions to be shown on an MSC.

Figure 3 shows an illustration of our approach on an example sentence. For the event pivot लिखा (likha; wrote), words गांधी (Gandhi) and पटेल (Patel) are its dependency children with relations *nsubj* and *dobj* respectively. They are also present in the list of extracted actors and hence are designated as sender and receiver of this event.

In Figure 4, the word छूट (chhuut; waiver) is dependent on the P-CONJ - मांग (maang; demand) through the dependency relation *nmod*, but is not a valid actor and hence not a valid receiver.

4 Experimentation Details

4.1 Datasets

We carry out our experiments on the four text narratives from Indian History, contributed by (Ramrakhiyani et al., 2018). We obtain the dataset text and gold actor annotations and we carry out the event annotations for these datasets with the help of three annotators. The statistics about the datasets are described in Table 2.

	sardar	emergency	plassey	shivaji
# Sentences	90	56	74	71
# Words	1661	1373	1361	1293
# Actors	115	78	79	112
# Interactions	88	74	57	69

Table 2: Dataset Statistics

4.2 Experimental Setup

We used the Google SyntaxNet[2] for dependency parsing the Hindi sentences. SyntaxNet is a TensorFlow toolkit for deep learning powered natural language understanding developed at Google. The *Parsey Universal* component of SyntaxNet supports NLP preprocessing tasks such as POS tagging, morphological analysis and dependency parsing for 40 different languages including Hindi.

We employed two different NER approaches proposed for Hindi and consider a word as part of a named entity if either or both of them identify it as a named entity. One of the approaches is Polyglot, proposed in (Al-Rfou et al., 2013). It is based on using language agnostic techniques involving Wikipedia and Freebase and no human annotated NER training data. The second approach is proposed by (Murthy et al., 2019) and is based on a supervised deep learning architecture for NER in Hindi. To access the Hindi WordNet (Narayan et al., 2002), we use the pyiwn toolkit (Panjwani et al., 2018) which is a python API to access Indian language WordNets.

We use the *Sardar* dataset as a training set to iteratively revise and improve the extraction algorithms while keeping the other datasets unseen.

4.3 Evaluation and Results

The approach comprises of multiple facets like actor identification, actor coreference resolution, event extraction and event argument finding. To assess each of these facets, we carry out evaluation of the proposed approach at multiple levels.

As the first level, we check the performance of actor identification and coreference resolution. If an actor predicted by the approach is present in the gold standard, it is marked as a true positive. False positives and false negatives are computed accordingly. We report the F1 scores for actor mention identification for each dataset in Table 3. At this level, we also report the MUC (Vilain et al., 1995), the B^3 (Bagga and Baldwin, 1998) and the

[2]https://github.com/tensorflow/models/tree/master/research/syntaxnet

92

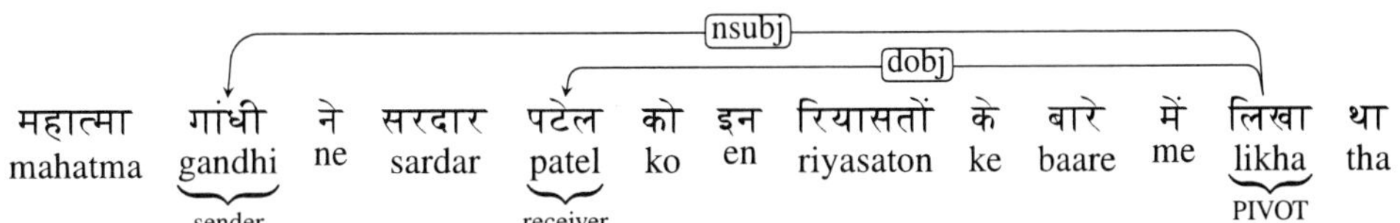

Figure 3: Example of event argument identification from a sentence (only relevant dependencies are shown for the sake of brevity)

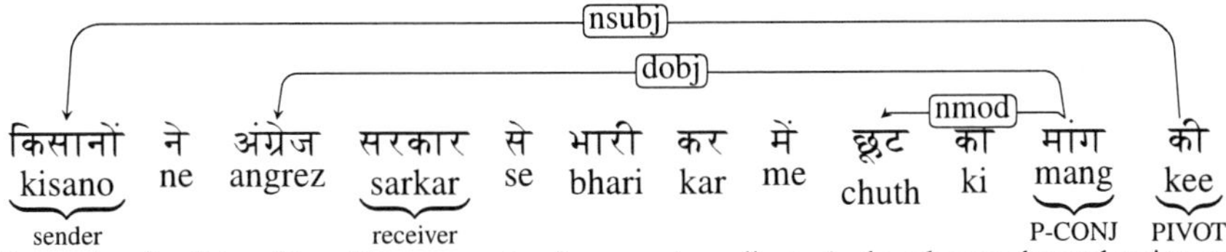

Figure 4: Example of valid and invalid arguments of an event predicate (only relevant dependencies are shown for the sake of brevity)

CEAFe (Luo, 2005) scores to measure the coreference resolution performance.

Dataset	Participant mentions	Canonical mentions & aliases		
		BCUB	MUC	CEAFe
sardar	68.2	45.7	51.0	48.6
emergency	71.0	41.2	44.1	43.1
plassey	68.5	40.6	50.4	34.6
shivaji	62.1	42.8	48.7	38.9

Table 3: Performance of Actor Identification and Coreference Resolution (F_1 metric in %).

At the next level, we check the correctness of events which are basis for interactions. If the predicted pivot is present in the gold standard, it is counted as a true positive and the false positives and false negatives are computed accordingly. In a similar way, true positives, false positives and false negatives are computed for P-CONJ and P-COMP parts. We report F1 scores for each of PIVOT, P-CONJ and P-COMP separately and the three combined i.e. the complete event, in Table 4.

At the final level, we check correctness of the extracted interactions which involves checking the correctness of both the event and its actor arguments. In Table 5, we report F1 scores for three settings namely Sender+Pivot (combination of both event pivot and corresponding sender should be correct), Receiver+Pivot (combination of both event pivot and corresponding receiver should be correct), Complete interaction (complete combination of event pivot, corresponding sender and corresponding receiver should be correct).

4.4 Analysis

From the low to moderate results, it can be observed that each stage of the approach is challenging. It is important to note here that this is a pipeline based approach and errors propagate from one stage to the next. A considerable number of errors is also attributed to the performance of linguistic tools such as SyntaxNet and Hindi NER.

We now discuss some error cases for the actor extraction stage. In the sentence इसके चलते कई अवसरों पर दोनो ने ही अपने पद का त्याग करने की धमकी दे दी थी (iske chalte kai avsaro par dono ne hi apne pad ka tyaag karne ki dhamki de di thi; *Meanwhile, on multiple occasions both had threatened to resign from their posts*), the gold actor दोनो (dono; both) is a noun but is not tagged as a valid actor. This is because none of the hypernyms of दोनो carry a PERSON sense and hence, our WordNet based approach fails to identify दोनो as a valid actor. This example highlights the need of a more richer knowledge resource that can disambiguate words like दोनो as an actor from its quantifier sense. Another error case is regarding pronouns like इसको (isko; this/him/her) which can be used to refer to events or actors. Pronouns like these are present in our pronoun list because of their actor referring property, but at places in the text when it appears referring a non-actor it is still considered as an actor leading to a false positive.

We also discuss error cases for the interaction extraction stage. In the sentence लन्दन जाकर उन्होंने बैरिस्टर की पढाई की और वापस आकर अहमदाबाद में वकालत करने लगे (landan jakar unhone baristri ki padhai ki aur wapas aakar ahmedabad me vakalat karne lage; *He went to London, studied law, came back and started practising law in Ahmedabad.*), the PIVOT आकर (aakar; came) does not find the right sender argument उन्होंने (unhone; he) using the dependency

	Sardar Patel	Emergency	Battle of Plassey	Shivaji Maharaj
PIVOT	0.82	0.82	0.64	0.79
P-CONJ	0.72	0.69	0.55	0.53
P-COMP	0.83	0.84	0.64	0.81
PIVOT+P-CONJ+P-COMP	0.66	0.62	0.47	0.46

Table 4: F1 scores - Event Evaluation

	Sardar Patel	Emergency	Battle of Plassey	Shivaji Maharaj
Sender+PIVOT	0.54	0.43	0.43	0.55
Receiver+PIVOT	0.50	0.39	0.35	0.48
Complete Interaction	0.38	0.30	0.25	0.41

Table 5: F1 scores - Interaction Evaluation

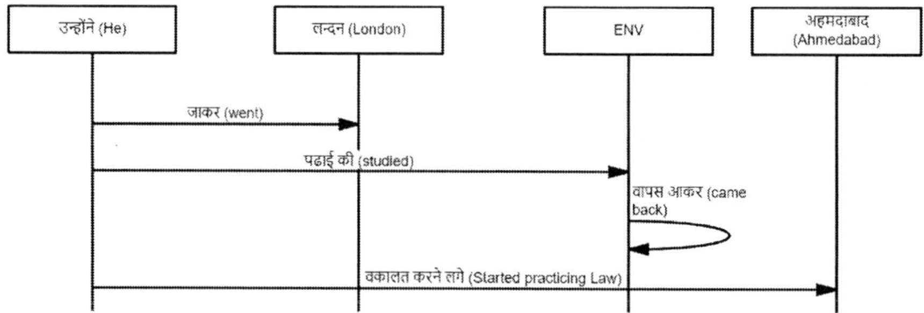

Figure 5: Predicted MSC of the example sentence "लन्दन जाकर उन्होंने बैरिस्टर की पढाई की और वापस आकर अहमदाबाद में वकालत करने लगे" (*He went to London, studied law, came back and started practising law in Ahmedabad.*)

parse based argument finding approach. This highlights the importance of more robust approach to identify arguments of events.

As part of the analysis, we show the visual MSC based depiction of the earlier sentence लन्दन जाकर उन्होंने बैरिस्टर की पढाई की और वापस आकर अहमदाबाद में वकालत करने लगे in Figure 5. As pointed out, the event आकर does not form a valid interaction because of absence of correct arguments.

5 Related Work

Automatic extraction of MSCs from narratives is studied for English language. Recently, (Palshikar et al., 2019) proposed a semantic role labelling and dependency parsing based approach to extract messages discussed in a narrative. They further use the Document Level Time-anchors algorithm for temporal ordering of extracted messages.

Several researchers such as (Rao and Devi, 2017, 2018) have focused on extraction of events from Hindi. However, these works are focused on news and social media texts. (Kuila et al., 2018) propose a neural network based approach for event extraction. However, the approach is supervised and needs labelled data. On the other hand, our approach does not need labelled data.

6 Conclusions

In this paper we proposed the use of a knowledge representation known as Message Sequence Charts (MSC) for visualizing Hindi narratives by identifying and depicting the multiple actors and interactions involved. As per our knowledge this is the first attempt to visualize Hindi narratives and represent them formally. We extend a set of annotation guidelines for marking events and their arguments pivoted on verbs. We also propose linguistic knowledge based approach for actor and interaction identification. We report results on four state-of-the-art Hindi narrative datasets and present a brief analysis of the approaches. As future work, we would like to extend this work on lines of Semantic Role Labelling (SRL) for Hindi including nominal predicates and more arguments. We also aim to work on the temporal ordering aspect of Hindi narratives which would allow us to depict interactions in the true chronological order.

References

Rami Al-Rfou, Bryan Perozzi, and Steven Skiena. 2013. Polyglot: Distributed Word Representations for Multilingual NLP. In *Proceedings of the Seventeenth Conference on Computational Natural Language Learning*, pages 183–192, Sofia, Bulgaria. Association for Computational Linguistics.

Amit Bagga and Breck Baldwin. 1998. Algorithms for Scoring Coreference Chains. In *The first international conference on language resources and evaluation workshop on linguistics coreference*, volume 1, pages 563–566. Granada.

Harsimran Bedi, Sangameshwar Patil, Swapnil Hingmire, and Girish Keshav Palshikar. 2017. Event Timeline Generation from History Textbooks. In *Proceedings of the 4th Workshop on Natural Language Processing Techniques for Educational Applications, NLP-TEA@IJCNLP 2017, Taipei, Taiwan, December 1, 2017*, pages 69–77.

Seymour Chatman. 1975. Towards a Theory of Narrative. *New literary history*, 6(2):295–318.

Wei-Te Chen, Claire Bonial, and Martha Palmer. 2015. English Light Verb Construction Identification using Lexical Knowledge. In *Twenty-Ninth AAAI Conference on Artificial Intelligence*.

Pranav Goel, Alok Debnath, Suhan Prabhu, and Manish Shrivastava. 2020. Hindi TimeBank: An ISO-TimeML Annotated Reference Corpus. In *Workshop on Interoperable Semantic Annotation (ISA-16)*.

Jaipal Singh Goud, Pranav Goel, Alok Debnath, Suhan Prabhu, and Manish Shrivastava. 2019. A Semantico-Syntactic Approach to Event-Mention Detection and Extraction In Hindi. In *Proceedings 15th Joint ACL-ISO Workshop on Interoperable Semantic Annotation*, pages 63–76.

Roderick Kay and Ruth Aylett. 1996. Transitivity and Foregrounding in News Articles: Experiments in Information Retrieval and Automatic Summarising. In *34th Annual Meeting of the Association for Computational Linguistics, 24-27 June 1996, University of California, Santa Cruz, California, USA, Proceedings.*, pages 369–371.

Alapan Kuila, Sarath chandra Bussa, and Sudeshna Sarkar. 2018. A Neural Network based Event Extraction System for Indian Languages. In *FIRE (Working Notes)*, pages 291–301.

Xiaoqiang Luo. 2005. On Coreference Resolution Performance Metrics. In *HLT/EMNLP 2005*, pages 25–32. Association for Computational Linguistics.

Christopher D. Manning, Mihai Surdeanu, John Bauer, Jenny Finkel, Prismatic Inc, Steven J. Bethard, and David Mcclosky. 2014. The Stanford CoreNLP Natural Language Processing Toolkit. In *In ACL, System Demonstrations*.

Teruko Mitamura, Zhengzhong Liu, and Eduard H. Hovy. 2015. Overview of TAC KBP 2015 Event Nugget Track. In *Proceedings of the 2015 Text Analysis Conference, TAC 2015, Gaithersburg, Maryland, USA, November 16-17, 2015, 2015*.

V. Rudra Murthy, Mitesh M. Khapra, and Pushpak Bhattacharyya. 2019. Improving NER Tagging Performance in Low-Resource Languages via Multilingual Learning. *ACM Trans. Asian & Low-Resource Lang. Inf. Process.*, 18(2):9:1–9:20.

Dipak Narayan, Debasri Chakrabarti, Prabhakar Pande, and Pushpak Bhattacharyya. 2002. An Experience in Building the Indo WordNet-a WordNet for Hindi. In *First International Conference on Global WordNet, Mysore, India*.

Girish Palshikar, Sachin Pawar, Sangameshwar Patil, Swapnil Hingmire, Nitin Ramrakhiyani, Harsimran Bedi, Pushpak Bhattacharyya, and Vasudeva Varma. 2019. Extraction of Message Sequence Charts from Narrative History Text. In *Proceedings of the First Workshop on Narrative Understanding*, pages 28–36, Minneapolis, Minnesota. Association for Computational Linguistics.

Ritesh Panjwani, Diptesh Kanojia, and Pushpak Bhattacharyya. 2018. pyiwn: A Python-based API to access Indian Language WordNets. In *Proceedings of the Global WordNet Conference*, volume 2018.

Nitin Ramrakhiyani, Swapnil Hingmire, Sachin Pawar, Sangameshwar Patil, Girish K. Palshikar, Pushpak Bhattacharyya, and Vasudeva Varma. 2018. Resolving Actor Coreferences in Hindi Narrative Text. In *Proceedings of the 15th International Conference on Natural Language Processing, ICON 2018, Patiala, India, December 15-18, 2018*.

Pattabhi RK Rao and Sobha Lalitha Devi. 2017. EventXtract-IL: Event Extraction from Social Media Text in Indian Languages@ FIRE 2017-An Overview. In *FIRE (Working Notes)*, pages 130–135.

Pattabhi RK Rao and Sobha Lalitha Devi. 2018. EventXtract-IL: Event Extraction from Newswires and Social Media Text in Indian Languages@ FIRE 2018-An Overview. In *FIRE (Working Notes)*, pages 282–290.

Ekkart Rudolph, Peter Graubmann, and Jens Grabowski. 1996. Tutorial on Message Sequence Charts. *Computer Networks and ISDN Systems*, 28(12):1629–1641.

Roger C. Schank and Gary Saul Morson. 1995. *Tell Me a Story: Narrative and Intelligence*. Northwestern University Press.

Ashwini Vaidya. 2015. *Hindi Complex Predicates: Linguistic and Computational Approaches*. Ph.D. thesis, University of Colorado at Boulder.

Ashwini Vaidya, Sumeet Agarwal, and Martha Palmer. 2016. Linguistic Features for Hindi Light Verb Construction Identification. In *Proceedings of COLING 2016, the 26th International Conference on Computational Linguistics: Technical Papers*, pages 1320–1329.

Josep Valls Vargas. 2017. *Narrative Information Extraction with Non-Linear Natural Language Processing Pipelines*. Ph.D. thesis, Drexel University, Drexel University.

Marc Vilain, John Burger, John Aberdeen, Dennis Connolly, and Lynette Hirschman. 1995. A Model-theoretic Coreference Scoring Scheme. In *Proceedings of the 6th conference on Message understanding*, pages 45–52. Association for Computational Linguistics.

Emotion Arcs of Student Narratives

Swapna Somasundaran, Xianyang Chen, and Michael Flor
Educational Testing Service
660 Rosedale Road, Princeton
NJ 08541, USA
{ssomasundaran,xchen,mflor}@ets.org

Abstract

This paper studies emotion arcs in student narratives. We construct emotion arcs based on event affect and implied sentiments, which correspond to plot elements in the story. We show that student narratives can show elements of plot structure in their emotion arcs and that properties of these arcs can be useful indicators of narrative quality. We build a system and perform analysis to show that our arc-based features are complementary to previously studied sentiment features in this area.

1   Introduction

This work deals with the study of emotion arcs in student narratives. Plots (Lehnert, 1981) and emotion arcs (Vonnegut, 1995; Reagan et al., 2016; Chu and Roy, 2017) form the foundations of story-telling.

Story-telling is an important literacy skill. Children are taught to understand and write narratives in school, and literacy standards[1] require students to write increasingly competent narratives.

While researchers have already introduced analysis of plots in well-written stories and emotion arcs in novels, not much attention has been paid to these phenomena in narratives written by novices. In this work we study student narratives along the dimension of emotion arcs. We show that even novice writing can show plot elements. We then investigate if the quality of narratives can be determined by measuring properties of the emotion arcs.

There has been work investigating scoring of student narratives (Somasundaran et al., 2018). However, previous focus has been on other aspects of the narrative, such as event progression, organization, vividness, detailing and subjectivity. We investigate if emotion arc characteristics can help to improve automated narrative scoring systems.

Plot analyses and research on constructing shapes of stories have considered the general sentiment or affect present in the text. In our work we focus on a specific type of sentiment/affect that we believe is closer to plot structure: events that produce good/bad effect, affective events and sentiment connotations. We show that while there is overlap with subjectivity and sentiment, our approach captures a different dimension of narrative quality.

We believe that our work advances the understanding of plots elements in narratives written by novices. Our work connects evidence of plots elements to the quality of narratives as judged by human raters using standard scoring rubrics. Specifically, the contributions of our work can be summarized as follows: 1. We show that emotion arcs can be seen even in simple narratives written by novice writers. 2. Our experiments show that emotion arc properties are indicative of the quality of narratives. They are related to other sentiment factors in narratives, but are distinct in what they capture about the narrative quality. 3. We show that encoding emotion arc characteristics help to improve narrative essay scoring systems.

2   Narrative Data

As our focus is student narratives, we use the annotated narrative dataset from Somasundaran et al. (2018). The data comprises of 942 narrative essays written by school students from the Criterion® program[2]. Criterion is an online writing evaluation service from Educational Testing Service[3]. It is a web-based, instructor-led writing tool that helps students plan, write and revise their essays. Nar-

---

[1] http://www.corestandards.org/ ELA-Literacy/W/11-12

[2] https://criterion.ets.org/criterion
[3] www.ets.org

Proceedings of the 1st Joint Workshop on Narrative Understanding, Storylines, and Events, pages 97–107
July 9, 2020. ©2020 Association for Computational Linguistics

rative essays in this dataset belong to writers from three grade levels: grades 7, 10 and 12. Each essay is in response to one of 18 story-telling prompts; prompts belong to topics related to personal experiences, hypothetical situations, and fictional stories. Given below are example prompts:

[Personal Experience] There are moments in everyone's lives when they feel pride and accomplishment after completing a challenging task. These moments can happen in the classroom, on the field, or in their personal lives. Write a story about one of your proudest moments.

[Hypothetical Situation] Pretend that one morning you wake up and find out that you've become your teacher for a day! What happened? What do you do? Do you learn anything? Write a story about what happens. Use your imagination!

[Fictional Story] While some well-loved films feature sequels, many do not. These movies can leave the audience wanting to know more about the plot and characters they've enjoyed. Is there a film you've wanted to continue past the ending? Write a synopsis of your own "sequel" to a beloved movie using the same characters and settings as the real film. Remember to include a summary of the previous title and plot, as well as specific new details to draw the reader into your continuation of the movie.

The average essay length in the data is 320 words, with a range of 3 to 1310 words and a standard deviation of 195. The rubric used for scoring the essays was created by education experts and teachers. It defines a separate score (0-4) each for essay organization and essay development. The dataset also provides a *Narrative Score* for each essay, which is the sum of the organization and development scores. The score is an integer value from 0 to 8, with 8 corresponding to perfect organization and development of the narrative. The human inter-annotator agreement for the narrative quality score is 0.76 QWK[4]. We use this score for our work. We refer the reader to the original paper for details on the data, rubrics and annotation.

3 Emotion Arc

An emotion arc involves the plotting or tracking of sentiment valence of some form along the time axis (Vonnegut, 1995; Reagan et al., 2016; Chu and Roy, 2017; Del Vecchio et al., 2018). However, we observed that sentiment words and phrases occurring in narratives serve different *purposes*, such as describing character and settings, embellishing the story, advancing the plot, etc. For example, senti-

ment words may be used to describe a scene (e.g. "beautiful house"), a character (e.g. "smart girl"), a character's private state (e.g. "Peter thought that was foolish") or emotions (e.g. "Sally was furious").

In our work, we are primarily interested in sentiments and emotions as they relate to the plot. Thus our focus is mainly on events and implicit sentiments. Events are the core building blocks of narratives, and positive and negative events are closely tied to plot progression. This intuition is in line with Lehnert's work on plot units (Lehnert, 1981), which also focuses on positive/negative events (called *events that please*, and *events that displease*). Additionally, much of the plot movement is brought about by elements that have implicit sentiment value. For example, if "A kills B" in a story, it indicates an objective event on the surface, but denotes a conflict (or resolution, depending on whether B is an antagonist) in the story. Given this focus, our emotion arcs are constructed based on the following phenomena that have been previously developed for other purposes in computational linguistics:

Good-for and bad-for events: Good-for and Bad-for events, also known as benefactive and malefactive events, positively/negatively affect the entities on which they act (Deng et al., 2013). These events indicate someone (or something) doing something that affects someone (or something) in a positive or negative manner. In the context of stories, we hypothesize that such events can indicate elements of a plot, such as conflict, resolution and goal achievement.

Affective events: These are events that affect an experiencer in positive or negative ways (Ding and Riloff, 2016) even though they do not, in their surface form, hold a valence. The events are implicitly affective based on the human knowledge of the event itself, such as going on a vacation or breaking a record.

Sentiment Connotation : These are words that imply a positive or negative sentiment even though they appear objective on the surface (Feng et al., 2013). For example, a gun-shot invariably indicates a conflict in the plot, even though it is objective on the surface.

3.1 Constructing Emotion Arcs

In order to construct the emotion arcs, we first extract the elements of interest described above. For

---

[4]Quadratic Weighted Kappa (Cohen, 1968) is a standard metric in essay evaluation

this we use the EffectWordNet (Choi and Wiebe, 2014) for extracting good-for/bad-for events, event polarity lexicon (Ding and Riloff, 2018) for extracting affective events, and a connotation lexicon (Feng et al., 2013) for extracting sentiment connotation words. Once the elements are extracted for each sentence, they are aggregated to obtain a valence-token offset plot with a sliding window. This process is detailed below:

Preprocessing For a given student essay, we first get the tokenization, part-of-speech tags and dependency parse of each sentence with ZPar[5]. Then we lemmatize the words with NLTK[6].

Good-for/Bad-for Event extraction The EffectWordnet lexicon is a subset of WordNet, with an extra effect polarity annotation for every synset. The effects are either positive, negative or neutral. We pick out all the verbs by POS tags and exclude the stopwords. Then for each verb, we look up its synset(s) in WordNet, and if the synsets are covered in EffectWordnet, we look up its effect polarity. One verb can have multiple senses, and thus multiple synsets in WordNet, with potentially contradicting effect polarities. Here, we take the majority voting approach. For example, if a verb has 3 positive senses, 1 negative sense and 2 neutral senses, we treat it as having a positive effect.

Affective Event extraction The Affective Event lexicon is a mapping from event templates to their polarities. An event template is a verb frame, with optional subject/object/prepositional phrase contexts. For example, *@I@,love,@my@ partner*. We pick out verbs from the sentences by their POS tag, then find out their subject/object by dependency parse, and match with the lexicon.

Sentiment Connotation extraction The Connotation lexicon is a mapping from verbs/nouns/adjectives to their connotation polarities. We simply traverse through all tokens with relevant POS tag, lemmatize them and look up their connotation polarity from the lexicon.

Arc Generation After the above extraction steps we associate every token with a set of extracted polarities. We quantify each token by the following rules: a positive polarity equals +1, a negative polarity equals -1, and a neutral polarity equals 0.

The score of a token is the sum of all its associated polarities from different sources. If a token has no associated polarity, it's score is 0. Once the sentiment score for each token is determined, we use a sliding window to slide over the whole narrative, moving by one token at a time, and aggregate the scores within the window. The scores are weighted with Gaussian distribution, with the center of the sliding window being the mean of distribution, and 1/4 of window size as standard derivation. We use a fixed window size of 50, and essays shorter than that are dropped (25 out of 942 total essays). We plot the aggregated scores against the sliding window position, and smooth it with the Savitsky-Golay filter[7] to fit a smooth curve over the narrative. As will be detailed in Section 4, this smoothing is very important for feature extraction on the arcs.

3.2 Emotion Arcs in Student Narratives

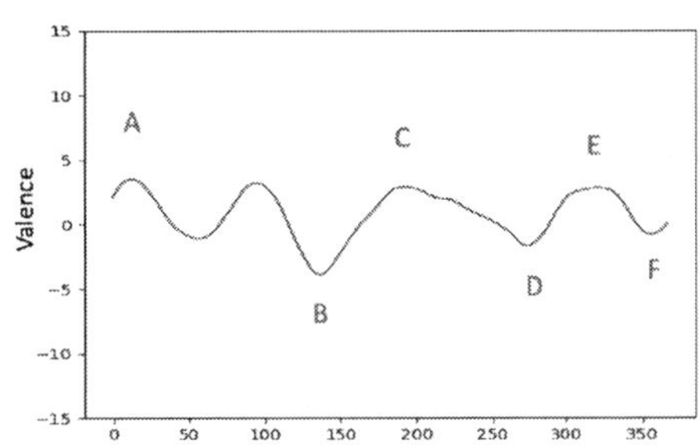

Figure 1: Emotion arc for a narrative on *Proudest Moment*. The Y-axis represents positive/negative valence while the story time-line is along the X-axis

Figure 1 shows the emotion arc constructed for a first person narrative describing The Proudest Moment (an essay written in response to the prompt "Write a story about one of your proudest moments."). In this narrative, the writer talks about her tryout for a marching band performance. The narrator begins with a statement that qualifying for the marching band was her proudest moment. She describes "flagline", the marching band ("Flagline is a group of 10 to 30 girls and they perform in costumes that show school colors."). This story setup and the writer's aspiration is seen in the region (A) of Figure 1. The narrator then goes on to describe how her friends and family thought she could not do it ("My family and friends didn't take me seriously.") and how that created self-doubt ("I started

[5]https://www.sutd.edu.sg/cmsresource/faculty/yuezhang/zpar.html
[6]https://www.nltk.org/
[7]https://plotly.com/python/smoothing/

doubting myself."). This conflict in the plot is evidenced as a dip into negative valence in region (B) in the figure. Then she went to her grandmother for advice ("She gave me the best advice.", "...god will always answer your prayers.). This is evidenced in part (C) where the emotion arc peaks on the positive side of the graph. When the narrator finally goes to the tryout, she is extremely nervous ("It felt like my knees were going to fall off", "It felt like I was going to faint ."). Corresponding to this suspense in the plot, the arc dips again at (D). Finally her name gets called by the judges, and she is extremely elated ("... hugging everyone around me ", "It was the proudest day of my life."). This happy resolution is corroborated by the arc at region (E). The narrative concludes with a reflective note that she remembers this day later on in life when she faces a tough situation (F).

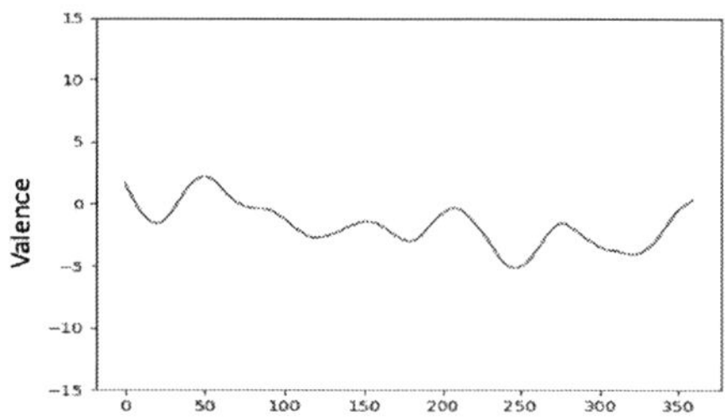

Figure 2: Emotion arc for a narrative on *Movie Sequel* The Y-axis represents positive/negative valence while the story time-line is along the X-axis

Figure 2 shows the emotion arc for a third person fictional narrative. This essay was written in response to the prompt *Write a synopsis of your own "sequel" to a beloved movie using the same characters and settings as the real film.* The student chose to write a sequel to the movie "The Grey" starring Liam Neeson. Similar to the original movie, the sequel too is a survival thriller and follows Ottway, the character from the original. The story is full of adversities, such as vicious wolves, harsh climate of the Alaskan wilderness and starvation. The emotion arc correspondingly, remains in the negative valence area, with the small wave-like fluctuations to the neutral (relatively less negative) side for small victories. Towards the end of the climax, the protagonist is critically wounded. In the last sentence, the narrative says that a rescue team is coming his way, indicating a positive ending.

We noticed that short narrative essays written by school students show variations in the emotion arc corresponding to elements of a plot such as setting, conflict, suspense, resolution and reflection. Overall, emotion arcs vary across narrative genres, topics, and even within a topic due to creative variety. Nevertheless, the basic elements of a good story can still be found across all narrative types. For example, a plot almost always requires an emotional variation and an effective narrative will have some form of conflict or dip in emotional valence.

4   Relationship to Narrative Quality

We saw in the previous section that well-written student narratives generally tend to have emotion arcs corresponding to plot elements. The next question is whether these elements can be indicators of narrative quality score as defined by standardized essay scoring rubrics. In order to answer this, we study the relationship of narrative quality scores to properties of the emotion arcs. Note that the narrative quality score is a function of a number of factors, such as organization of the story, effective use of transitioning, clear opening and closing, vivid description, character development, use of dialog, event sequencing, effective use of figurative language and other narrative techniques. Hence we expect presence of plot element in a story to be just a component that would contribute to the determination of the score.

While individual creativity makes it difficult to directly equate emotion arcs to scores, we can extract features that represent arc characteristics. We extract the following features from the arcs. For the ease of explanation, we denote the arc value at position i as $d(i)$. We define *local maximum* as positions where $d(i-1) < d(i) > d(i+1)$, and *local minimum* as points where $d(i-1) > d(i) < d(i+1)$. The *slope* at each point is calculated as $d(i) - d(i-1)$.

1. **Max Peak**: We find the "peaks" in the arc by looking for local maximums. And we choose the maximum among the local maximums as Max Peak.

2. **Second Max Peak**: Similar to Max Peak, but the second greatest one of the local maximums.

3. **Min Valley**: The minimum of local minimums.

4. **Second Min Valley**: The second least local minimum.

5. **Number of Peaks**: Number of identified local maximums.

6. **Number of Valleys** : Number of identified local minimums.

7. **Positive Slope**: The slope where the arc is most steep and going upward, i.e. $\max_i d(i) - d(i-1)$.

8. **Negative slope**: The slope where the arc is most steep and going downward, i.e. $\min_i d(i) - d(i-1)$.

The plots generated by sliding windows are noisy and contain lots of spurious local maximums/minimums. So we apply Savitsky-Golay filter to smooth the high-frequency variations in the plots, as we are not interested in the fine-grained perturbations, but in how valence emerges or drops in at a coarser granularity.

The maximum peak and minimum valley capture the height of happiness and depth of despair in the story. The second max peak (and min valley) capture the second highest points. Presumably, narratives with non-trivial story-lines will show multiple significant peaks and valleys. The number of peaks and valleys try to capture the emotional variance in the story. The positive and negative slopes try to capture the emotional pace of the story.

4.1 Correlation with Narrative Quality

Using the scored essays, we compute correlation (Pearson's r) for each of our features to the Narrative Quality score. Previous studies on essay scoring (Chodorow and Burstein, 2004) have found that essay length is strongly correlated with its score. Thus, for each of our features, we calculate correlation with score after accounting for length, in order to see its effect on the narrative quality independent of essay length.

Table 1 presents the Pearson's correlation r (sorted in ascending order) and partial correlation with narrative score. Observe that the number of peaks and valleys are strongly correlated with score – having more peaks and valleys is related to higher the score. However, such stories are also relatively longer, and hence correlation drops dramatically when the length factor is removed. The slope-based features (Positive Slope and Negative Slope) show

Feature	Pearson's r	r After controlling length
Max Peak	0.151	0.006
Second Max Peak	0.184	-0.003
Positive Slope	0.307	0.155
Negative Slope	0.312	0.136
Min Valley	0.412	0.202
Second Min Valley	0.431	0.193
Num of Peaks	0.538	-0.016
Num of Valleys	0.541	-0.011

Table 1: Correlation (Pearson's r) of each feature with score.

moderate correlation with score. The features related to negative dips in the story (Min Valley and Second Min Valley) show moderately strong correlation with score, and have a relatively smaller drop after accounting for length. This indicates that elements corresponding to strong adversities are effective narrative techniques even in short stories.

4.2 Narrative Quality Prediction

The next question we explore is if and by how much the emotion arc features, individually or as a group, are useful for predicting narrative quality. Given that there has been previous work on developing narrative quality features, our focus is on how much the emotion arc features can help to improve a system based on previous narrative features. For this, we closely follow the procedure from (Somasundaran et al., 2018): we build a Linear regression model using scikit-learn toolkit (Pedregosa et al., 2011), with 10-fold cross-validation. Trimming of the predicted output is performed; that is, if the predicted score was above the max score (8), or below the min score (0), it is assigned the max or the min score, respectively. Bootstrapping experiments (Berg-Kirkpatrick et al., 2012; Efron and Tibshirani, 1994) were performed to test for statistical significance. We used 10,000 bootstrap samples.

The system using the *best narrative features* from previous work is our baseline. Thus the baseline comprises of the following features: Details+ Modal+ Pronoun+ Content+ Graph+ Statives+ Subjectivity+ Transition + Quote[8]. We build prediction models by (1) adding one emotion arc-based fea-

---

[8]This feature, capturing the presence of dialog or air quotes, was added by the authors after the publication of their paper. It produces a small improvement in performance.

ture at a time to the baseline (2) adding all of our
features to baseline

Feature	QWK
Baseline	0.656
+ Negative Slope	0.652
+ Max Peak	0.657
+ Second Max Peak	0.657
+ Number of Valleys	0.661
+ Second Min Valley	0.663
+ Number of Peaks	0.666 *
+ Positive Slope	0.667 **
+ Min Valley	0.669 **
+ All	0.668

Table 2: Performance of the system when new features
are added to the baseline.
$*$ indicates $p < 0.1$; $** = p < 0.05$

Table 2 reports the performance of the resulting
systems sorted in ascending order (for individual
feature additions). Features corresponding to the
positive emotional peaks in the story (Max Peak
and Second Max Peak) add only minor improvements. Features corresponding to negative valence
(Min Valley, Second Min Valley) help to improve
the performance, indicating that detecting negative
dips can improve the reliability of scoring. With
respect to pacing, moving from a negative point
to a positive point (Positive slope) seems to be indicative of narrative quality. However, adding all
features together seems to produce no improvement indicating that while some individual features
show promise, others tend to bring the performance
down.

We performed a detailed ablation study (8 features resulted to 256 experiments) to find the subset
of features that can be used together. The resulting
feature combination that gave the best performance
was [Max Peak + Min Valley + Second Max Peak
+ Number of Peaks + Positive Slope] and had a
QWK value of 0.676.

4.3 Correlation with Other Sentiment Features

Somasundaran et al. (2018) have explored
subjectivity-based features for predicting narrative
score. Their motivation was to capture evaluative and subjective language that is used to describe characters, situations, and characters' private
states (Wiebe, 1994). While our features are also
sentiment-based, we believe that our arc-based fea-

tures capture a different dimension of the narrative
and are complementary in nature.

In order to investigate this, we compared our
features with the following subjectivity-based features in the baseline system: count of MPQA (Wilson et al., 2005) polar words (CMP), count of
MPQA neutral words (CMN), presence of MPQA
neutral words (PMN), presence of MPQA polar
words (PMP), count of ASSESS (Beigman Klebanov et al., 2012) polar words (CAP), count of
unique ASSESS polar words (UAP).

Table 3 presents the Pearson's correlation r between our features and subjectivity features from
the baseline system. Values of r greater than 0.5
are shown in **bold**.

As expected, there is strong correlation between
the emotion arc features and subjectivity/sentiment.
We believe that this is because (1) There are events
that are *also* clearly sentiment-bearing words (e.g.,
"failing"), (2) Good/bad events and feeling about
them would co-occur in the story. For example,
if something adverse happens to a character, he
might feel bad about it. (3) It is very likely that
there is overlap between the lexical resources we
use for constructing emotion arcs and the subjec-
tivity/sentiment features.

However, the correlation values also indicate
that there is some separation between our plot-
motivated features and the subjectivity features
– except for the high correlation between count-
based subjectivity features and number-based arc
features (all of which also correlate with length),
the rest have $r < 0.5$.

5   Related Work

Narratives can be analyzed along many different
dimensions, such as sentiment, emotion, plot, characters, engagement, creativity, and success of stories. Computational linguistic analyses started with
shorter texts, concentrating mostly on fables, folk
stories and fairy tales. In the last decade they fully
embraced analysis of full length novels and movie
scripts.

Several studies focused on character traits and
personas in stories. Elsner (2012) proposed a rich
representation of story-characters for summarizing
and representing novels. Bamman et al. (2014)
automatically inferred character types in English
novels.Valls-Vargas et al. (2014) extracted character roles from Russian folk tales, based on character
actions. Chaturvedi et al. (2015) analyzed short sto-

Emotion arc feature	CMP	CMN	PMN	PMP	CAP	UAP
Max Peak	0.34	0.19	0.07	0.05	0.33	0.34
Second Max Peak	0.40	0.23	0.06	0.03	0.39	0.40
Min Valley	0.38	0.31	0.13	0.00	0.41	0.43
Second Min Valley	0.43	0.35	0.08	0.00	0.46	0.47
Num of peaks	**0.73**	**0.61**	0.19	0.04	**0.78**	**0.73**
Num of Valleys	**0.73**	**0.60**	0.19	0.05	**0.78**	**0.73**
Positive Slope	0.38	0.23	0.14	0.08	0.39	0.42
Negative Slope	0.42	0.27	0.12	0.10	0.41	0.45

Table 3: Correlation (Pearson's r) of each feature with previously explored subjectivity features: count of MPQA polar words (CMP), count of MPQA neutral words (CMN), presence of MPQA neutral words (PMN), presence of MPQA polar words (PMP), count of ASSESS polar words (CAP), count of unique ASSESS polar words (UAP)

ries for characters' desires and desire fulfillment.

Researchers have also studied social networks and have modeled relationships in stories (Elson et al., 2010; Celikyilmaz et al., 2010; Agarwal et al., 2013). Iyyer et al. (2016); Chaturvedi et al. (2016) modeled character inter-relations and their development in novels. Evolving relations were represented as *relationship sequences/trajectories* and learned using structured prediction techniques.

Ouyang and McKeown (2015) analyzed personal narratives from a blogging platform for automatic detection of *turning points* in stories. Papalampidi et al. (2019) presented the task of detecting turning points in movie scripts, as a particular way for analyzing narrative structure. They used neural network models for automatically detecting sequences of major explicit events in stories.

Sentiment analysis has been employed for narrative analysis in many studies. Goyal et al. (2010a,b) analyzed Aesop's fables, producing automatic plot-unit representations (Lehnert, 1981), using task-specific knowledge base of affect. Several studies focused on annotation of folk stories and fairy tales for emotions (Francisco et al., 2012; Volkova et al., 2010; Alm and Sproat, 2005). Alm et al. (2005) described a machine learning approach for multi-class classification of sentences for their emotional content.

Piper and So (2015) used a sentiment lexicon and compared the proportion of sentiment words between several groups of novels. They found that, on average, 19th century novels have a larger proportion of sentiment words (7%) than modern novels (about 5.5%). Bostan and Klinger (2018) presented a survey of recent corpora annotated for emotion classification in text, with a variety of clas-

sification schemata. Liu et al. (2019) present a new dataset of classic and modern novels, with passages (sections of 40 to 200 words) manually annotated for emotion classes based on Plutchik's eight basic emotions. The data was used for training and evaluating Deep Learning architectures for emotion classification. Kim and Klinger (2019, 2018) presented a novel challenge and datasets for affect and emotion detection in text, calling it *emotional relationships* classification: which character feels which emotion to which character.

The idea that, in stories, emotion and sentiment is not static, but changes dynamically, is an old one. It is often presented as practical advice in writing guides for aspiring screenwriters and novelists (McKee, 1997). The idea of actually charting the emotional progression of scenes and stories (*emotion arcs*) is attributed to Kurt Vonnegut (see e.g. Vonnegut (1995, 2004), described by Jockers (2014) and Del Vecchio et al. (2018)).

The annotation study of Alm and Sproat (2005) was one of the earliest computational studies that considered a notion of *emotional trajectory* - plotting the emotional values for sequences of text segments in 22 Grimms' fairy tales. Reagan et al. (2016) used sentiment analysis to generate emotional profiles for full-length English novels. They implemented the notion of emotion arcs, tracking the level of emotion-laden content through consecutive segments (10K-long word segments) of literary works (from Project Gutenberg), using a lexicon of words with ratings on a single positive-negative scale - a sentiment polarity lexicon. They found that large-scale arcs cluster into six common arc shapes. A similar approach was described by Jockers (2014) and Gao et al. (2016).

Del Vecchio et al. (2018) used a similar technique to track emotion arcs in about 6000 movie scripts. That study also found that large-scale arcs cluster into six common shapes. The study went further, relating the arc shapes to movie success, using movie gross revenue as success indicator.

Chu and Roy (2017) performed a multi-modal analysis of emotion arcs. They used neural network models to construct emotional arc representations from movie clips, audio clips, images and two-word image captions (the latter analyzed with SentiWordNet lexicon, (Baccianella et al., 2010)). They applied clustering to find major groupings of emotional arcs. They evaluated their models by predicting viewer engagement with short online videos (measured as number of comments the videos received).

Kim et al. (2017) used lexical expressions of emotion for genre-classification of whole novels. They extended the *emotion arc* approach, by using eight fundamental emotions defined by Plutchik (2001), instead of a single sentiment valence dimension. Thus, their tracking reflects the development of each of the eight emotions throughout the time course of the narrative. Overall, this method contributes to significant improvement of genre classification over a strong lexical baseline.

6 Discussion

To the best of our knowledge, our work is a first attempt in exploring emotion arcs and plot elements in student writing via event affect and implied sentiment. The exploration is by no means complete. In this section we discuss the rationale of our choices, some limitations of the current study and challenges in this task.

In order to construct emotion arcs in Section 3 we relied on a number of resources and made a number of choices, which has influenced the precision of the resulting arcs. First, we used (semi) automatically created lexicons, and these have issues with both noise and coverage. We did not combine the lexicons or remove duplicates between lexicons. This could have led to a single instance of an easily recognizable emotional element in a sentence being counted more strongly than it otherwise should have. Contextual polarity resolution was not performed, which could have influenced the determination of the sentence-level valence. Finally, when employing the EffectWordnet, we simply used the most frequent sense instead of performing complete word sense disambiguation. Our curve-fitting function might have dampened some of the spurious errors, but there is obviously scope for improvement.

In Section 4 we sampled arc properties and employed them as features. Our choices were driven by the requirements that the properties should be efficiently extracted, and be generalizable across narrative sub-genres and writing proficiency. More constrained environments/applications could afford closer modeling of arcs (e.g. finding components of the curve equation).

In our work, we have used the simplifying assumption that there are emotional correlates to plot elements, and by tracking the emotion arc, we are able to capture some elements of the plot. While this assumption may hold for simple short stories, it is likely to collapse for stories from creative authors. Accomplished authors can create tension and resolution without emotional accompaniment.

Finally, it is important to note that plot and components of a plot, such as rising action, conflict, falling action, resolution, etc., while easily discernible to human readers, pose significant challenges for a machine. World knowledge, human experiences, interpretation of motivations, inferences of human actions and context of the story, play an important part in the recognition. Consequently, automated methods too will need to look beyond words, sentences and paragraphs.

7 Conclusion

In this work, we studied emotion arcs in student narratives, and explored ways to harness them for automatically determining narrative quality.

We showed that emotion arcs are manifest in student writing and intuitively correspond to plot elements. Our analyses showed that simple arc properties correlate with narrative quality score, and that the features derived from the arcs are similar to, yet distinguished from previously explored subjectivity features. We built scoring systems and showed that adding our arc-based features have the potential to improve the scoring performance.

Our future work will include addressing the limitations and challenges discussed in Section 6.

References

Apoorv Agarwal, Anup Kotalwar, and Owen Rambow. 2013. Automatic extraction of social networks from literary text: A case study on Alice in Wonderland. In *IJCNLP*, pages 1202–1208.

Cecilia Ovesdotter Alm, Dan Roth, and Richard Sproat. 2005. Emotions from text: Machine learning for text-based emotion prediction. In *Proceedings of Human Language Technology Conference and Conference on Empirical Methods in Natural Language Processing*, pages 579–586, Vancouver, British Columbia, Canada. Association for Computational Linguistics.

Cecilia Ovesdotter Alm and Richard Sproat. 2005. Emotional sequencing and development in fairy tales. In *International Conference on Affective Computing and Intelligent Interaction*, pages 668–674. Springer.

Stefano Baccianella, Andrea Esuli, and Fabrizio Sebastiani. 2010. Sentiwordnet 3.0: an enhanced lexical resource for sentiment analysis and opinion mining. In *Lrec*, volume 10, pages 2200–2204.

David Bamman, Ted Underwood, and Noah A. Smith. 2014. A Bayesian mixed effects model of literary character. In *Proceedings of the 52nd Annual Meeting of the Association for Computational Linguistics*, pages 370–379, Baltimore, MA, USA.

Beata Beigman Klebanov, Jill Burstein, Nitin Madnani, Adam Faulkner, and Joel Tetreault. 2012. Building subjectivity lexicon (s) from scratch for essay data. *Computational Linguistics and Intelligent Text Processing*, pages 591–602.

Taylor Berg-Kirkpatrick, David Burkett, and Dan Klein. 2012. An empirical investigation of statistical significance in NLP. In *Proceedings of the 2012 Joint Conference on Empirical Methods in Natural Language Processing and Computational Natural Language Learning*, pages 995–1005. Association for Computational Linguistics.

Laura Ana Maria Bostan and Roman Klinger. 2018. An analysis of annotated corpora for emotion classification in text. In *Proceedings of the 27th International Conference on Computational Linguistics*, pages 2104–2119. Association for Computational Linguistics.

Asli Celikyilmaz, Dilek Hakkani-Tur, Hua He, Greg Kondrak, and Denilson Barbosa. 2010. The actor-topic model for extracting social networks in literary narrative. In *NIPS Workshop: Machine Learning for Social Computing*.

Snigdha Chaturvedi, Dan Goldwasser, and Hal Daume III. 2015. Ask, and shall you receive?: Understanding desire fulfillment in natural language text. *arXiv preprint arXiv:1511.09460*.

Snigdha Chaturvedi, Shashank Srivastava, Hal Daumé III, and Chris Dyer. 2016. Modeling evolving relationships between characters in literary novels. In *Proceedings of the Thirtieth AAAI Conference on Artificial Intelligence (AAAI-16)*, pages 2704–2710.

Association for the Advancement of Artificial Intelligence.

Martin Chodorow and Jill Burstein. 2004. Beyond essay length: evaluating e-rater®'s performance on toefl® essays. *ETS Research Report Series*, 2004(1):i–38.

Yoonjung Choi and Janyce Wiebe. 2014. +/-effectwordnet: Sense-level lexicon acquisition for opinion inference. In *Proceedings of the 2014 Conference on Empirical Methods in Natural Language Processing (EMNLP)*, pages 1181–1191.

Eric Chu and Deb Roy. 2017. Audio-visual sentiment analysis for learning emotional arcs in movies. In *2017 IEEE International Conference on Data Mining (ICDM)*, pages 829–834. IEEE.

Jacob Cohen. 1968. Weighted kappa: Nominal scale agreement provision for scaled disagreement or partial credit. *Psychological Bulletin*, 70(4):213.

Marco Del Vecchio, Alexander Kharlamov, Glenn Parry, and Ganna Pogrebna. 2018. The data science of hollywood: Using emotional arcs of movies to drive business model innovation in entertainment industries. *Available at SSRN 3198315*.

Lingjia Deng, Yoonjung Choi, and Janyce Wiebe. 2013. Benefactive/malefactive event and writer attitude annotation. In *Proceedings of the 51st Annual Meeting of the Association for Computational Linguistics (Volume 2: Short Papers)*, pages 120–125.

Haibo Ding and Ellen Riloff. 2016. Acquiring knowledge of affective events from blogs using label propagation. In *Thirtieth AAAI Conference on Artificial Intelligence*.

Haibo Ding and Ellen Riloff. 2018. Weakly Supervised Induction of Affective Events by Optimizing Semantic Consistency. In *Proceedings of the Thirty-Second AAAI Conference on Artificial Intelligence (AAAI-18)*.

Bradley Efron and Robert J Tibshirani. 1994. *An introduction to the bootstrap*. CRC press.

Micha Elsner. 2012. Character-based kernels for novelistic plot structure. In *Proceedings of the 13th Conference of the European Chapter of the Association for Computational Linguistics*, pages 634–644. Association for Computational Linguistics.

David K. Elson, Nicholas Dames, and Kathleen R. McKeown. 2010. Extracting social networks from literary fiction. In *Proceedings of the 48th Annual Meeting of the Association for Computational Linguistics*, pages 138–147. Association for Computational Linguistics.

Song Feng, Jun Sak Kang, Polina Kuznetsova, and Yejin Choi. 2013. Connotation lexicon: A dash of sentiment beneath the surface meaning. In *Proceedings of the 51th Annual Meeting of the Association for Computational Linguistics (Volume 2: Short*

Papers), Sofia, Bulgaria. Association for Computational Linguistics.

Virginia Francisco, Raquel Hervás, Federico Peinado, and Pablo Gervás. 2012. Emotales: creating a corpus of folk tales with emotional annotations. *Language Resources and Evaluation*, 46(3):341–381.

Jianbo Gao, Matthew L. Jockers, John Laudun, and Timothy Tangherlini. 2016. A multiscale theory for the dynamical evolution of sentiment in novels. In *2016 International Conference on Behavioral, Economic and Socio-cultural Computing (BESC)*, pages 1–4.

Amit Goyal, Ellen Riloff, and Hal Daumé III. 2010a. Automatically producing plot unit representations for narrative text. In *Empirical Methods in Natural Language Processing (EMNLP)*, Boston, MA.

Amit Goyal, Ellen Riloff, Hal Daumé III, and Nathan Gilbert. 2010b. Toward plot units: Automatic affect state analysis. In *Proceedings of the NAACL HLT 2010 Workshop on Computational Approaches to Analysis and Generation of Emotion in Text*, pages 17–25. Association for Computational Linguistics.

Mohit Iyyer, Anupam Guha, Snigdha Chaturvedi, Jordan Boyd-Graber, and Hal Daumé III. 2016. Feuding families and former Friends: Unsupervised learning for dynamic fictional relationships. In *Proceedings of the 2016 Conference of the North American Chapter of the Association for Computational Linguistics: Human Language Technologies*, pages 1534–1544, San Diego, California. Association for Computational Linguistics.

Matthew L. Jockers. 2014. A novel method for detecting plot.

Evgeny Kim and Roman Klinger. 2018. Who feels what and why? annotation of a literature corpus with semantic roles of emotions. In *Proceedings of the 27th International Conference on Computational Linguistics*, pages 1345–1359, Santa Fe, New Mexico, USA. Association for Computational Linguistics.

Evgeny Kim and Roman Klinger. 2019. Frowning Frodo, wincing Leia, and a seriously great friendship: Learning to classify emotional relationships of fictional characters. In *Proceedings of the 2019 Conference of the North American Chapter of the Association for Computational Linguistics: Human Language Technologies, Volume 1 (Long and Short Papers)*, pages 647–653, Minneapolis, Minnesota. Association for Computational Linguistics.

Evgeny Kim, Sebastian Padó, and Roman Klinger. 2017. Investigating the relationship between literary genres and emotional plot development. In *Proceedings of the Joint SIGHUM Workshop on Computational Linguistics for Cultural Heritage, Social Sciences, Humanities and Literature*, pages 17–26, Vancouver, Canada. Association for Computational Linguistics.

Wendy G Lehnert. 1981. Plot units and narrative summarization. *Cognitive Science*, 5(4):293–331.

Chen Liu, Muhammad Osama, and Anderson De Andrade. 2019. DENS: A dataset for multi-class emotion analysis. In *Proceedings of the 2019 Conference on Empirical Methods in Natural Language Processing and the 9th International Joint Conference on Natural Language Processing (EMNLP-IJCNLP)*, pages 6293–6298, Hong Kong, China. Association for Computational Linguistics.

Robert McKee. 1997. *Story: Substance, Structure, Style and the Principles of Screenwriting*. Regan Books, Harper-Collins Publishers.

Jessica Ouyang and Kathleen McKeown. 2015. Modeling reportable events as turning points in narrative. In *Proceedings of the 2015 Conference on Empirical Methods in Natural Language Processing*, pages 2149–2158.

Pinelopi Papalampidi, Frank Keller, and Mirella Lapata. 2019. Movie plot analysis via turning point identification. In *Proceedings of the 2019 Conference on Empirical Methods in Natural Language Processing and the 9th International Joint Conference on Natural Language Processing (EMNLP-IJCNLP)*, pages 1707–1717, Hong Kong, China. Association for Computational Linguistics.

Fabian Pedregosa, Gaël Varoquaux, Alexandre Gramfort, Vincent Michel, Bertrand Thirion, Olivier Grisel, Mathieu Blondel, Peter Prettenhofer, Ron Weiss, Vincent Dubourg, et al. 2011. Scikit-learn: Machine learning in python. *the Journal of machine Learning research*, 12:2825–2830.

Andrew Piper and Richard Jean So. 2015. Quantifying the weepy bestseller. *New Republic*.

Robert Plutchik. 2001. The nature of emotions. *American Scientist*, 89(4):344–350.

Andrew J. Reagan, Lewis Mitchell, Dilan Kiley, Christopher M. Danforth, and Peter Sheridan Dodds. 2016. The emotional arcs of stories are dominated by six basic shapes. *EPJ Data Science*, 5(1):31.

Swapna Somasundaran, Michael Flor, Martin Chodorow, Hillary Molloy, Binod Gyawali, and Laura McCulla. 2018. Towards evaluating narrative quality in student writing. *Transactions of the Association for Computational Linguistics*, 6:91–106.

Josep Valls-Vargas, Jichen Zhu, and Santiago Ontanón. 2014. Toward automatic role identification in unannotated folk tales. In *Proceedings of the Tenth AAAI Conference on Artificial Intelligence and Interactive Digital Entertainment*, pages 188–194. AAAI Press.

Ekaterina P. Volkova, Betty J. Mohler, Detmar Meurers, Dale Gerdemann1 Heinrich H, and Bülthoff. 2010. Emotional perception of fairy tales: Achieving agreement in emotion annotation of text. In

Proceedings of the NAACL HLT 2010 Workshop on Computational Approaches to Analysis and Generation of Emotion in Text, pages 98–106. Association for Computational Linguistics.

Kurt Vonnegut. 1995. Kurt Vonnegut on the Shapes of Stories. YouTube.

Kurt Vonnegut. 2004. Kurt Vonnegut Lecture. YouTube.

Janyce M. Wiebe. 1994. Tracking point of view in narrative. *Computational Linguistics*, 20(2):233–287.

Theresa Wilson, Janyce Wiebe, and Paul Hoffmann. 2005. Recognizing contextual polarity in phrase-level sentiment analysis. In *Proceedings of the Conference on Human Language Technology and Empirical Methods in Natural Language Processing*, pages 347–354. Association for Computational Linguistics.

Frustratingly Hard Evidence Retrieval for QA Over Books

Xiangyang Mou
Rensselaer Polytechnic Institute
Troy, NY 12180
moux4@rpi.edu

Mo Yu
IBM Research
USA
yum@us.ibm.com

Bingsheng Yao
Rensselaer Polytechnic Institute
Troy, NY 12180
yaob@rpi.edu

Chenghao Yang
Columbia University
New York, NY 10027
chenghao.yang@columbia.edu

Xiaoxiao Guo
IBM Research
USA
xiaoxiao.guo@ibm.com

Saloni Potdar
IBM Watson
USA
potdars@us.ibm.com

Hui Su
IBM Research
USA
huisuibmres@us.ibm.com

Abstract

A lot of progress has been made to improve question answering (QA) in recent years, but the special problem of QA over narrative book stories has not been explored in-depth. We formulate BookQA as an open-domain QA task given its similar dependency on evidence retrieval. We further investigate how state-of-the-art open-domain QA approaches can help BookQA. Besides achieving state-of-the-art on the NarrativeQA benchmark, our study also reveals the difficulty of evidence retrieval in books with a wealth of experiments and analysis - which necessitates future effort on novel solutions for evidence retrieval in BookQA.

1 Introduction

The task of question answering has benefited largely from the advancements in deep learning, especially from the pre-trained language models(LM) (Radford et al., 2019; Devlin et al., 2019). While question answering over single passage (reading comprehension datasets) and over the large-scale open-domain corpora (open-domain QA) have largely benefited from these, the performance of QA over book stories (BookQA) lags behind. For example, the most representative benchmark in this direction, the NarrativeQA (Kočiský et al., 2018) which was released three years ago - the current state-of-the-art methods only show marginal improvement over the first baselines.

There are several challenges in NarrativeQA which slow down the research progress. First, the narrative stories lead to a new writing style which differs from previous works over formal texts like Wikipedia. Second, the long inputs of books are beyond the processing ability of neural models so evidence identification from a whole book is critical. Third, NarrativeQA is a generative task, and many of the answers cannot be exactly matched in the original books. Hence, the generative QA models are required. Finally and most importantly, the dataset does not provide annotations of the supporting evidence. While this makes it a realistic setting like open-domain QA, together with the generative nature of the answers, also makes it difficult to infer the supporting evidence similar to most of the extractive open-domain QA tasks.

The requirements around evidence identification and the missing supporting evidence annotation make BookQA task similar to open-domain QA. In this paper, we first study whether the ideas used in state-of-the-art open-domain QA systems can be extended to improve BookQA including: (1) the neural ranker-reader pipeline (Wang et al., 2018), where a neural ranker is used to select related passages (evidence) given a question from a large candidate sets; (2) the usage of pre-trained LMs as reader and ranker, such as GPT (Radford et al., 2019), BERT (Devlin et al., 2019) and their follow-up work; (3) the distantly supervised and unsupervised training techniques (Wang et al., 2018; Lee et al., 2019; Min et al., 2019; Guu et al., 2020; Karpukhin et al., 2020) that help rankers learn more from noisy gold data.

By training a ranker-reader framework on BookQA, we successfully achieve a new state-of-the-art on NarrativeQA using both generative and extractive readers. Based on these results and our

Proceedings of the 1st Joint Workshop on Narrative Understanding, Storylines, and Events, pages 108–113
July 9, 2020. ©2020 Association for Computational Linguistics

analysis, we observe the followings:

- Using the pre-trained LMs as the reader model, such as BERT and GPT, improves the NarrativeQA performance. With the same BM25 IR baseline, they give 5-6% improvement on Rouge-L over their non-pre-trained counterparts.

- Our specifically designed distant supervision signals improve the neural ranker significantly, but the improvement is small compared to the upper bound. Further analysis of the ranker module confirms the difficulty in training, as the improvement from the pre-trained LM BERT is marginal in it.

2 Proposed Method

2.1 Task Definition

Following (Kočiský et al., 2018), we define the task of **BookQA** as finding the answer $\mathbf{A}$ to a question $\mathbf{Q}$ from a book $\mathbf{B}$,[1] where each book contains a number of consecutive paragraphs $\mathcal{C}$ (usually hundreds or more). $\mathbf{A}$ is a free-form answer that can be concluded from the book but may not appear in it in an exact form.

In this paper we propose an open-domain QA formulation and solution to the task of BookQA. Specifically, the task consists of (1) an evidence retrieval step that selects evidence from $\mathbf{B}$ for $\mathbf{Q}$, which in our case is a collection of paragraphs $\mathcal{C}_{\mathbf{Q}} = \{\mathbf{C_i}\} \subset \mathbf{B}$; and (2) a question-answering step that predicts an answer given $\mathbf{Q}$ and $\mathcal{C}_{\mathbf{Q}}$.

In the state-of-the-art open-domain QA systems, the aforementioned two steps are modeled by two learnable models (usually based on pre-trained LMs), namely the **ranker** and the **reader**. The ranker predicts the relevance of each paragraph $\mathbf{C} \in \mathbf{B}$ to the question, where the top ranked paragraphs form the $\mathcal{C}_{\mathbf{Q}}$; and the reader predicts the answer following $P(\mathbf{A}|\mathbf{Q}, \mathcal{C}_{\mathbf{Q}})$.

In the following subsections, we describe our solution to make the training of pre-trained LM-based ranker and reader work for the BookQA task.

2.2 Reader (QA Model)

Extractive Reader We use a pre-trained BERT model (Devlin et al., 2019; Wolf et al., 2019) to predict the answer span given the query and the context. One challenge of training an extraction model in BookQA is that there is no annotation of true spans because of its generative nature. Our solution is to find the most likely span as answer

supervision. Specifically, we compute the Rouge-L score (Lin, 2004) between the true answer and each candidate span of the same length, and finally take the span with the maximum Rouge-L score as our weak label. We initially tried the exact-answer spans but failed to find many due to its low coverage in BookQA.

Generative Reader Considering the GPT memory limitation, we use the `GPT-2-medium` model as our pre-trained generative model and fine-tune it on BookQA using default training parameters[2].

2.3 Book Paragraph Ranker

We fine-tune another BERT binary classifier for paragraph retrieval, following the usage of BERT on text similarity tasks. In BookQA, training such a classifier is challenging because of the lack of evidence-level supervision. We deal with this problem by using an ensemble method to achieve distant supervision. We build two weak BM25 retrievers with one using only $\mathbf{Q}$ and the other using both $\mathbf{Q}$ and true $\mathbf{A}$. Denoting the correspondent rough-grained retrievals as $\mathcal{C}_{\mathbf{Q}}$ and $\mathcal{C}_{\mathbf{Q+A}}$, we then tutor a model to select their intersection $\mathcal{C}_{\mathbf{Q}} \cap \mathcal{C}_{\mathbf{Q+A}}$ by sampling the positive samples from $\mathcal{C}_{\mathbf{Q}} \cap \mathcal{C}_{\mathbf{Q+A}}$ and the negative ones from $(\mathcal{C}_{\mathbf{Q}} \cap \mathcal{C}_{\mathbf{Q+A}})^{\mathsf{c}}$. In order to encourage the ranker to select passages that have better coverage of the answers, we further apply a **Rouge-L filter** upon the previous sampling results, and only select the positive samples whose answer-related Rouge-L score is higher than the upper threshold and the negative samples lower than the lower threshold[3].

3 Experiments

3.1 Settings

Dataset We conduct experiments on NarrativeQA dataset (Kočiský et al., 2018), which has a collection of 783 books and 789 movie scripts and their summaries, with each having on average 30 question-answer pairs. Each book or movie script contains an average of 62k words. NarrativeQA provides two different settings, the **summary** setting and the **full-story** setting. Our BookQA task corresponds to the full-story setting that finds answers from books or movie scripts. Note that the NarrativeQA is a *generative* QA task. The answers are not guaranteed to appear in the books.

---

[1] To be more accurate, the question should be denoted as $\mathbf{Q_B}$ but we use $\mathbf{Q}$ for simplicity.

[2] https://huggingface.co/transformers/model_doc/gpt2.html

[3] In practice, we set the hyperparameters 0.7 and 0.4

System	w/ trained ranker	w/ pre-trained LM	w/ extra training data
Attention Sum (Kočiskỳ et al., 2018)			
BiDAF (Kočiskỳ et al., 2018)			
IAL-CPG (Tay et al., 2019)			
R^3 (Wang et al., 2017)	✓		
BERT-heur (Frermann, 2019)	✓	✓	✓
Our generative/extractive systems	✓	✓	

Table 1: Summary of the characteristics of the compared systems. Red/blue color refers to generative/extraction QA systems. In addition to the standard techniques, (Wang et al., 2017) uses reinforcement learning to train the ranker; and (Tay et al., 2019) uses curriculum to train the reader to overcome the divergence of evidence retrieval qualities between training and testing.

We preprocess the raw data with SpaCy[4] tokenization. Then following (Kočiskỳ et al., 2018), we cut the books into non-overlapping paragraphs with a length of 200 each for the full-story setting.

Baseline We conduct experiments with both generative and extractive readers, and compare with the competitive baseline models from (Kočiskỳ et al., 2018; Tay et al., 2019; Frermann, 2019) in the full-story setting. Meanwhile, we take a BM25 retrieval as the baseline ranker and evaluate our distantly supervised BERT rankers. We also compare to the strong results from (Frermann, 2019), which constructed evidence-level supervision with the usage of book summaries. However, the summary is not considered available by design (Kočiskỳ et al., 2018) in the general full-story scenario where questions should be answered solely from books.[5]

Although not the focus of the paper, our reader performance in the summary setting is also reported (Section 3.2), to show the properties of the readers.

Metrics Because of the generative nature of the task, following previous works (Kočiskỳ et al., 2018; Tay et al., 2019; Frermann, 2019), we evaluate the QA performance with Bleu-1, Bleu-4 (Papineni et al., 2002), Meteor (Banerjee and Lavie, 2005), Rouge-L (Lin, 2004).[6] We also report the Exact Match(EM) and F1 scores[7] that are commonly used in open-domain QA evaluation. We convert both hypothesis and reference to lowercase and remove the punctuation before evaluation.

Model Selection We select the best models on the development set according to its average score of Rouge-L and EM. For ranker model selection, we use the average score of upper bound EM and Rouge-L of top-5 ranked paragraphs.

3.2 Reader Model Validation (the QA-over-Summary Setting)

First, we compare our readers under the summary setting, to verify the correctness of our readers. Our BERT reader achieves performance close to the public state-of-the-art in this setting.

Our GPT-2 reader outperforms the existing systems without usage of pointer generators (PG), but is behind the state-of-the-art with PG. Despite the large gap between systems with and without PG in this setting, (Tay et al., 2019) demonstrates that it didn't contribute much in the full-story setting in the ablation study. Nonetheless, we will investigate the usage of PG in pre-trained LMs in the future work.

3.3 Main Results (the QA-over-Book Setting)

We then experimented our whole QA pipelines in the full-story setting. Table 3 and Table 4 compare our results with public state-of-the-art generative and extractive QA systems.

Our pipeline system with the baseline BM25 ranker outperforms the existing state-of-the-art, confirming the advantage of pre-trained LMs as observed in most QA tasks. Our distantly supervised ranker adds another 1-2% of improvement to all the metrics, bringing both our generative and extractive models with the best performance. It also helps outperform (Frermann, 2019) on multiple metrics without the usage of the strong extra supervision from the summaries.

3.4 Ablation of Ranker Performance

To take a deeper look at the challenges in ranker training, we conduct an ablation study on the ranker independently. The quality of a ranker is measured

---

[4]https://spacy.io/

[5]In NarrativeQA, the summary has a good coverage of the answers due to the data collection procedures; also, summaries can be viewed as humans' comprehension of the books.

[6]We used an open-source evaluation library (Sharma et al., 2017): https://github.com/Maluuba/nlg-eval.

[7]The squad/evaluate-v1.1.py script is used.

System	Bleu-1	Bleu-4	Meteor	Rouge-L
Extractive Readers				
BERT + Hard EM (Min et al., 2019)	-	-	-	**58.1/58.8**
BERT-only (Min et al., 2019)	-	-	-	55.8/56.1
BERT w/ full training signals [**Ours**]	49.35/49.02	25.76/25.85	23.93/24.14	52.62/52.02
BERT w/ exact answer match only [**Ours**]	**49.78/49.64**	**27.01/28.94**	**25.22/25.12**	57.19/56.35
Generative Readers				
Attention Sum (Kočiskỳ et al., 2018) (w/o PG)	23.54/23.20	5.90/6.39	8.02/7.77	23.28/22.26
Masque (Nishida et al., 2019) (w/ PG)	**-/48.70**	**-/20.98**	**-/21.95**	**-/54.74**
GPT-2 Reader(w/o PG) [**Ours**]	**33.63/35.49**	**11.87**/14.33	**13.71**/14.36	**34.32/35.65**

Table 2: Results under NarrativeQA summary setting on dev/test set (%). PG refers to the usage of pointer generator. For extractive model, we compare with the best public result (Min et al., 2019) and its BERT-only ablation. The latter corresponds to the same setting as ours. For generative model, we compare with the best public models with and without pointer generators.

System	Bleu-1	Bleu-4	Meteor	Rouge-L	EM	F1
Public Generative Baselines						
AttSum (top-10) (Kočiskỳ et al., 2018)	20.00/19.09	2.23/1.81	4.45/4.29	14.47/14.03	-	-
AttSum (top-20) (Kočiskỳ et al., 2018)	19.79/19.06	1.79/2.11	4.60/4.37	14.86/14.02	-	-
IAL-CPG (Tay et al., 2019)	23.31/22.92	2.70/2.47	5.68/5.59	17.33/17.67	-	-
- curriculum	20.75/-	1.52/-	4.65/-	15.42/-		
Our Generative QA Models						
BM25 + GPT-2 Reader	24.54/24.43	4.74/4.37	7.32/7.32	20.25/21.04	5.12/5.22	17.72/18.38
+ BERT Ranker	**24.94/25.03**	**4.76/4.42**	**7.74/7.81**	**21.89/22.36**	**6.79/6.31**	**19.67/19.94**
+ Oracle IR (BM25 w/ Q+A)	*33.18/32.95*	*8.16/7.70*	*12.35/12.47*	*34.83/34.96*	*17.09/15.98*	*33.65/33.75*

Table 3: Generative performance in NarrativeQA full-story setting (BookQA setting) dev/test set(%). *Oracle IR* utilizes question and true answers for retrieval.

System	Bleu-1	Bleu-4	Meteor	Rouge-L	EM	F1
Public Extractive Baselines						
BiDAF (Kočiskỳ et al., 2018)	5.82/5.68	0.22/0.25	3.84/3.72	6.33/6.22	-	-
R^3 (Wang et al., 2017)	**16.40/15.70**	0.50/0.49	3.52/3.47	11.40/11.90	-	-
Our Extractive QA Models						
BM25 + BERT Reader	13.27/13.84	0.94/1.07	4.29/4.59	12.59/13.81	4.67/5.26	11.57/12.55
+ BERT Ranker	14.60/14.46	**1.81**/1.38	**5.09**/5.03	**14.76/15.49**	**6.79/6.66**	**13.75/14.45**
+ Oracle IR (BM25 w/ Q+A)	*23.81/24.01*	*3.54/4.01*	*9.72/9.83*	*28.33/28.72*	*15.27/15.39*	*28.42/28.55*
Extractive Models w/ additional supervision						
BERT-heur (Frermann, 2019)	-/12.26	-/2.06	-/5.28	-/15.15	-	-

Table 4: Extractive performance in NarrativeQA full-story setting (BookQA setting) dev/test set(%). *Oracle IR* utilizes question and true answers for retrieval.

by the answer coverage of its top-5 selections on the basis of the top-32 candidates from the baseline. The answer coverage is estimated by the maximum Rouge-L score of the subsequences of the selected paragraphs of the same length as the answers; and whether the answer can be covered by any of the selected paragraphs (EM).

Our BERT ranker together with supervision filtering strategy has a significant improvement over the BM25 baseline. Our BERT ranker improves by 0.7%, compared with MatchLSTM (Wang and Jiang, 2016) or an improved BiDAF architec-ture (Clark and Gardner, 2018). On the other hand, comparing the benefits that BERT brings to open-domain QA tasks, the relatively small improvement demonstrates the difficulty of evidence retrieval in BookQA. This shows the potential room for future novel improvements, which is also exhibited by the large gap between our best rankers and either the upper bound or the oracle.

3.5 Discussion of Future Improvement

We can see a considerable gap between our best models (ranker and readers) and their correspond-

Question	Gold Answer 1	Gold Answer 2	Generative Result
Where is Millicent sent to boarding school?	Millicent is sent to a boarding school in France	France	France
What is Morgan's relationship to Wyatt?	Morgan is Wyatt's brother	Brothers	Brother
What illness does Doc Holiday suffer from?	Tuberculosis	Tuberculosis	Lung cancer
How does Carl make his house fly?	He attaches thousands of helium balloons to it	Balloons	He uses a parachute to climb up the side of the dirigible
How does Felipe die?	Suicide	He suffers a physical breakdown	He is killed by a bullet in the head
What was the great stone face and how did it appear?	A natural rock formation on the side of a mountain	A natural rock formation which appeared when viewed at a proper distance	It was a stone face

Table 5: Generative result examples. The model tends to generate shorter answers in general. The longer answer it generates, the less likely the answer tends to be correct. The grammatical correctness and fluency of the long generative answers are approaching to human level, regardless of the problematic logic between the generated answer and question. The majority of the generative results do not make sense logically which leads to the low scores in different metrics.

IR Method	EM	Rouge-L
BM25	18.99	47.48
BERT ranker	**24.26**	**52.68**
- Rouge-L filtering	22.63	51.02
Repl BERT w/ BiDAF	21.88	50.64
Repl BERT w/ MatchLSTM	21.97	50.39
Upperbound (BM25 top-32)	30.81	61.40
Oracle (BM25 w/ Q+A)	35.75	63.92

Table 6: IR Evaluation on NarrativeQA dev set(%).

ing oracles in Table 3, 4, and 6. One difficulty that limits the effectiveness of ranker training is the noisy annotation resulted from the nature of the free-form answers. Our filtering technique helps significantly but is still not sufficient. One way we believe that can improve the distant supervision signals is by iteratively updating the ranker and reader like in Hard-EM (Min et al., 2019; Guu et al., 2020). Another possible direction is to extend the idea of inferring evidence on training data with game-theoretic approaches (Perez et al., 2019; Feng et al., 2020), then use the inferred evidence paragraph as labels to train the ranker.

4 Conclusion

We explored the BookQA task and systemically tested on NarrativeQA dataset different types of models and techniques from open-domain QA. Our proposed approaches bring significant improvements to the state-of-the-art across different metrics. Our insight and analysis lay the path for excit-

ing future work in this domain.

Acknowledgment

This work is supported by Cognitive and Immersive Systems Lab (CISL), a collaboration between IBM and RPI, and also a center in IBM's AI Horizons Network.

References

Satanjeev Banerjee and Alon Lavie. 2005. Meteor: An automatic metric for mt evaluation with improved correlation with human judgments. In *Proceedings of the acl workshop on intrinsic and extrinsic evaluation measures for machine translation and/or summarization*, pages 65–72.

Christopher Clark and Matt Gardner. 2018. Simple and effective multi-paragraph reading comprehension. In *Proceedings of the 56th Annual Meeting of the Association for Computational Linguistics (Volume 1: Long Papers)*, pages 845–855.

Jacob Devlin, Ming-Wei Chang, Kenton Lee, and Kristina Toutanova. 2019. Bert: Pre-training of deep bidirectional transformers for language understanding. In *Proceedings of the 2019 Conference of the North American Chapter of the Association for Computational Linguistics: Human Language Technologies, Volume 1 (Long and Short Papers)*, pages 4171–4186.

Yufei Feng, Mo Yu, Wenhan Xiong, Xiaoxiao Guo, Junjie Huang, Shiyu Chang, Murray Campbell, Michael Greenspan, and Xiaodan Zhu. 2020. Learning to recover reasoning chains for multi-hop question answering via cooperative games. *arXiv preprint arXiv:2004.02393*.

Lea Frermann. 2019. Extractive NarrativeQA with heuristic pre-training. In *Proceedings of the 2nd Workshop on Machine Reading for Question Answering*, pages 172–182, Hong Kong, China. Association for Computational Linguistics.

Kelvin Guu, Kenton Lee, Zora Tung, Panupong Pasupat, and Ming-Wei Chang. 2020. Realm: Retrieval-augmented language model pre-training.

Vladimir Karpukhin, Barlas Oğuz, Sewon Min, Ledell Wu, Sergey Edunov, Danqi Chen, and Wentau Yih. 2020. Dense passage retrieval for open-domain question answering. *arXiv preprint arXiv:2004.04906*.

Tomáš Kočiskỳ, Jonathan Schwarz, Phil Blunsom, Chris Dyer, Karl Moritz Hermann, Gábor Melis, and Edward Grefenstette. 2018. The narrativeqa reading comprehension challenge. *Transactions of the Association for Computational Linguistics*, 6:317–328.

Kenton Lee, Ming-Wei Chang, and Kristina Toutanova. 2019. Latent retrieval for weakly supervised open domain question answering. *Proceedings of the 57th Annual Meeting of the Association for Computational Linguistics*.

Chin-Yew Lin. 2004. Rouge: A package for automatic evaluation of summaries. page 10.

Sewon Min, Danqi Chen, Hannaneh Hajishirzi, and Luke Zettlemoyer. 2019. A discrete hard em approach for weakly supervised question answering. In *Proceedings of the 2019 Conference on Empirical Methods in Natural Language Processing and the 9th International Joint Conference on Natural Language Processing (EMNLP-IJCNLP)*, pages 2844–2857.

Kyosuke Nishida, Itsumi Saito, Kosuke Nishida, Kazutoshi Shinoda, Atsushi Otsuka, Hisako Asano, and Junji Tomita. 2019. Multi-style generative reading comprehension. *arXiv preprint arXiv:1901.02262*.

Kishore Papineni, Salim Roukos, Todd Ward, and Wei-Jing Zhu. 2002. Bleu: a method for automatic evaluation of machine translation. In *Proceedings of the 40th annual meeting on association for computational linguistics*, pages 311–318. Association for Computational Linguistics.

Ethan Perez, Siddharth Karamcheti, Rob Fergus, Jason Weston, Douwe Kiela, and Kyunghyun Cho. 2019. Finding generalizable evidence by learning to convince q&a models. In *Proceedings of EMNLP 2019*.

Alec Radford, Jeff Wu, Rewon Child, David Luan, Dario Amodei, and Ilya Sutskever. 2019. Language models are unsupervised multitask learners.

Shikhar Sharma, Layla El Asri, Hannes Schulz, and Jeremie Zumer. 2017. Relevance of unsupervised metrics in task-oriented dialogue for evaluating natural language generation. *CoRR*, abs/1706.09799.

Yi Tay, Shuohang Wang, Anh Tuan Luu, Jie Fu, Minh C Phan, Xingdi Yuan, Jinfeng Rao, Siu Cheung Hui, and Aston Zhang. 2019. Simple and effective curriculum pointer-generator networks for reading comprehension over long narratives. In *Proceedings of the 57th Annual Meeting of the Association for Computational Linguistics*, pages 4922–4931.

Shuohang Wang and Jing Jiang. 2016. Learning natural language inference with lstm. In *Proceedings of the 2016 Conference of the North American Chapter of the Association for Computational Linguistics: Human Language Technologies*, pages 1442–1451.

Shuohang Wang, Mo Yu, Xiaoxiao Guo, Zhiguo Wang, Tim Klinger, Wei Zhang, Shiyu Chang, Gerald Tesauro, Bowen Zhou, and Jing Jiang. 2017. R^3: Reinforced reader-ranker for open-domain question answering.

Shuohang Wang, Mo Yu, Xiaoxiao Guo, Zhiguo Wang, Tim Klinger, Wei Zhang, Shiyu Chang, Gerry Tesauro, Bowen Zhou, and Jing Jiang. 2018. R 3: Reinforced ranker-reader for open-domain question answering. In *Thirty-Second AAAI Conference on Artificial Intelligence*.

Thomas Wolf, Lysandre Debut, Victor Sanh, Julien Chaumond, Clement Delangue, Anthony Moi, Pierric Cistac, Tim Rault, R'emi Louf, Morgan Funtowicz, and Jamie Brew. 2019. Huggingface's transformers: State-of-the-art natural language processing. *ArXiv*, abs/1910.03771.

On-The-Fly Information Retrieval Augmentation for Language Models

Hai Wang David McAllester
Toyota Technological Institute at Chicago, Chicago, IL, USA
{haiwang,mcallester}@ttic.edu

Abstract

Here we experiment with the use of information retrieval as an augmentation for pre-trained language models. The text corpus used in information retrieval can be viewed as form of episodic memory which grows over time. By augmenting GPT 2.0 with information retrieval we achieve a zero shot 15% relative reduction in perplexity on Gigaword corpus without any re-training. We also validate our IR augmentation on an event co-reference task.

1 Introduction

We are interested in exploring the value of long term episodic memory in language modeling. For example, a language model can be used in January to assign a probability distribution over the statements that will appear in the newspaper in March. But one month later, in February, the distribution over the predictions for March should be updated to take into account factual developments since the previous prediction. Long term episodic memory should be taken into account when assigning a probability to a statement.

Here we take a simple approach in which a pre-trained GPT language model (Radford et al., 2018a, 2019) is zero-shot augmented with an episodic memory consisting simply of a corpus of past news articles. Conceptually the past news articles are viewed as additional training data which can be legitimately accessed when evaluating on future text. In our most basic experiment we calculate the probability of a future article by first calculating the probability of its first k sentences using the pre-trained GPT model. We then use the first k sentences as a query in an information retrieval system to extract a relevant past article. We then insert the past article following the first k sentences when calculating the probability of the remainder

of the future article using the same pre-trained GPT model. This is a zero-shot augmentation in the sense that there is no additional training or fine tuning of the pre-trained model. Our results show that this augmentation significantly reduces perplexity. We also present various other experiments including results on fine-tuning the model in the presence of the memory and the effect of this memory on event co-reference.

2 Related Work

Various language models have utilized external knowledge or long contexts (Paperno et al., 2016; Yang and Mitchell, 2017; Peng et al., 2019; Khandelwal et al., 2018; Ghosh et al., 2016; Lau et al., 2017; Grave et al., 2016; Parthasarathi and Pineau, 2018). But these papers do not address the question of whether additional context or external knowledge is useful as a zero-shot augmentation of large scale pre-trained NLP models.

The value of external knowledge has previously been demonstrated for NLP tasks such as natural language inference (Chen et al., 2018; Yang et al., 2019), language generation (Parthasarathi and Pineau, 2018), knowledge base completion (Toutanova et al., 2015; Das et al., 2017) and question answering (Sun et al., 2019, 2018; Dhingra et al., 2017). However, all those prior works assume the model is small and trained from scratch.

As large scale pre-trained models have become more powerful it is not immediately clear whether external resources can still add value. The only work we know of on using external resources in modern large scale models is Yang et al. (2019) where a human curated external lexical resource is used to improve BERT.

Our approach bears some resemblance to neural cache models (Grave et al., 2016). However, neural cache models store past hidden states as memory

Proceedings of the 1st Joint Workshop on Narrative Understanding, Storylines, and Events, pages 114–119
July 9, 2020. ©2020 Association for Computational Linguistics

and accesses them through a dot product with the current hidden states. This is different from retrieving knowledge from a corpus-sized memory.

Our approach is also somewhat related to memory networks (Weston et al., 2014). Memory networks have a memory module which can be learnt jointly with other components. It has shown success in applications such as machine reading comprehension (Kumar et al., 2016a,b; Shi et al., 2016) and visual question answering (Na et al., 2017; Ma et al., 2018; Su et al., 2018). Significant progress in memory networks has been achieved in both architecture (Chandar et al., 2016; Miller et al., 2016; Gulcehre et al., 2017) and model scale (Rae et al., 2016; Lample et al., 2019).

Several papers have formulated, and experimented with, scalable memory networks — memory networks that employ some method of efficiently reading and writing to very large neural memories. This is done with approximate nearest neighbor methods in Rae et al. (2016) and with product keys in Lample et al. (2019). These large memories are used to provide additional model capacity where the memory contents are trained over a large data set using gradient descent training, just as one would train the parameters of a very large network. It is shown in Lample et al. (2019) that it is possible to insert a large memory as a layer in a transformer architecture resulting a model where the same number of parameters and the same performance can be achieved with half the layers and with much faster training time than a standard transformer architecture. Here, however, we are proposing zero-shot augmentation with an external data source used as an episodic memory.

The use of key-value memories in Miller et al. (2016) is particularly similar to our model. Key-value memories were used there in treating a corpus of Wikipedia movie pages as a memory for answering questions about movies. As in our system, articles were extracted using word based information retrieval. Each article was encoded as a vector which was then given to a question answering architecture. This was shown to improve on automated knowledge base extraction from the same corpus but was still not competitive with human curated knowledge graphs for movies. Here we give the text of the retrieved article directly to the language model architecture and focus on augmenting large scale language models.

3 Model

We use the pre-trained transformer GPT 2.0 (Radford et al., 2019). Let W_w and W_p be the subword and position embeddings respectively. Let M denote the total number of layers, for a token at time step t, the m-th layer's hidden state h_t^m is given by:

$$h_t^m = \begin{cases} W_w + W_p & \text{if } m = 0 \\ \text{TB}(h_t^{m-1}) & \text{if } 1 \leq m \leq M \end{cases}$$

where TB stands for Transformer Block. We use last layer's hidden state h_t^M as the presentation H_t for the token at time step t. We augment GPT 2.0 with a large episodic memory component, and the overall architecture is shown in Figure 1.

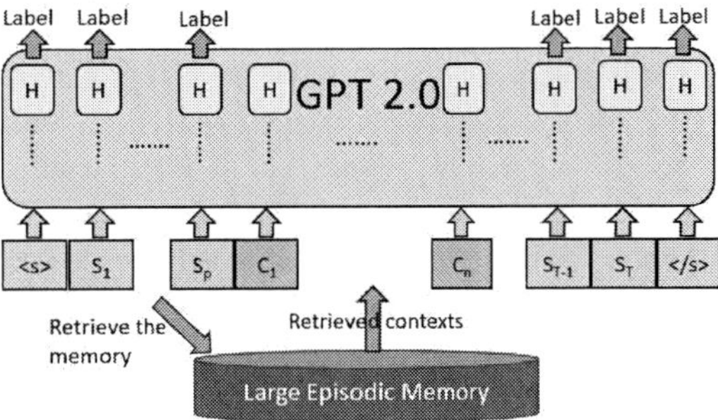

Figure 1: GPT with large episodic memory component

For a sequence S with T tokens, let $S_1, \ldots, S_p$ be the tokens of the first k sentences. Let C be a sequence (article) retrieved from memory using the first k sentences as the query, the vector H_t is:

$$H_t = \begin{cases} \text{GPT}(S_1, \ldots, S_t), \text{if } t \leq p \\ \text{GPT}(S_1, \ldots, S_p, C, \ldots, S_t), \text{otherwise} \end{cases}$$

That's to say, for the first k sentences, we directly feed them to GPT to obtain their representations. For remaining sentences, their representations are conditioned on both the first k sentences and the retrieved context C. Table 1 compares features of our simple memory augmentation with those of other memory models.

4 Experiments

We focus on two tasks: document level language modelling and event co-retrieved . In both tasks we take a document as input and use first k sentences to query the memory. To calculate the perplexity of a document, we compute the log-probability of a document by multiplying byte level probability,

Model	episodic	search	memory size
DMN	yes	exact	∼1K words
SAM:	no	approx	∼100K slots
KVM:	yes	exact	≤ 1M slots
LMN:	no	exact	∼1M slots
Ours:	yes	approx	∼10M documents

Table 1: Comparison between different models. DMN: Dynamic Memory Network (Kumar et al., 2016b); SAM: Sparse Access Memory (Rae et al., 2016); KVM: Key Value Memory (Miller et al., 2016); LMN: Large Memory Network (Lample et al., 2019). Memory size is measured in their own words.

then divide the log-probability by the actual word count in the *query* document.

We use Gigaword (Parker et al., 2011) as both our language modeling test set and as our external memory. Gigaword contains news from different sources such as NY Times and XinHua News etc. For language modelling we use the NY Times portion because it is written by native English speakers. Since GPT 2.0 is trained on Common Crawl which contains news collections started from 2008. To avoid testing on GPT-2 training data, we use Gigaword articles collected prior to 2008. For the pre-trained language model we use GPT 2.0 (Radford et al., 2019) [1]. It contains three pre-trained models: GPT Small, Medium and Large.

For information retrieval we use Lucene due to its simplicity. Given a query document we first do sentence and word tokenization and then use the first k sentences to retrieve top 20 retrieved documents with the default TF-IDF distance metric provided by Lucene. Since too distant document pairs are uninformative and too related document pairs tends to be duplicates of the test article, we further filter those top ranked documents by time stamp, news source and cosine similarity. More specifically, we choose the highest ranked retrieved document that simultaneously satisfies the following three conditions: it comes from a different news source; it appears earlier but within two weeks time window of the test document, and the bag of word cosine similarity between the test and the retrieved cannot be larger than 0.6α where α is the largest bag of word cosine similarity between the test article and any retrieved articles. To support fine-tuning experiments we constructed a corpus of pairs of a *query* article and a cached *retrieved*

document. We split the dataset into train/dev/test by query document's time stamp. The train/dev/test size is: 79622,16927,8045. For zero-shot experiments we use the test set of 8045 articles. We do experiments with $k \in \{1, 2, 5\}$.

To check the quality of *query-retrieved* pairs, we randomly sample 100 pairs from dev set and compute the bag of word cosine similarity between the two documents. The mean cosine similarity is 0.15. We also manually inspect them: we ask two NLP researchers to annotate the *query-retrieved* pair as "BAD" or "OK" independently, i.e., if two documents are almost duplicates or totally unrelated, then it's "BAD", otherwise, it's "OK". Among 100 pairs, 83 pairs are "OK", 17 pairs are "BAD" due to irrelevance. The Cohen's kappa coefficient between two annotations is 0.94.

4.1 Language modelling

For language modeling we try zero-shot memory augmentation, fine-tuned memory augmentation, and training a small memory-augmented network from scratch. When training, we use the Adam optimizer from GPT 1.0 (Radford et al., 2018b). The learning rate is 0.001, weight decay parameter is 0.01, the warm up proportion is 0.1. For other parameters, we use the default values from GPT 2.0. The fine-tuning on Gigaword takes less than one day with a single GPU.

Zero-shot and fine-tuning results Following Radford et al. (2019), we first evaluate our model on Gigaword with zero-shot setting and then fine-tune the model. The results are given in Table 2.

Model Size	woc	k=1	k=2	k=5
GPT-Small	35.15	29.29	30.54	32.38
GPT-Medium	22.78	19.84	20.54	21.48
GPT-Large	19.90	17.41	18.00	18.80
GPT-Small	23.03	21.01	21.89	22.66

Table 2: Perplexity for zero-shot (top 3 rows) and fine-tuning (last row) settings when use different k to retrieve the context. **woc**: without retrieved context.

From Table 2, we see that with additional context retrieved from episodic memory, for all different GPT models, we obtain significantly lower perplexity than using original GPT 2.0. When fine tuning the model with context, we can further reduce the overall perplexity. We only fine tune GPT small due to our GPU memory constraints. Preliminary

---

[1] https://github.com/huggingface/pytorch-transformers

analysis indicates that most of the perplexity reduction comes at content words and semantically rich words where predictions require broader context. This is consistent with the phenomena found in Khandelwal et al. (2018). We further find that smaller k leads to slightly worse retrieval quality, however, more continued sentences will benefit from the retrieved context. Since Gigaword contains newswire, the first several sentences usually are importation summarizations, thus overall, smaller k will result in lower perplexity.

Train from scratch We also investigate training this form of memory-augmented model from scratch on our query-retrieved pairs. For these experiments we train smaller transformers and the results are given in Table 3. From Table 3, we see that additional context still helps and we can get decent perplexity even with quite small models.

Model Config	woc	k=1	k=2	k=5
E=384,H=6,L=6	35.62	31.94	33.18	35.26
E=384,H=8,L=8	33.67	29.62	30.76	32.73
E=576,H=8,L=8	31.32	27.38	28.54	30.63

Table 3: Perplexity when train from scratch. E: hidden states dimensionality; H: # of head; L: # of layer. GPT-Small has the configuration: E=764, H=12, L=12.

When context is irrelevant We also evaluate our method on Wikitext-2/103, in which the retrieved context is irrelevant due to domain difference between Wikipedia and Gigaword. In this case, we use the most top ranked document from Gigaword as reference. Table 4 shows that irrelevant contexts have very little impact on perplexity.

Dataset	woc	k=1	k=2	k=5
Wikitext-2	28.67	28.96	28.95	28.70
Wikitext-103	25.38	25.68	25.56	25.39

Table 4: Zero-shot perplexity using GPT-Small

4.2 Event Co-reference

Intuitively episodic memory is useful because it contains information about the particular events mentioned in the test document. With this in mind we evaluate our approach on the event co-reference dataset ECB+ (Cybulska and Vossen, 2014). ECB+ contains 982 documents clustered into 43 topics, and has two evaluation settings: coreferring mentions occurring within a single document (within

document) or across a document collection (cross document). For the event co-reference pipeline, we follow the joint modeling method of Barhom et al. (2019) where they jointly represented entity and event mentions with various features and learned a pairwise mention/entity scorer for coreference classification. We augment their mention features with the mention's vector representations extracted from either GPT 2.0 or our zero-shot augmented GPT 2.0. For event co-reference, we use the whole test document to retrieve the context from Gigaword. From Table 5, we see that the context can help boost the CONLL F1 score.

System	MUC	B^3	CONLL
Within Document			
KCP	63.0	92.0	81.0
JM	70.9	93.5	85.1
JM+GPT	80.1	93.5	85.2
JM+GPT+CTX♣	80.2	93.9	85.4
Combined Within and Cross Document			
CV	73.0	74.0	73.0
KCP	69.0	69.0	69.0
JM	80.9	80.3	79.5
JM+GPT	81.2	80.2	79.6
JM+GPT+CTX♣	81.3	80.5	79.8

Table 5: F1 score on ECB+ dataset. KCP: Kenyon-Dean et al. (2018) where they add a clustering-oriented regularization term; CV: Cybulska and Vossen (2015) where they add the feature calculated from "event template"; JM: Barhom et al. (2019). ♣: we also feed the retrieved context to GPT to get the representation.

5 Conclusion

In this paper we propose a method to augment a pre-trained NLP model with a large episodic memory. Unlike previous work, we use information retrieval to handle a large external corpus of text and feed retrieved documents directly to language models. Evaluation results on language modelling and event co-reference show the promise of our method. To the best of our knowledge, this is the first work that augments pre-trained NLP models with large episodic memory. In principle, the memory-augmented GPT-2 can be used as a variant of GPT-2 for any downstream tasks, such as GLUE tasks (Wang et al., 2018), although we have not experimented with that here.

References

Shany Barhom, Vered Shwartz, Alon Eirew, Michael Bugert, Nils Reimers, and Ido Dagan. 2019. Revisiting joint modeling of cross-document entity and event coreference resolution. pages 4179–4189.

Sarath Chandar, Sungjin Ahn, Hugo Larochelle, Pascal Vincent, Gerald Tesauro, and Yoshua Bengio. 2016. Hierarchical memory networks. *arXiv preprint arXiv:1605.07427*.

Qian Chen, Xiaodan Zhu, Zhen-Hua Ling, Diana Inkpen, and Si Wei. 2018. Neural natural language inference models enhanced with external knowledge. In *Proceedings of the 56th Annual Meeting of the Association for Computational Linguistics (Volume 1: Long Papers)*, pages 2406–2417.

Agata Cybulska and Piek Vossen. 2014. Using a sledgehammer to crack a nut? lexical diversity and event coreference resolution. In *Proceedings of the Ninth International Conference on Language Resources and Evaluation (LREC-2014)*, pages 4545–4552.

Agata Cybulska and Piek Vossen. 2015. Translating granularity of event slots into features for event coreference resolution. In *Proceedings of the the the 3rd Workshop on EVENTS: Definition, Detection, Coreference, and Representation*, pages 1–10.

Rajarshi Das, Shehzaad Dhuliawala, Manzil Zaheer, Luke Vilnis, Ishan Durugkar, Akshay Krishnamurthy, Alex Smola, and Andrew McCallum. 2017. Go for a walk and arrive at the answer: Reasoning over paths in knowledge bases using reinforcement learning. *arXiv preprint arXiv:1711.05851*.

Bhuwan Dhingra, Zhilin Yang, William W Cohen, and Ruslan Salakhutdinov. 2017. Linguistic knowledge as memory for recurrent neural networks. *arXiv preprint arXiv:1703.02620*.

Shalini Ghosh, Oriol Vinyals, Brian Strope, Scott Roy, Tom Dean, and Larry Heck. 2016. Contextual lstm (clstm) models for large scale nlp tasks. *arXiv preprint arXiv:1602.06291*.

Edouard Grave, Armand Joulin, and Nicolas Usunier. 2016. Improving neural language models with a continuous cache. *arXiv preprint arXiv:1612.04426*.

Caglar Gulcehre, Sarath Chandar, and Yoshua Bengio. 2017. Memory augmented neural networks with wormhole connections. *arXiv preprint arXiv:1701.08718*.

Kian Kenyon-Dean, Jackie Chi Kit Cheung, and Doina Precup. 2018. Resolving event coreference with supervised representation learning and clustering-oriented regularization. In *Proceedings of the Seventh Joint Conference on Lexical and Computational Semantics*, pages 1–10.

Urvashi Khandelwal, He He, Peng Qi, and Dan Jurafsky. 2018. Sharp nearby, fuzzy far away: How neural language models use context. In *Proceedings of the 56th Annual Meeting of the Association for Computational Linguistics (Volume 1: Long Papers)*, pages 284–294.

Ankit Kumar, Ozan Irsoy, Peter Ondruska, Mohit Iyyer, James Bradbury, Ishaan Gulrajani, Victor Zhong, Romain Paulus, and Richard Socher. 2016a. Ask me anything: Dynamic memory networks for natural language processing. In *International conference on machine learning*, pages 1378–1387.

Ankit Kumar, Ozan Irsoy, Peter Ondruska, Mohit Iyyer, James Bradbury, Ishaan Gulrajani, Victor Zhong, Romain Paulus, and Richard Socher. 2016b. Ask me anything: Dynamic memory networks for natural language processing. In *International conference on machine learning*, pages 1378–1387.

Guillaume Lample, Alexandre Sablayrolles, Marc'Aurelio Ranzato, Ludovic Denoyer, and Hervé Jégou. 2019. Large memory layers with product keys. In *Advances in Neural Information Processing Systems*, pages 8546–8557.

Jey Han Lau, Timothy Baldwin, and Trevor Cohn. 2017. Topically driven neural language model. In *Proceedings of the 55th Annual Meeting of the Association for Computational Linguistics (Volume 1: Long Papers)*, pages 355–365.

Chao Ma, Chunhua Shen, Anthony Dick, Qi Wu, Peng Wang, Anton van den Hengel, and Ian Reid. 2018. Visual question answering with memory-augmented networks. In *Proceedings of the IEEE Conference on Computer Vision and Pattern Recognition*, pages 6975–6984.

Alexander Miller, Adam Fisch, Jesse Dodge, Amir-Hossein Karimi, Antoine Bordes, and Jason Weston. 2016. Key-value memory networks for directly reading documents. In *Proceedings of the 2016 Conference on Empirical Methods in Natural Language Processing*, pages 1400–1409.

Seil Na, Sangho Lee, Jisung Kim, and Gunhee Kim. 2017. A read-write memory network for movie story understanding. In *Proceedings of the IEEE International Conference on Computer Vision*, pages 677–685.

Denis Paperno, Germán Kruszewski, Angeliki Lazaridou, Ngoc Quan Pham, Raffaella Bernardi, Sandro Pezzelle, Marco Baroni, Gemma Boleda, and Raquel Fernandez. 2016. The lambada dataset: Word prediction requiring a broad discourse context. In *Proceedings of the 54th Annual Meeting of the Association for Computational Linguistics (Volume 1: Long Papers)*, pages 1525–1534.

Robert Parker, David Graff, Junbo Kong, Ke Chen, and Kazuaki Maeda. 2011. English gigaword. *Linguistic Data Consortium*.

Prasanna Parthasarathi and Joelle Pineau. 2018. Extending neural generative conversational model using external knowledge sources. In *Proceedings of the 2018 Conference on Empirical Methods in Natural Language Processing*, pages 690–695.

Haoruo Peng, Qiang Ning, and Dan Roth. 2019. KnowSemLM: A Knowledge Infused Semantic Language Model. In *Proc. of the Conference on Computational Natural Language Learning (CoNLL)*.

Alec Radford, Karthik Narasimhan, Tim Salimans, and Ilya Sutskever. 2018a. Improving language understanding by generative pre-training. *OpenAI Blog*.

Alec Radford, Karthik Narasimhan, Tim Salimans, and Ilya Sutskever. 2018b. Improving language understanding by generative pre-training. In *Preprint*.

Alec Radford, Jeffrey Wu, Rewon Child, David Luan, Dario Amodei, and Ilya Sutskever. 2019. Language models are unsupervised multitask learners. *OpenAI Blog*, 1(8).

Jack Rae, Jonathan J Hunt, Ivo Danihelka, Timothy Harley, Andrew W Senior, Gregory Wayne, Alex Graves, and Timothy Lillicrap. 2016. Scaling memory-augmented neural networks with sparse reads and writes. In *Advances in Neural Information Processing Systems*, pages 3621–3629.

Jing Shi, Yiqun Yao, Suncong Zheng, Bo Xu, et al. 2016. Hierarchical memory networks for answer selection on unknown words. In *Proceedings of COLING 2016, the 26th International Conference on Computational Linguistics: Technical Papers*, pages 2290–2299.

Zhou Su, Chen Zhu, Yinpeng Dong, Dongqi Cai, Yurong Chen, and Jianguo Li. 2018. Learning visual knowledge memory networks for visual question answering. In *Proceedings of the IEEE Conference on Computer Vision and Pattern Recognition*, pages 7736–7745.

Haitian Sun, Tania Bedrax-Weiss, and William W Cohen. 2019. Pullnet: Open domain question answering with iterative retrieval on knowledge bases and text. *arXiv preprint arXiv:1904.09537*.

Haitian Sun, Bhuwan Dhingra, Manzil Zaheer, Kathryn Mazaitis, Ruslan Salakhutdinov, and William Cohen. 2018. Open domain question answering using early fusion of knowledge bases and text. In *Proceedings of the 2018 Conference on Empirical Methods in Natural Language Processing*, pages 4231–4242.

Kristina Toutanova, Danqi Chen, Patrick Pantel, Hoifung Poon, Pallavi Choudhury, and Michael Gamon. 2015. Representing text for joint embedding of text and knowledge bases. In *Proceedings of the 2015 Conference on Empirical Methods in Natural Language Processing*, pages 1499–1509.

Alex Wang, Amanpreet Singh, Julian Michael, Felix Hill, Omer Levy, and Samuel Bowman. 2018. Glue: A multi-task benchmark and analysis platform for natural language understanding. In *Proceedings of the 2018 EMNLP Workshop BlackboxNLP: Analyzing and Interpreting Neural Networks for NLP*, pages 353–355.

Jason Weston, Sumit Chopra, and Antoine Bordes. 2014. Memory networks. *arXiv preprint arXiv:1410.3916*.

Bishan Yang and Tom Mitchell. 2017. Leveraging knowledge bases in lstms for improving machine reading. In *Proceedings of the 55th Annual Meeting of the Association for Computational Linguistics (Volume 1: Long Papers)*, pages 1436–1446.

Xiaoyu Yang, Xiaodan Zhu, Huasha Zhao, Qiong Zhang, and Yufei Feng. 2019. Enhancing unsupervised pretraining with external knowledge for natural language inference. In *Canadian Conference on Artificial Intelligence*, pages 413–419. Springer.

Detecting and Understanding Moral Biases in News

Usman Shahid, Barbara Di Eugenio, Andrew Rojecki, Elena Zheleva
University of Illinois at Chicago
Chicago, IL
{hshahi6,bdieugen,arojecki,ezheleva}@uic.edu

Abstract

We describe work in progress on detecting and understanding the moral biases of news sources by combining framing theory with natural language processing. First we draw connections between issue-specific frames and moral frames that apply to all issues. Then we analyze the connection between moral frame presence and news source political leaning. We develop and test a simple classification model for detecting the presence of a moral frame, highlighting the need for more sophisticated models. We also discuss some of the annotation and frame detection challenges that can inform future research in this area.

1 Introduction

While much attention has focused on the role of fake news in political discourse, comparatively little attention has been paid to the dissemination of news frames. Framing in news coverage–highlighting certain aspects of an issue or event–can have a significant impact on public opinion formation (Callaghan, 2014). Framing theory posits that preference formation depends on which subset of relevant considerations or beliefs–"frame in mind"–are activated by a particular message–"frame in communication." Scholars refer to the power of such a frame as a framing effect, a phenomenon widely reported in academic scholarship on domestic and foreign issues alike (Jacob, 2000; Grant and Rudolph, 2003; Nicholson and Howard, 2003; Baumgartner and Boydstun, 2008; Perla, 2011). If one-sided and morally charged, it can exacerbate polarization and post-truth politics.

According to the most widely cited model used by social scientists (Entman, 1993), the essential components of a frame include problem definition, diagnosis of cause, moral judgment, and prescribed remedy. For example, obesity may be defined as a significant national health problem, diagnosed as the result of increasingly passive lifestyles judged as detrimental to the strength of society and individuals, and effectively treated by increased physical activity. Such an emphasis on individual choice redirects attention from other possible causes such as genetic disposition or advertising campaigns for caloric rich foods.

Even though moral judgment is central to frame analysis, much of the frame analysis research neglects the moral dimension. Our work responds to this gap by adapting Moral Foundations Theory (MFT) which proposes a set of five modalities–each with a virtue and vice binary partner–that underlie moral thinking (Graham et al., 2013). Morally-inflected frames follow the contours of political ideology (Graham et al., 2009), are more likely to be shared on social media (Valenzuela et al., 2017), and, most importantly, reinforce attitudes, making compromise more difficult (Koleva et al., 2012).

Technology offers little solution to mitigate these framing effects at the scale and speed of modern information networks. Our work responds to the need for cross-disciplinary frameworks that enable the early detection, propagation, and influence of moral frames in such networks. In this paper, we offer an initial analysis on the steps necessary for detecting and understanding the prominence of moral frames in news. We annotate a small corpus of news articles with moral frames and look into their connection to issue-specific frames and news source leaning, together with models for detecting them.

2 Related work

In the last few years, a number of NLP approaches have been devised for frame identification in text: most focus on coarser-grained primary frame identification (Card et al., 2016; Ji and Smith, 2017; Johnson et al., 2017a), possibly based on a probabilistic distribution (Burscher et al., 2014); few

Proceedings of the 1st Joint Workshop on Narrative Understanding, Storylines, and Events, pages 120–125
July 9, 2020. ©2020 Association for Computational Linguistics

Statistics	Values
Sentences with at least one moral frame	2.81 %
Articles with at least one moral frame	20.61 %
Article frame presence agreement alpha	0.0485
Sentence frame presence agreement alpha	-0.0264
Article frame type agreement alpha	0.8435
Sentence frame type agreement alpha	0.8525

Table 1: Dataset annotation statistics.

address finer-grained frame tagging at the paragraph level (Tsur et al., 2015). Most research relies on word-based approaches, from direct keyword matching to latent representations (Boydstun et al., 2013; Burscher et al., 2014; Baumer et al., 2015; Tsur et al., 2015; Johnson et al., 2017a,b). Few studies use rhetorical information such as discourse structure (Ji and Smith, 2017).

Additionally, work has been done on general frames, such as *economy* or *law and order* (Card et al., 2016; Burscher et al., 2014) that can apply across issues, or on issue-specific (also called topical) frames, such as *innocence* as concerns capital punishment; than on identifying moral foundations. Approaches to the latter mostly rely on moral foundation keyword dictionaries, again directly (Fulgoni et al., 2016) or via latent representations (Kaur and Sasahara, 2016; Garten et al., 2016).

3   Datasets and annotation

Since there is no existing corpus with moral frame annotations for news articles, we put together a small initial dataset to help us understand the intricacies of moral frame annotation and analysis. Our dataset contains 400 articles on four different issues. 300 articles are from a previously collected corpus (Card et al., [n. d.]), 100 articles for each of immigration, smoking and same-sex marriage issues from 13 news sources. Another set of 100 articles was collected on the racial unrest in Baltimore from 16 national and local newspaper sources.

Three undergraduate student annotators were hired as summer interns for this project. Each article was independently annotated with sentence-level and article-level moral frames by all three annotators based on the 10 moral foundations (Graham et al., 2013) – Care/Harm, Fairness/Cheating, Loyalty/Betrayal, Authority/ Subversion, Sanctity/Degradation – or with NA. The annotators used the BRAT software to perform the annotations (https://brat.nlplab.org/).

The annotation process proceeded in two stages, each of which involved a detailed annotation man-

ual, that was modified in the second stage [1].

Stage 1.   The annotation manual instructed the annotators to proceed with coding in 3 ordered steps: (1) to identify the moral frame type; (2) to decide whether the author supports or rejects the frame; and (3) to decide whether the author explicitly favors or opposes the specific issue the article is about. The annotators were also instructed to do so for both sentences and the whole article; at the article-level, the annotators were asked to evaluate the entire article and specify what they regarded as its main moral frame. The annotators were told to first annotate the sentences in an article and then the article as a whole, but no explicit written guidelines were provided in this regard.

Stage 2.   After the initial set of annotations from Stage 1 (which were discarded), the protocol was adjusted based on annotator feedback, with the goal of making the annotation process less ambiguous. First, a preliminary step was added to the three annotation steps, a.k.a step 0: annotators were instructed to identify the presence or absence of any moral frame before embarking in the subsequent three steps. Second, the sentence and article annotation were clearly separated, and for the article annotation specific guidelines were provided: *Evaluate the entire article and specify what you regard is its main moral claim. Keep in mind that it may or may not be the most frequent one (based on counting sentences with moral claims).*

Another main adjustment was providing the annotators with a list of keywords associated with each moral foundation developed by Graham et al. (Graham et al., 2013). The annotators were instructed to use such sets as keywords as guidance, but were warned that (a) a moral frame may contain none of the keywords listed in the codebook, and that (b) the presence of a keyword does not necessarily indicate the presence of a moral frame. The annotators were provided with examples of both (a) and (b).

We refer to the dataset with sentence-level annotations as ***mf-sent*** and with article-level annotations as ***mf-art***. 116 articles have both an article-level frame and at least one sentence-level frame, as annotated by at least one annotator. The percentage of articles whose moral frame is different from the most frequent moral frame among the article's sentences is 14.3%.

---

[1] Annotation manual: https://bit.ly/2LXiiR5

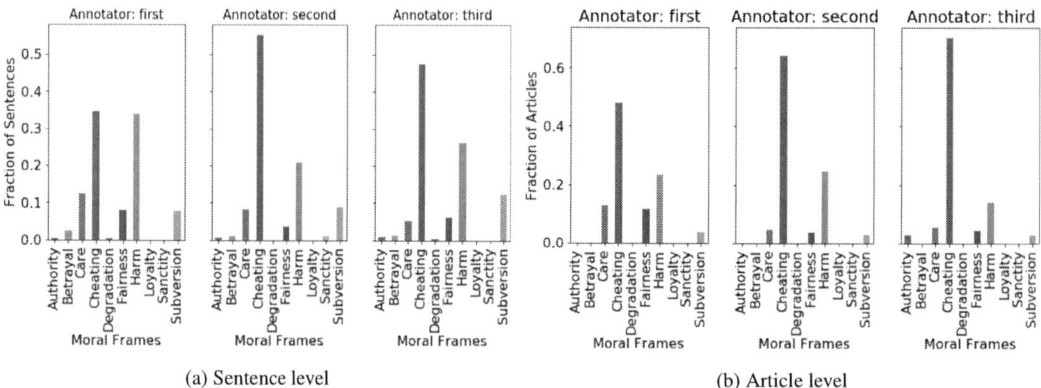

(a) Sentence level   (b) Article level

Figure 1: Moral frame distribution for each annotator in moral frames datasets

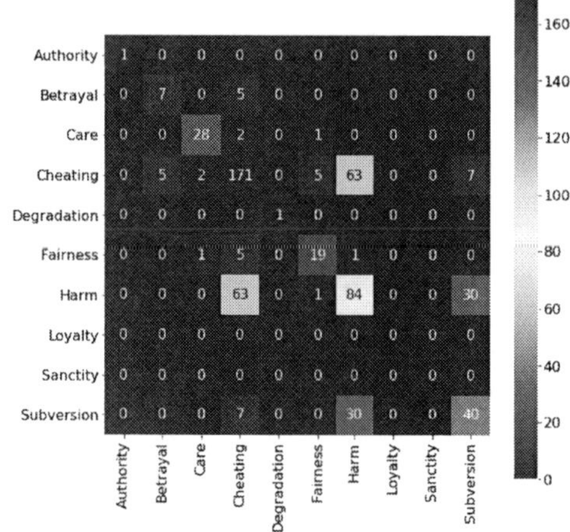

Figure 2: Coincidence matrix showing number of times annotators (dis)agree on sentence-level frame types.

To study the connection between issue-specific frames and more general, moral frames, a domain expert annotated a subset of 48 Baltimore unrest articles from *mf-sent* with issue-specific frames at the sentence level following (Rojecki, 2017): Black Criminality, Police Racism, Rogue Cops, and Structural Inequality. We refer to this dataset as ***ol-sent***.

Subjectivity in Moral Frame Annotation. Table 1 shows dataset annotation statistics including Krippendorff's alpha for inter-annotator agreement. Despite the protocol iterations, the annotators had a fairly low level of agreement on the presence/absence of a moral frame both at the article level (alpha=0.0485) and the sentence level (alpha=-0.0264). However, when at least two annotators agreed that a moral frame is present, the frame type agreement was relatively high both at the article level (alpha=0.8435) and at the sentence level (alpha=0.8525). Figure 1 shows the distri-

bution of frames for each annotator at article and sentence level. While some frames like Cheating and Harm are prevalent across annotators, the actual distributions are different. Figure 2 shows the frame confusion matrix at the sentence level. Each box represents the number of times a moral frame disagreement occurred at the sentence level. The figure shows that annotators often disagree on the most frequent frames, Harm, Subversion and Cheating.

These results reflect the challenges in using non-experts for moral frame annotation. A number of annotation studies have analyzed the reliability of non-expert annotations, and investigated whether corrections need to be applied to the annotation process and / or to the models derived from the non-expert annotated datasets (Snow et al., 2008; Welinder and Perona, 2010; Patton et al., 2019; Lavee et al., 2019). However, many of these studies can actually compare the performance of non-expert and expert annotation, since datasets annotated by experts for the phenomenon of interest did exist; this was not the case for us. In fact, this initial effort of ours at annotation can be taken as an indication of how difficult annotating for moral frames is for non-experts; it remains to be seen how expert annotators would fare on this task. This is part of the future research we will undertake to understand whether this task can be crowdsourced successfully at scale or whether it requires expert annotators.

4 Moral frame analysis

4.1 Issue-specific vs. moral frames

We analyze the connection between issue-specific and moral frames in the Baltimore unrest articles (*ol-sent* dataset). When a sentence is annotated with multiple frames, we consider the one with the

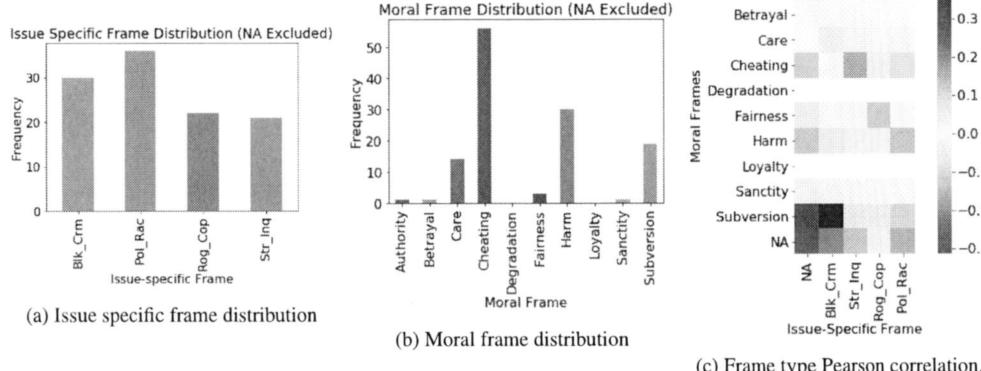

(a) Issue specific frame distribution

(b) Moral frame distribution

(c) Frame type Pearson correlation.

Figure 3: Frame distributions for different types of frames in *ol-sent* dataset.

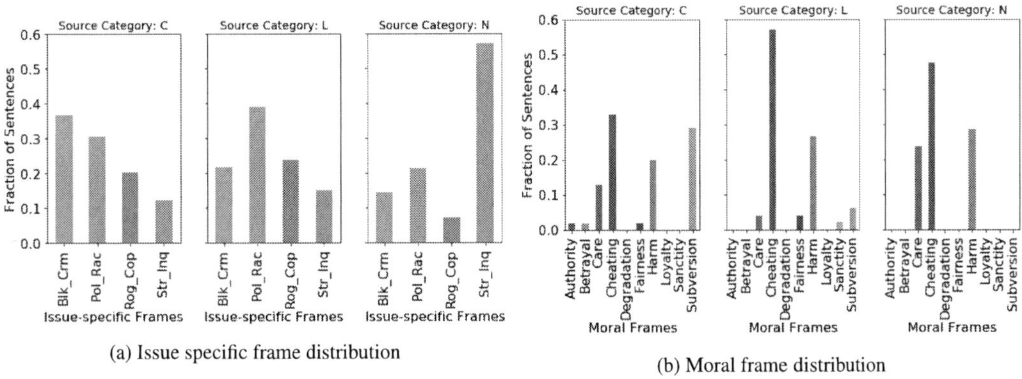

(a) Issue specific frame distribution

(b) Moral frame distribution

Figure 4: Frame type distributions in *ol-sent* dataset based on news source type (**C**onservative, **L**iberal, **N**eutral).

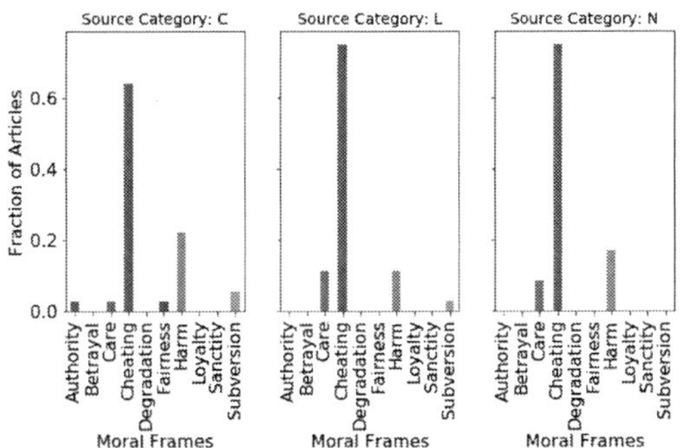

Figure 5: Moral frame distributions for different types of sources in Baltimore articles from *mf-art* dataset.

highest agreement. The sentence-level distribution of issue-specific and moral frames is given in Figure 3. While issue-specific frames are more evenly distributed, moral frames have a skewed distribution with Cheating and Harm being the dominant frames. The most likely reason for this is that, the Care/Harm and Fairness/Cheating foundations are valued by conservatives and liberals alike and is therefore more likely to be present in news frames.

We computed the Pearson correlation between different frame labels, and their heat-map representation can be found in Figure 3c. It is interesting to note that for most moral frames, there is a dominant corresponding issue-specific frame. For Subversion, it is Black Criminality (Blk_Crm), for Fairness, it is Rogue Cops (Rog_Cop), for Cheating/Injustice it is Structural Inequality (Str_Inq).

4.2 Moral frames and news source leaning

In order to understand whether moral frames can explain the political leanings of news sources, a domain expert labeled each news source based on the history of their support for a liberal/conservative candidate. [2] We use the *ol-sent* dataset for this purpose since it has both issue-specific and moral frame labels. The sentence-level distributions for liberal/conservative/neutral news sources can be seen in Figure 4. Issue-specific frame distributions (Fig. 4(a)) are very revealing and consistent

---

[2] Other possible news-source leaning annotations (e.g., (Wihbey et al., 2017)) can be considered in future work.

Model	Precision	Recall	F-score
Keyword match	0.08	0.65	0.14
SVM	0.20	0.41	0.27

Table 2: Moral frame presence classification results.

with previous work (Rojecki, 2017): conservative sources tend to criminalize the protesters while liberal sources focus more on police racism and rogue cops. Neutral sources are harder to explain, however, according to the domain expert, the structural inequality in issue-specific frames can be explained by the fact that these sources are more likely to be aligned with the liberal sources.

Since Black Criminality strongly correlates with Subversion as shown in Figure 3c, we can see in Figure 4(b) that subversion frame is heavily used by conservatives as opposed to liberals. Cheating or Injustice is heavily used by liberal sources as opposed to conservative. Authority and Betrayal are present in conservative sources and absent in the liberal ones. Liberal sources have some sentences labeled as Sanctity which is missing from conservative sources.

Figure 5 shows the distribution of article-level moral frames for the 100 Baltimore articles in the *mf-art* dataset. It shows similar patterns as the sentence-level annotations, except that the differences between news source categories are not as pronounced.

4.3 Moral frame detection

We train a binary classifier to detect whether a moral frame is present or absent in a sentence using all articles in *mf-sent*. Each sentence is represented by a normalized sum of its *word2vec* word vectors. A balanced SVM classifier is tuned and trained using 5-fold stratified cross-validation. Its accuracy is reported in Table 2. It is compared to a baseline *Keyword match* which reports a frame present if at least one of the MFT keywords (Graham et al., 2013) is present in the sentence. The relatively poor results partially reflect the class skew (95% of sentences do not have a moral frame present). For the subset of sentences with moral frames present (396 in total), we used the same methods and evaluation mechanism as above to classify sentences in specific moral frame categories. The only exception is that we used frame-specific MFT keywords and SVM is trained using a one-versus-one multi-class classification setup. The weighted-average results are reported in Table 3.

Model	Precision	Recall	F-score
Keyword match	0.69	0.29	0.31
SVM	0.68	0.70	0.68

Table 3: Multi-class moral frame classification results.

5 Conclusion

We presented a small-scale study of moral frames in news showing that moral frames have the potential to explain issue-specific frames and the biases of their news sources. In order to increase the analysis scale and reliability, we need to collect a larger dataset covering more issues and news sources. We also need to improve the annotation protocol and overcome the challenges associated with annotator subjectivity. Future directions include improving on the machine learning models for predicting moral frames in news articles and studying their impact on opinions expressed in social media.

Acknowledgments

The authors would like to thank Sumayya Siddiqui, Navya Reddy and Hasan Sehwail for their help with annotating the data.

References

Eric Baumer, Elisha Elovic, Ying Qin, Francesca Polletta, and Geri Gay. 2015. Testing and comparing computational approaches for identifying the language of framing in political news. In *NAACL*. 1472–1482.

De Boef Suzanna L. Baumgartner, Frank R. and Amber E. Boydstun. 2008. *The decline of the death penalty and the discovery of innocence*. Cambridge University Press, Cambridge ; New York.

Amber E. Boydstun, Justin H. Gross, Philip Resnik, and Noah A. Smith. 2013. Identifying media frames and frame dynamics within and across policy issues. In *New Directions in Analyzing Text as Data Workshop, London*.

Björn Burscher, Daan Odijk, Rens Vliegenthart, Maarten De Rijke, and Claes H De Vreese. 2014. Teaching the computer to code frames in news: Comparing two supervised machine learning approaches to frame analysis. *Communication Methods and Measures* 8, 3 (2014), 190–206.

Karen Callaghan. 2014. *Framing American Politics*. University of Pittsburgh Press, Pittsburgh PA.

Dallas Card, Amber E Boydstun, Justin H Gross, Philip Resnik, and Noah A Smith. [n. d.]. The media frames corpus: Annotations of frames across issues. In *ACL*.

Dallas Card, Justin Gross, Amber Boydstun, and Noah A Smith. 2016. Analyzing framing through the casts of characters in the news. In *EMNLP*. 1410–1420.

Robert M Entman. 1993. Framing: Toward clarification of a fractured paradigm. *Journal of Communication* 43, 4 (1993), 51–58.

Dean Fulgoni, Jordan Carpenter, Lyle H Ungar, and Daniel Preoţiuc-Pietro. 2016. An Empirical Exploration of Moral Foundations Theory in Partisan News Sources. In *LREC*.

Justin Garten, Reihane Boghrati, Joe Hoover, Kate M Johnson, and Morteza Dehghani. 2016. Morality between the lines: Detecting moral sentiment in text. In *IJCAI workshop on Computational Modeling of Attitudes*.

Jesse Graham, Jonathan Haidt, Sena Koleva, Matt Motyl, Ravi Iyer, Sean P Wojcik, and Peter H Ditto. 2013. Moral foundations theory: The pragmatic validity of moral pluralism. In *Advances in Experimental Social Psychology*. Vol. 47. Elsevier, 55–130.

Jesse Graham, Jonathan Haidt, and Brian A. Nosek. 2009. Liberals and conservatives rely on different sets of moral foundations. *Journal of Personality and Social Psychology* 96, 5 (2009), 1029.

J. Tobin Grant and Thomas J. Rudolph. 2003. Value Conflict, Group Affect, and the Issue of Campaign Finance. *American Journal of Political Science* 47, 3 (2003), 453.

William G. Jacob. 2000. Issue Framing and Public Opinion on Government Spending. *American Journal of Political Science* 44, 4 (2000), 750.

Yangfeng Ji and Noah Smith. 2017. Neural discourse structure for text categorization. In *ACL*.

Kristen Johnson, Di Jin, and Dan Goldwasser. 2017a. Leveraging Behavioral and Social Information for Weakly Supervised Collective Classification of Political Discourse on Twitter. In *ACL (Volume 1: Long Papers)*, Vol. 1. 741–752.

Kristen Johnson, I-Ta Lee, and Dan Goldwasser. 2017b. Ideological Phrase Indicators for Classification of Political Discourse Framing on Twitter. In *Proceedings of the Second Workshop on NLP and Computational Social Science*. 90–99.

Rishemjit Kaur and Kazutoshi Sasahara. 2016. Quantifying moral foundations from various topics on Twitter conversations. In *IEEE BigData*. 2505–2512.

Spassena P. Koleva, Jesse Graham, Ravi Iyer, Peter H. Ditto, and Jonathan Haidt. 2012. Tracing the threads: How five moral concerns (especially Purity) help explain culture war attitudes. *Journal of Research in Personality* 46, 2 (2012), 184 – 194.

Tamar Lavee, Lili Kotlerman, Matan Orbach, Yonatan Bilu, Michal Jacovi, Ranit Aharonov, and Noam Slonim. 2019. Crowd-sourcing annotation of complex NLU tasks: A case study of argumentative content annotation. In *Proceedings of the First Workshop on Aggregating and Analysing Crowdsourced Annotations for NLP*. Association for Computational Linguistics, Hong Kong, 29–38. https://doi.org/10.18653/v1/D19-5905

Stephen P. Nicholson and Robert M. Howard. 2003. Framing Support for the Supreme Court in the Aftermath of Bush v. Gore. *The Journal of Politics* 65, 3 (2003), 676–695.

Desmond Patton, Philipp Blandfort, William Frey, Michael Gaskell, and Svebor Karaman. 2019. Annotating social media data from vulnerable populations: Evaluating disagreement between domain experts and graduate student annotators. In *Proceedings of the 52nd Hawaii International Conference on System Sciences*.

Héctor Perla. 2011. Explaining Public Support for the Use of Military Force: The Impact of Reference Point Framing and Prospective Decision Making. *International Organization* 65, 1 (2011), 139–167.

Andrew Rojecki. 2017. Racial Threat and Local Framing of Baltimores Unrest. In *News of Baltimore: race, rage and the city*, Linda Steiner and Silvio R. Waisbord (Eds.). Routledge, New York.

Rion Snow, Brendan OConnor, Dan Jurafsky, and Andrew Y. Ng. 2008. Cheap and Fast–but is it Good? Evaluating Non-Expert Annotations for Natural Language Tasks. In *Proceedings of the 2008 conference on empirical methods in natural language processing*. 254–263.

Oren Tsur, Dan Calacci, and David Lazer. 2015. A frame of mind: Using statistical models for detection of framing and agenda setting campaigns. In *ACL (Volume 1: Long Papers)*. 1629–1638.

Sebastin Valenzuela, Josefina Ramrez, and Martina Pia. 2017. Behavioral Effects of Framing on Social Media Users: How Conflict, Economic, Human Interest, and Morality Frames Drive News Sharing. *Journal of Communication* 67, 5 (8 2017), 803–826.

P. Welinder and P. Perona. 2010. Online crowdsourcing: Rating annotators and obtaining cost-effective labels. In *2010 IEEE Computer Society Conference on Computer Vision and Pattern Recognition - Workshops*. 25–32.

John Wihbey, Thalita Dias Coleman, Kenneth Joseph, and David Lazer. 2017. Exploring the Ideological Nature of Journalists' Social Networks on Twitter and Associations with News Story Content. *KDD Workshop on Data Science + Journalism* (2017).